THE LEAST AMONG THEM

THE LEAST AMONG THEM

29 PLAYERS,
THEIR BRIEF MOMENTS IN THE BIG LEAGUES,
AND A UNIQUE HISTORY
OF THE NEW YORK YANKEES

Paul Russell Semendinger

Artemesia
Publishing

ISBN: 978-1-951122-16-4 (paperback)
ISBN: 978-1-951122-27-0 (ebook)
LCCN: 2021936587
Copyright © 2021 by Paul Semendinger, Ed.D.
First Edition

Cover Design: Geoff Habiger

Artemesia Publishing
9 Mockingbird Hill Rd
Tijeras, New Mexico 87059
www.apbooks.net
info@artemesiapublishing.com

Contact the author at: drpaulsem@hotmail.com

Praise for *The Least Among Them*

"True Yankee fans, those who have attained a virtual Ph.D. level of fandom, can address each other in code. They can say "34" and know they are referring to Tony Kubek's rookie uniform number. So now comes this, perhaps the ultimate insider book. If you say 'Loyd Colson' to a Yankee fan and get a knowing wink in return, with a reminder that there is only one 'L' in Loyd, you know you are talking to someone worthy. Otherwise, send them home to read Paul Semendinger's book of one-game wonders and tell them not to return until they have mastered it. Only then can they write 'Ph.D. NYY' after their names."

Marty Appel, Yankee historian and former team executive, and author of *Pinstripe Empire: The New York Yankees from Before the Babe to After the Boss.*

"Forget Babe, Lou, and the Mick for a moment, and enjoy the stories of Honey, Rugger, and Clem. This charming and meticulously researched book will remind you of baseball's power to change and enrich lives far beyond the diamond."

Jonathan Eig, New York Times best-selling author of *Luckiest Man*, *Opening Day*, and *Ali: A Life*

"In the United States, there are surely more books written about baseball than any other sport. Even Amazon can't keep a tally. When you type 'baseball books' into the search window, Amazon has the total narrowed to "over 20,000." So you'd think all the good baseball-book ideas have been used up by now. But here comes author Paul Russell Semendinger with a fresh angle. His new book, *The Least Among Them: 29 Players, Their Brief Moments in the Big Leagues, and A Unique History of the New York Yankees*, is a fascinating study of luck, timing and the unpredictable, arduous, near-impossible path to the Major Leagues. These are the stories of men who spent a single day with the Yankees. Elvio Jimenez in 1964 was fortunate enough in his one game to play 13 innings. Frank Verdi in 1953 played one, never touching the ball and never stepping to the plate. Charlie Fallon in 1905 was a pinch runner in the last inning back when the Yankees were the Highlanders. Floyd Newkirk in 1934 pitched a solid ninth inning despite having just three fingers on his pitching hand. That's another thing I like about the book—the short history lessons interspersed with the players' stories. Most of us know that Derek Jeter had the longest tenure as Yankees team captain with 12. But did you know Babe Ruth had the shortest with just five games? Semendinger is a fine writer and his passion for the game—and its players—shine through every page of *The Least Among Them*."

Joan Ryan, award-winning journalist and New York Times bestselling author of five books including *Intangibles*

"The most impressive scholarship on the Yankees I have read, *The Least Among Them* literally fills the gaping hole between biographies of famous Yankees of world fame and national attention, like *Dinner with DiMaggio*, with genuinely profound sketches of lesser-known Yankees who could have nudged the likes of the Yankee Clipper but could not. It reads like a good novel. It's a page turner mainly because the writing is superb, the scholarship involved impeccable, and the author sticks to his narrative in spite of a bewildering history of Minor, Major and international League involvement of his many profiles. It is a back door history: we get the origin of the Seventh Inning Stretch, three fingered ball players, a history of varied "Docs" (ball players with that nickname and why) and other social histories. If you are a Yankee fan, and want a good read, *The Least Among Them* is a mandatory purchase."

Dr. Rock Positano and John Positano, award-winning authors of *Dinner With DiMaggio*

"I am an admirer of deep dives when it comes to baseball, and Paul splashes elegantly into the pool in this regard. Exhaustively researched and very well-crafted, even a Mets guy like me can appreciate his work! This is for fans who want to fill their curiosity gaps; Paul has done the work and done it well. If you like learning things you never knew, and if the Yankees are your team, jump on in."

Josh Lewin, Sportscaster (Fox Sports, and various teams including the Mets, Red Sox, Cubs, Rangers, Orioles, and Tigers)

"I don't think I've ever seen a book quite like it—the least storied players on baseball's most storied team. Paul Semendinger digs deep to find not the hidden gems of the Yankee organization but the fool's gold—players who for one reason or another lasted but a single game with the Bombers. It's a fascinating concept and Semendinger's book delivers. Semendinger manages to pull off the seemingly impossible—a deep dive into the shallow waters of these most minor Yankees. Pick up a copy and I promise that you'll stick with it longer than these guys did in pinstripes."

Mitchell Nathanson, author of *Bouton: The Life of a Baseball Original* and *God Almighty Hisself: The Life and Legacy of Dick Allen*

"*The Least Among Them* is a treasure trove of fascinating stories about lesser known Yankees, lovingly researched and crafted by writer/historian Paul Semendinger. A must-read for Yankee fans and the baseball cognoscenti."

Jon Leonoudakis, Baseball Documentarian

"*The Least Among Them* is a unique and fascinating work, a look at the greatest of sports franchises through its most marginal players. Here are the good, the bad, the ugly, and even the (briefly) perfect, men who for one reason or another lasted just one game for the New York Yankees. Paul Semendinger pivots from their individual stories—poignant, tragic, uplifting—to tell the extraordinary story of baseball."

Kevin Baker, author of *Sometimes You See It Coming and Becoming Mr. October (with Reggie Jackson)*

"Paul Semendinger cleverly unravels New York Yankees history by pulling on the string of 29 players whose Major League careers consisted of one game with the club. While telling their unknown stories, he finds connections with other Yankees and events. *The Least Among Them* is a delightful journey into the past of baseball's most hallowed franchise."

Barry Sparks, author of *Frank "Home Run" Baker: World Series Hero and Hall of Famer*

"*The Least Among Them* provides an original look into 29 unique threads that contribute to the fabric of the game's most storied franchise—The New York Yankees. Inside this well researched book you'll be amazed by the stories within the stories, and come away with a new appreciation for the "cup of coffee" ballplayer. Semendinger delivers a fun and thoughtful book; an enjoyable read for not only passionate Yankee fans, but for any lover of the history of the game."

Matt Dahlgren, author of *Rumor In Town: A Grandson's Promise to Right a Wrong* and *The Flannel Past.*

"Every guy who spends just one day on an MLB team's 25-man roster represents the dreams of tens of thousands of boys. With meticulous research and clever storytelling, Paul Semendinger pays homage to the 29 lucky ones who were able to live out that dream for one afternoon in Pinstripes. *The Least Among Them* promises to be the best among choices for Yankees' fans looking to add to their baseball libraries."

David Ostrowsky, author of *Pro Sports in 1993*

"Semendinger has made remarkable the seemingly unremarkable moments of 29 players who had less than a cup of coffee in the majors. Through his story telling, we learn the names of Batten, Newkirk and Marsonek while also enjoying their everlasting connection to legends like Babe Ruth, Lou Gehrig and Mickey Mantle. A great read for anyone who has ever dreamed of playing in the big leagues, if only for just one game."

Chris Donnelly, author of *Doc, Donnie, the Kid, and Billy Brawl: How the 1985 Mets and Yankees Fought For New York's Baseball Soul*

"There's a love song by Luther Vandross entitled, "If Only for One Night." The equivalent for baseball love might be, for the average Joe Ballplayer/Dreamer, "If Only for One Day." Paul Semendinger highlights these 'one day in MLB' stories, even better that they are all in Yankees pinstripes, in a totally entertaining read. The reality is one day in "the Show" would never be enough for most and reflect shattered dreams. But for these ballplayers, they have bragging rights that most of us, especially Yankees fans, can only dream about. Thank you, Paul, for finding and telling these unique stories worthy of engaging our imaginations and tugging on our emotions."

Robert Skead, author of *Safe at Home, a baseball card mystery*, and other popular children's books

"Earl Warren, Chief Justice of the Supreme Court once wrote: "I always turn to the sports section first. The sports page records people's accomplishments.". Paul Semendinger in his fine new tome has recorded details on those special New York Yankees or Highlanders who had one and only one game in the major leagues. Most of us can only dream of what these people did, and the details Paul brings to each story brings them all to life. Fun read and even as a long-time SABR member, I learned plenty about both baseball and Yankees history!"

Rich Klein, 3-Time SABR National Trivia Champion,40 Years on writing about the Sports Collecting Hobby

"You know the greats from the Yankees history: Ruth. Mantle. DiMaggio. Jeter. A hundred more names every casual baseball fan knows. But the men in this collection are the lesser-known. The men who had their one brief shining moment. Their cup of coffee in pinstripes. Their stories are equally important and definitely fascinating."

Armand Rosamilia, author of *A View From My Seat: My Baseball Season With the Jumbo Shrimp*

"A poignant look at 29 men, from 1903 to 2011, whose entire Major League career consisted of but one game, and that was with the Yankees. This was their moment in the sun, and Paul Semendinger brings them back to life. Each of their sketches has an "Extra Innings" coda that tells relevant stories of far more famous Yankees. Taken together, a wonderfully refreshing angle to view America's most famous sports club."

Steve Steinberg, baseball historian and co-author of books on the Yankees of Babe Ruth's era, *1921* and *The Colonel and Hug*

"There are scores of books on Yankee icons—Ruth, Mantle, Berra, et al. Paul Semendinger hits the opposite way and highlights the tiniest bit players in the Yankee saga, guys who played but a single game for sport's most famous franchise. The result: a parade of twenty-nine Moonlight Grahams, some of them literally one-hit wonders (I'm looking at you, Heinie Odom), whose stories are fresh to even the most dedicated and well-read of baseball fanatics. These are guys who got a sip, not even a full cup of coffee in the major leagues. I found myself downing the book in large gulps for both the fine storytelling and the deep research that went into it. Some of these players were lucky to get their line in a Yankee box score; others could have had so much more, like the prospect who tore his rotator cuff hurling his first inning in the big leagues. Make room on your reading list for this one. You'll come back to it again and again."

Dan Joseph, author of *Last Ride of the Iron Horse: How Lou Gehrig Fought ALS to Play One Last Championship Season.*

"How nice to read a book about the Yankees that is not centered around Babe Ruth, Lou Gehrig, Joe DiMaggio, Mickey Mantle, Derek Jeter, or any of the other legendary members of the game's most legendary team. Instead, Paul Semendinger brings to life a bevy of men who appeared in just one game for the Yankees. Men such as Eddie Quick, Honey Barnes, George Batten, Larry McClure, and George Washburn—players with interesting stories whom even the most devoted Yankees-follower would have trouble identifying.

"In addition to bringing these players to life, Semendinger adds context to their stories with a highly informative treatise devoted to one or another interesting aspect of baseball. This book is a wonderful read for any historian or fan of the game, and a must-have if your team is the Yankees."

Lyle Spatz, Chairman of SABR's Baseball Records Committee and the author of *New York Yankees Openers, Yankees Coming... Yankees Going*

TABLE OF CONTENTS

Chapter 1 Elvio Jimenez (1964)..1
Extra Innings: Tommy John and his Surgery
Chapter 2 Frank Verdi (1953)..12
Extra Innings: The Story of Orlando "El Duque" Hernandez
Chapter 3 Charlie Fallon (1905)..23
Extra Innings: A History of the NY Yankees Captains
Chapter 4 Art Goodwin (1905)..31
Extra Innings: The Top Yankees' Minor League Affiliates
Chapter 5 Phil Cooney (1905)..38
Extra Innings: The Unassisted Triple Play
Chapter 6 Roger Slagle (1979)..45
Extra Innings: The Longest-Tenured Yankees Teammates
Chapter 7 Floyd Newkirk (1934)..54
Extra Innings: Yankees in Combat in World War II
Chapter 8 Honey Barnes (1926)..63
Extra Innings: Mark Koenig and The Babe's Called Shot
Chapter 9 Steve Garrison (2011)..70
Extra Innings: Yankees Who Came from Japan
Chapter 10 Eddie Quick (1903)..79
Extra Innings: Some Yankees Who Changed Their Names
Chapter 11 Homer Thompson (1912)..86
Extra Innings: Yankee Brothers
Chapter 12 George Batten (1912)..95
Extra Innings: A Void in Monument Park
Chapter 13 Harry Hanson (1913)..104
Extra Innings: A Watershed Year
Chapter 14 Jim Hanley (1913)..111
Extra Innings: The Seventh-Inning Stretch
Chapter 15 Rugger Ardizoia (1947)..118
Extra Innings: Yankees Born in Europe
Chapter 16 Stefan Wever (1982)..127
Extra Innings: The Tallest Yankees of All Time
Chapter 17 Sam Marsonek (2004)..136
Extra Innings: A Forgotten Two-Sport Legend

Chapter 18 Christian Parker (2001)......................146
Extra Innings: How Yaz Almost Became a Yankee
Chapter 19 Hal Stowe (1960)......................153
Extra Innings: Dave Righetti's Move to the Bullpen
Chapter 20 Walter Bernhardt (1918)......................159
Extra Innings: Doctors Who Played for the Yankees
Chapter 21 Jack Enright (1917)......................167
Extra Innings: Babe Ruth and Ty Cobb Compete at Golf
Chapter 22 Larry McClure (1910)......................173
Extra Innings: The Shortest Yankees All-Stars
Chapter 23 Tom Burr (1914)......................180
Extra Innings: Sad Tales of Airplanes and Yankees
Chapter 24 Heinie Odom (1925)......................186
Extra Innings: The True Story of Wally Pipp's Headache
Chapter 25 Clem Llewellyn (1922)......................193
Extra Innings: The Least Among Them Managers
Chapter 26 George Washburn (1941)......................201
Extra Innings: The End of Joe DiMaggio's Streak
Chapter 27 Bob Davidson (1989)......................209
Extra Innings: Position Players Who Pitched
Chapter 28 Loyd Colson (1970)......................218
Extra Innings: The First Designated Hitter
Chapter 29 Two Who Might Join the Team (2015)......................225
Extra Innings: An Amazing Comeback
Chapter 30 Andy O'Connor (1908)......................231
Extra Innings: A "Casey At The Bat" Moment
Chapter 31 The Most Famous *Least Among Them*
   Players of All Time (1947)......................239
Notes, Sources and References......................242
About the Author......................251

AUTHOR'S NOTE

Baseball is a game that is beloved by so many, including myself, who spend countless hours reading and researching the players, the games, and the events that tell the history of this great sport. Organizations like the Society of Baseball Research (SABR), Retrosheet, and others continue to find new information, undiscovered box scores, and more that sometimes change well-known (or little-known) statistics. This is especially true with statistics from baseball's earliest days when the record-keeping was not as precise. For example, early in my research, it was reported that Ty Cobb had a batting average of over .400 at the Polo Grounds, the ballpark the early Yankees played in. With subsequent research, the number has been modified to .395. It may change again. In my research for this book, I have also found and corrected numerous errors in the annals of baseball. I even corrected an important document in the research library at the Baseball Hall of Fame.

In this text, I will share where I have uncovered new truths about the game and its players. I am sure there is more to do! I love discussing baseball history with fans and experts. I welcome and appreciate all feedback. I hope for future updates of this text as new information comes forward through my continued research and the research of others.

All of the information and statistics, to the best of my knowledge, were accurate at the time when this text went into final publication.

ACKNOWLEDGEMENTS

Throughout the writing of this text, one person stood as the Largest Among Them—my father, Paul Semendinger. I doubt anyone knows more about baseball or loves the sport more than my dad. Each time I reached out, he was able to provide facts, information, and resources. Dad also proved to be a great editor who helped turn my initial writings into a coherent and interesting book. I am thrilled that we have had the opportunity to collaborate on this project.

This book would not have been possible without the great work of Cassidy Lent the head researcher at the National Baseball Hall of Fame in Cooperstown, New York who was so tremendously helpful to me in my research and visits to the great library there. I look forward to donating all the papers of my research for this project to this great library.

Special thanks go to my friend Dr. Paul Amoroso who read through much of the early manuscript and who provided necessary guidance, suggestions, and encouragement.

My work as editor-in-chief of *Start Spreading the News* has brought me in contact with many great writers. Special and great thanks to Don Burke, Steve Steinberg, Chris Donnelly and Colin Cerniglia for their careful review of the manuscript and all the edits, suggestions, and such that added greatly to the finished product. I cannot thank each of you enough for the vast amount of time you spent poring over my words.

Special thanks go to my Mom and Dad and my good friend Dave Connelly for taking the time to give the manuscript one last final review. I appreciate all the time you spent on this project.

I am thrilled to be publishing this book through Artemesia Publishing. Geoff Habiger is a class act and one of the finest people in publishing. He shares my passion for writing and baseball.

His leadership and support were essential components of this project.

Thank you also to all my friends at the *Start Spreading the News* Yankees blog. The writers who work with me there inspire me on a daily basis.

My three wonderful sons are each, in his own way, the very best. I love each of them more than words can say. And a special thank you to Ethan for all his work in helping me with those box scores (and for often being my catcher when we play baseball for the Ridgewood Maroons).

No man has a better wife than I do. Laurie, you're the love of my life. I am truly blessed. Your support, encouragement, and smiles, even as I write and write and write always inspire me. Nothing of this would be possible without you and your support—and love. You're the best.

And, of course, I must thank God for the love and goodness he shares with all of us. Always.

INTRODUCTION

T he history of baseball can, in large part, be told through the exploits of the New York Yankees. The Yankees are Major League Baseball's most successful franchise having won 40 pennants and 27 World Series. No other franchise comes close to this record of dominance. Some of the greatest players in baseball history established their legends while wearing the Yankee pinstripes: Babe Ruth, Lou Gehrig, Joe DiMaggio, Mickey Mantle, Reggie Jackson, Mariano Rivera, and Derek Jeter. In addition, there were other players, probably not quite as great, but just as notable who also brought glory to the franchise. Every thorough history of baseball includes the names Yogi Berra, Whitey Ford, Roger Maris, and so many others. These players tower over the record books—their greatness unquestioned.

The Yankees also appear quite frequently in popular culture. When Ernest Hemingway referenced a baseball player in *The Old Man and the Sea*, he used Joe DiMaggio. Songwriter Paul Simon also wrote lyrics about Joe D. Other musicians, among them Les Brown, Billy Joel, Madonna, and Jay-Z have included Yankee references in some of their most famous songs. The Yankees have been featured in numerous feature films. The franchise has even appeared on Broadway in a number of stage productions, most notably in the hit play *Damn Yankees.* The Yankees are ubiquitous. They seem to be everywhere both in and out of the sports world.

Volumes have been written about the Yankees, yet there are some stories that have not been told—tales of men whom history seems to have forgotten. Alongside the legends who played for the Yankees were these ballplayers whose entire Major League career lasted for just one solitary game. For one day, just one, they played alongside some of baseball's greatest heroes. This book tells their stories.

Here are the stories of men whose names may be unfamiliar, but who were New York Yankees, if only for a day. The stories of these players are compelling. Some have great names like Homer Thompson, Rugger Ardizoia, and Eddie Quick. Numerous players including Frank Verdi and Floyd Newkirk are enshrined in lesser-known halls of fame. At least one of these players holds a unique Major League record. Some were perfect—others not so much. In the annals of baseball history their stories are rarely, if ever, shared. That changes with this text. Here I bring these players' stories to life.

The stories of these players though do not end with that lone Major League appearance. A single moment does not define a life. Five of these men served in the United States military during World War I or World War II with one dying in service to his country and one who served in both of the great wars. Many of the men stayed in the game as coaches, managers, and scouts, but others left to follow careers outside the game. Before and after their single day with the Yankees, these men found success in other areas. On the pages that follow, we will find doctors and leaders, community members, and fathers. These players might not have been big leaguers for long, but many were impressive individuals.

Through their stories, I will also explore additional baseball history, most often related in some way, to the history of the New York Yankees. Some myths are shattered as I tell the true stories behind some famous moments that have become part of the grand history of baseball.

Even today many children dream at one point or another about playing Major League Baseball. (I know some adults who still hold onto that dream.) These men lived it. They wore the Yankees uniform. They played professional baseball in front of paying customers. It may have been for a fleeting moment, but they each had their one day in the sun. In the pages that follow, I bring these players back and allow them to reside alongside their more famous teammates with whom they once spent a brief moment in time.

When comparing the players in this book to their more famous Yankees brethren, one might say that they were indeed *The Least Among Them...*

Courtesy of The Topps Company.

CHAPTER ONE
ELVIO JIMENEZ (1964)

For a man who appeared in only one game in his Major League career, Elvio Jimenez sure had promise. Numerous experts predicted stardom for this young outfield prospect signed as an amateur free agent by the Yankees in 1959. This potential is clearly seen in Jimenez's first appearance on a baseball card. In 1965, Elvio is depicted alongside catching prospect Jake Gibbs as a "Yankees Rookie Star." The chance for big league success for Elvio Jimenez seemed all but certain. Interestingly, the Topps Chewing Gum Company, who produced these popular baseball cards, did not have a great proofreader. On the front of the card Elvio's last name is spelled correctly, but on the reverse it is spelled Jiminez. Nonetheless, the card speaks to this player's potential as it states, *In seven campaigns in the minors, Elvio topped the .300 mark five times.* The man could certainly hit.

Born January 6, 1940 in the Dominican Republic, Jimenez reached the big leagues when he was twenty-four years old as a member of the 1964 New York Yankees. His performance on what would become his single day in the Major Leagues may

1

have influenced the Topps Company to highlight Jimenez again as a future star in its 1965 baseball card series, but, as we will see, it wasn't to be.

One can only imagine what that must have been like to join the Yankees franchise in 1964. At that time, the Yankees were in the midst of their greatest dynasty. Between 1949 and 1964, the Yankees appeared in every World Series save for two (1954 and 1959). They won nine of those World Series. The sports world had never seen anything like this dominance before and it has not since. This was the club, the mighty Yankees, that Jimenez joined that summer. It had been a long road for him to reach this pinnacle of his playing career.

Elvio Jimenez made it to the Yankees after a steady progression through the minor leagues. His career began in 1959 when he was nineteen years old playing for the St. Petersburg Saints, a Yankees affiliate in the D League, the lowest level of the minors at that time. Jimenez played 132 games that first year and accumulated an impressive .329 batting average to go along with 29 doubles, 17 triples, and 10 home runs. He led the league in triples, hits (181) and total bases (274). Elvio Jimenez earned recognition as an All-Star in the Florida State League. For the 1960 season, he was promoted to C Level baseball and played 105 games for the Modesto Reds of the California League. He again impressed with his batting skills, compiling a very impressive .368 batting average which was enough to place him second in the California League in batting and recognition once again as a league All-Star. 1961 saw Jimenez earn another promotion, this time to a Single-A ball club playing in New York, albeit, not the big city, but 183 miles to the northwest in Binghamton. His .299 batting average helped earn him a promotion the next year, 1962, to the Amarillo Gold Sox of the Double-A Texas League. His prolific batting continued as he posted a .310 batting average. Indeed, the man could certainly hit.

Along the way to the majors, as he toiled through the minors one step at a time, Jimenez played alongside numerous future Yankees. He was often a teammate of Yankees second baseman Horace Clarke; playing together in 1959 and again from 1961 through 1964. While playing in the bushes, Jimenez also played with future Yankee pitching stars Al Downing and Mel Stottle-myre. It is apparent that the Yankees were moving Elvio Jimenez on the same path with their most highly regarded prospects. In fact, by 1961, Jimenez was so well regarded, that he was invited to spring training. That year he roomed with Al Downing in the still-segregated South as the black players were not permitted to live with the rest of the team.

The most interesting teammate Jimenez may have had, though, was an infielder who no longer had much of a future as a player. Alongside Elvio Jimenez on the 1962 Gold Sox was a thir-ty-six-year-old light-hitting infielder named Frank Verdi. Verdi played in only 23 games that year hitting a paltry .192. At that point, Verdi had fewer than 33 minor league games left in his playing career. His dream had already passed. Once, for a single day in 1953, he had been a New York Yankee.

By 1963, it was evident that Jimenez was on the steady track to the Major Leagues. He began the season at Double-A with the Augusta Yankees in the Sally League, but after hitting .331 in 82 games, he was promoted to the Triple-A Richmond Virginians, the highest level of the minor leagues. There, Elvio Jimenez con-tinued to impress. He batted .316 for the Virginians. Jimenez was even called, the Yankees' "brightest rookie prospect."

Invited again to spring training in 1964, Elvio Jimenez forced new Yankees manager Yogi Berra into a difficult decision—carry Jimenez on the bench or send him back to Triple-A Richmond for some needed at-bats. At the time Berra commented, "Everybody knows he isn't going to break into my outfield—not with Roger Maris, Mickey Mantle, and Tom Tresh around. The big thing to see is how he does as a pinch hitter." Toward the end of spring training, Berra optioned Jimenez to the minors with some words of advice, "Work on your defense and we'll call you back up." At Richmond, Jimenez hit .296 and set the International League re-cord for best fielding average (1.000) for an outfielder. This per-formance placed him on the International League All-Star team. It was at the conclusion of that 1964 campaign that Jimenez final-ly earned his promotion to the Yankees.

October 4, 1964 was a dry but overcast day in New York City. The Yankees had already clinched the American League pennant and were finishing out the season before they would face the St. Louis Cardinals in the World Series. However, the last game of the regular season, against the Cleveland Indians, had to come first. Fewer than 11,000 fans came to the ballpark for the 1:30 p.m. game in the Bronx.

The 1964 Cleveland Indians were a mediocre team finishing the year with a 79-83 record which was good enough for sixth place in the ten-team American League. While there were numerous players of minor note on that Cleveland team, there were no standout players. Their only player on the All-Star team that year was Jack Kralick, a left-handed pitcher who didn't even appear in the game.

For this last game of the 1964 season, Elvio Jimenez was penciled in as the starting left fielder by Yogi Berra. He was placed in the third spot in the batting order. Since it was the last game of the season, most of the Yankees starters, including Bobby Richardson, Elston Howard, Tom Tresh, Roger Maris, and Mickey Mantle were given the day off. For Elvio Jimenez, his long, but steady climb through the minors seemed over. He had arrived.

On this day, Jim Bouton, at this point a highly touted young pitcher who had won 18 games that year, was making his league-leading 37th start of the year for the Yankees. After retiring the first batter, Vic Davalillo on a ground out to second base, Bouton faced Dick Howser, the Indians' shortstop. Howser, who would later coach and would, in 1980, manage the Yankees to a division title, singled to left field. This gave Jimenez his first opportunity to actively participate in a Major League game. He fielded the ball cleanly and returned it to the infield.

In the bottom of the first inning, Elvio Jimenez came to bat after the first two Yankee batters were retired. Elvio, a right-handed batter, stood in against Luis Tiant, the Indians' hard-throwing pitcher. This was the final game of Tiant's rookie season—a year that saw him win ten games which jump-started his very successful nineteen-year career. (Toward the end of his career, Tiant played for the 1979 and 1980 Yankees. His manager in 1980 was the man playing shortstop behind him who had singled in the top of the first inning, Dick Howser.)

In his first big league at-bat, Jimenez grounded out to Howser to end the first inning.

Then, with one out in the top of the second inning, Cleveland's third baseman, Max Alvis hit a fly ball to left field. Elvio Jimenez caught it for the second out and had recorded his first Major League putout.

By the time Jimenez came to bat in the bottom of the third inning, the game was tied 1-1. The only Cleveland run to this point was recorded on a home run, hit by none other than the Indians' pitcher, Luis Tiant. In this second at-bat of his career, Jimenez again placed his bat on the ball, but he flew out to right field ending the inning. He was now hitless in two tries.

Elvio Jimenez did not see any more action in the field until the top of the fifth inning when, with two outs, Vic Davalillo, a future All-Star, flied out to him to end the frame.

In the bottom of the sixth inning, with the score still tied, Jimenez came to bat for the third time. There was one out. Luis Tiant was still on the mound. For Jimenez, the third time was the charm. He took Tiant's offering and drove a single to centerfield for his first Major League hit. Jimenez then reached second base on a single by Johnny Blanchard, often a catcher, but on this day, the Yankees' right fielder. Following that single, the final two batters were retired.

As the game progressed, both Yogi Berra, the Yankees manager, and Birdie Tebbetts, the Indians manager, made frequent substitutions. Jim Bouton was replaced after three innings by Hal Rennif. Rennif was followed in succession by Mel Stottlemyre, Steve Hamilton, and Bill Stafford. After six innings of work for the Indians, Luis Tiant was replaced by another rookie, a left-handed pitcher named Tommy John. In John's future lay a 26-year career that included two tenures as a Yankee. Tommy John twice won over 20 games in New York. He would also pitch, with Tiant, as a member of the 1980 Yankees squad under manager Dick Howser.

In the eighth inning with the score tied 1 - 1, Jimenez came to bat in against Tommy John. This time he was batting with two outs. For the second consecutive time, Elvio Jimenez singled to center field. Johnny Blanchard again singled him to second, but again the other batters could get him no further.

Stan Williams came out of the Yankee bullpen to pitch

the ninth inning. With two outs, Tito Francona doubled over Jimenez's head in left field, but the Indians couldn't score him. The Yankees also couldn't score in their half of the ninth inning. In his first Major League game Elvio Jimenez was certainly getting his money's worth as the game went into extra innings.

In the top of the tenth inning, Jimenez once again tracked down a fly ball and recorded an out from the bat of Vic Davilillo. In the top of the eleventh, Leon Wagner also flew out to Jimenez. In the bottom of that frame, Jimenez came to bat again, this time against Sonny Siebert. Jimenez popped out to the third baseman.

The game continued.

Finally, in the top of the thirteenth inning, the Indians pushed across a run. Vic Davilillo had led off the inning with a bunt single. With one out, he was driven to third on a single by Fred Whitfield. It is interesting to note, that with Davilillo at third base, the game in extra innings, and the season coming to a close, manager Yogi Berra made two defensive changes. First, he brought Johnny Blanchard in from right field to catch (replacing Jake Gibbs who would appear on the 1965 Topps Future Stars baseball card with Elvio Jimenez) and placed the sure-handed Joe Pepitone in right field. The season might have been in its concluding moments but it is evident that Berra still wanted the victory. The next batter, Leon Wagner hit a groundball to first base where Mike Hegan attempted to start a double play by throwing to the shortstop. Wagner beat the return throw to first with Davilillo scoring giving Cleveland a 2-1 lead.

Hard-throwing "Sudden" Sam McDowell (a future Yankee himself) came out of the Indians' bullpen to close out the game and the season. Due to the many substitutions, McDowell would be facing mostly Yankees regulars who had anticipated having the day off. First came Elston Howard. He struck out. Bobby Richardson then grounded out to the pitcher. With two outs though, Joe Pepitone singled past the second baseman. This brought up Elvio Jimenez with the game on the line.

For Jimenez, this was his sixth at-bat of the day. He had already recorded two hits. With Pepitone leading off first base, Jimenez hit a ground ball to shortstop. The throw across the infield beat him to the bag. The game, the season, and Elvio Jimenez's Major League Baseball career all ended when the ball stuck in first baseman Fred Whitfield's glove.

In 1965, Elvio Jimenez returned to the minor leagues. He had a solid season, hitting .297 for the Toledo Mud Hens. His manager that year was his former minor league teammate, Frank Verdi. Mike Hegan, who wasn't able to turn the double play in that last game in 1964, was also on the team, as was Jimenez's baseball card companion Jake Gibbs.

The 1966 season saw Jimenez playing at both Double-A and Triple-A for Yankees affiliates, but by 1967, Elvio Jimenez was the property of the Pittsburgh Pirates organization. Jimenez's first minor league season for his new organization saw him hit .340 for the Columbus Jets. Playing alongside Elvio in that minor league outfield was a special person, his brother Manny. Manny Jiminez had been playing in the major and minor leagues for many years. He had seen a fair amount of big league time with stints on the Kansas City Athletics and the Pittsburgh Pirates. Manny would return to the Major Leagues in 1968 for the Pirates and in 1969 for the Chicago Cubs. Also on that 1967 minor league team was a pitcher named Jim Shellenback with whom Elvio Jimenez would forever share space on another baseball card. Still feeling that he was a player with great potential, the Topps Company again listed Jimenez as a Rookie Star; this time with the Pirates for their 1969 baseball card series. Jimenez never made good on those "future star" predictions.

After the 1971 season, Elvio Jimenez was out of professional baseball in the United States. In 1972, he began a four-year career in the Mexican League. He later served as a scout for the Dodgers and Red Sox organizations.

Jimenez's biggest claim to fame may have been the fact that he was the scout who signed pitching sensation Fernando Valenzuela for the Dodgers. In 1981, Valenzuela captured all of baseball's interest as he won the NL Rookie of the Year Award and helped propel the Dodgers to a world championship over the Yankees. For his contribution to that championship, Elvio Jimenez was awarded a World Series ring.

Elvio Jimenez sure could hit. Over the course of 17 minor league seasons, he batted .307 with 120 home runs and 783 runs batted in. He played over 1,600 minor league games with more than one thousand coming at Triple-A, the highest level of the minors.

Jimenez had a brief Major League career. Still, of all the players in the history of baseball who played only one game, he is tied for the record for the most at-bats (6). With two hits, both off of long-time Major League stars, he also retired with a batting average of .333.

Extra Innings
Tommy John and His Surgery

In his sole Major League game, Elvio Jiminez singled off of left-handed pitcher Tommy John. John was a rookie in 1964 and his career was a long one, lasting into the 1989 season. In total, Tommy John spent 26 years in the big leagues pitching for the Cleveland Indians, Chicago White Sox, Los Angeles Dodgers, New York Yankees, California Angels, and Oakland A's. John was a four-time All-Star and was twice (1977 and 1979) the runner-up for the Cy Young Award (once in the National League and once in the American League). Only twenty-five pitchers have won more games in their career than the 288 won by Tommy John. Yet, in spite of his overall success, Tommy John is best remembered not for what he did on the field; instead, he is best remembered for the surgery that is named after him.

After the 1964 season referenced above, Tommy John was part of a three-team trade that sent him to the Chicago White Sox and brought Cleveland favorite Rocky Colavito back to the Indians from whom he had been traded five long years before. Tommy John pitched for the White Sox for seven seasons winning 82 games against 80 losses. He was a solid pitcher winning in double figures every year but one while with Chicago. Still, there was a sense that he was an underachiever, and, at the conclusion of the 1971 season he was traded to the Los Angeles Dodgers in a deal that brought the controversial slugger Richie Allen to the White Sox. It was in Los Angeles that Tommy John started to pitch to his potential. (Of note Richie Allen won the American League Most Valuable Player Award for the White Sox immediately after this trade.) In 1973, Tommy John had his best season winning 16 games against only 7 defeats. By July 1974, Tommy John, with a 13-3 record, was widely considered one of the best pitchers in the National League. Yet, in a game against the Montreal Expos on

July 17, Tommy John tore a ligament in his left elbow. He was unable to pitch again that season. The prescribed rest that followed the injury did not help. He was unable to throw.

The type of injury Tommy John succumbed to was, until this point, a career-ending injury. During his failed rehabilitation period, Tommy John had talked with Dr. Frank Jobe, a member of the Dodgers' medical staff. Dr. Jobe recommended a surgery that had never been attempted before—taking a ligament from John's right arm and using it to replace the ruptured tendon in his left arm. Feeling that his career was over without the surgery, Tommy John agreed to the procedure not knowing if it would be successful enough to allow him to play baseball again.

For over a year after the surgery, Tommy John worked through a vigorous rehabilitation. Progress was slow, but John gave this process his very best efforts. By the end of the 1975 season, Tommy John was working his way back and was able to throw batting practice.

In 1976, Tommy John returned to the Major Leagues. He became known as the man with the bionic arm. In the next four seasons, Tommy John won 20 games three times, two of those seasons with the Yankees. His success following the surgery was remarkable. Tommy John actually won more games after his surgery (164) than before it (124). Amazingly, Tommy John pitched for thirteen seasons after the surgery. In his final season, 1989, Tommy John, at 46 years old, was the Yankees' Opening Day starting pitcher.

Tommy John's willingness to embrace an untried surgical procedure broke down the preconceived notions athletes had regarding what was once a career-ending injury. This new approach was simply revolutionary. It can be argued that no procedure has revolutionized baseball, or even all of sport as much as the procedure that has since become known as Tommy John surgery.

CLEVELAND INDIANS at NEW YORK YANKEES

Sunday, October 4, 1964 (Yankee Stadium)

	1	2	3	4	5	6	7	8	9	10	11	12	13	R	H	E
CLE	0	0	1	0	0	0	0	0	0	0	0	0	1	2	10	0
NY	0	1	0	0	0	0	0	0	0	0	0	0	0	1	8	1

CLE		AB	R	H	RBI	NY		AB	R	H	RBI
Davalillo	CF	6	1	1	0	Linz	SS	3	0	0	0
Howser	SS	4	0	2	0	Richardson	PH/SS	3	0	0	0
Banks	PH2B	2	0	0	0	Gibbs	C	5	0	0	0
Chance	1B	5	0	2	0	Pepitone	RF	1	0	1	0
Luplow	PR					**Jimenez**	LF	6	0	2	0
Whitfield	1B	1	0	1	0	Blanchard	RF/C	4	1	4	0
Wagner	LF	6	0	0	1	Lopez	3B	5	0	0	0
Held	LF					Hegan	1B	4	0	0	0
Francona	RF	4	0	1	0	Gonzalez	2B	5	0	0	0
Agee	PR/RF	2	0	1	0	Moore	CF	5	0	1	1
Alvis	3B	4	0	1	0	Bouton	P	1	0	0	0
Martinez	2B	3	0	0	0	Reniff	P				
John	P					Tresh	PH	1	0	0	0
Salmon	PH	0	0	0	0	Stottlemyre	P				
Siebert	P					Hamilton	P				
Dicken	PH	1	0	0	0	Boyer	PH	1	0	0	0
McDowell	P					Stafford	P				
Sims	C	5	0	0	0	Williams	P	1	0	0	0
Tiant	P	2	1	1	1	Howard	PH	1	0	0	0
Brown	2B/SS	3	0	0	0						

CLE	IP	H	R	BB	SO	NY	IP	H	R	BB	SO
Tiant	6	4	1	2	6	Bouton	3	3	1	0	3
John	2	2	0	0	2	Reniff	2	0	0	0	1
Siebert	3	1	0	0	3	Stottlemyre	1	1	0	0	1
McDowell - W	2	1	0	0	2	Hamilton	1	1	0	0	2
						Stafford	1	0	0	0	1
						Williams - L	5	5	1	2	1

Elvio Jimenez

FRANK VERDI   MGR

Courtesy of TCMA Ltd.

CHAPTER TWO
FRANK VERDI (1953)

F rank Verdi is best remembered for his long and notable
career as a minor league manager. Verdi managed for
twenty-one seasons working in the Yankees, New York
Mets, Houston Astros, and Baltimore Orioles organizations. He
also coached in the Houston Astros, Minnesota Twins, and Washington Senators organizations and also served as a scout. In total,
Verdi spent over fifty years in baseball. He was a successful minor
league manager winning three International League championships (1969, 1970, and 1981). Before all of that, Frank Verdi was
a *Least Among Them* player.

As Elvio Jimenez was working his way up the minor league
ladder, Verdi was struggling to hang on to his fleeting dream of
once again reaching the big leagues. He didn't make it back, and,

in spite of his long and successful career as a minor league manager, he also never made it to the Major Leagues in that capacity either. Frank Verdi's long baseball life brought him only one day in The Show.

Frank Verdi graduated Boys High School in Brooklyn, New York in 1944. That same year, he began attending New York University, but he also received another call—to serve with the United States Navy in World War II. This author was unable to locate any of the specifics related to Verdi's service in the war. After the war, in 1946, Frank Verdi signed with the Yankees organization beginning his career in the minor leagues.

Frank Verdi's climb through the minors was slow, but steady. His first assignment in 1946 was with the D-Level Wellsville Yankees in the PONY (Pennsylvania-Ontario-New York) League. Verdi was fortunate that he was an able fielder as he hit only .239 in 106 games. Partially because he was known for his good glove, he was promoted for the last few weeks of the season to the Class-B Sunbury Yankees. 1947 saw Verdi spend time between the Butler Yankees (Class-C) and Sunbury. His .319 batting average with Butler indicated that he also had some promise with the bat.

By 1949, Frank Verdi was making a name for himself during his progression through the bush leagues. That year he successfully performed a play called the "hidden ball trick" seven times while playing for the Binghamton Yankees, an A-Level team. This trick play involves a fielder pretending to throw the ball to a teammate, usually the pitcher, to confound the base runner who then leaves the safety of the base, only to be tagged out by the fielder still holding the baseball. Of note, Future Hall of Famer Edward Charles "Whitey" Ford was a star pitcher with a 16-5 record for that same Binghamton team.

The Yankees organization seemed to have reluctant hope for Frank Verdi as an eventual Major Leaguer. In each of his minor league seasons, he was shuttled between various teams at various levels. With Binghamton again in 1952, Verdi hit .313 and was an All-Star as a third baseman in the Eastern League. That same year, Verdi had his first taste of Triple-A baseball as he was promoted to the Kansas City Blues at the end of the season.

And so it was, that in 1953, Frank Verdi was slated to begin the season with the Syracuse Chiefs, the Yankees' top farm team. And then, better news! In May of that year Frank Verdi got the call to the majors.

Writers frequently refer to playing for the Yankees as "putting on the pinstripes." Unfortunately, for Frank Verdi, in his brief stay he didn't even get that opportunity. Verdi's lone Yankee appearance did not come at Yankee Stadium, rather it came in a rival city to the north, Boston. In Verdi's one Yankee game, he wore the road grays while playing at Fenway Park.

Among non-pitchers who had brief Major League careers, Frank Verdi's career must have been one of the shortest.

As the day began on May 10, 1953, the Yankees were sitting atop the American League with a 14-7 record. The Cleveland Indians were 12-6 and just a half game behind the Yankees. The Yankees' opponent on that day, the Boston Red Sox, were 11-9, two and one-half games off the pace. Sitting at the head of the American League was nothing new for these Yankees. They were baseball's best team in each of the previous four years, winning the World Series in 1949, 1950, 1951, and 1952. It was the desire, if not the expectation, of this team to win it all again in 1953. This squad was looking to become the first team ever to win five consecutive World Series. As such, every game, even against the Red Sox, mattered. The Red Sox finished the previous season at 76-78 in sixth place. (The 1953 Red Sox would eventually finish in fourth place with a respectable 84-69 record).

FRANK VERDI

Courtesy of TCMA Ltd.

This game was the last of a three-game set in Boston. The Red Sox had won the Friday game 2-1, while the Yankees took the Saturday game 6-4 with the assistance of a two-run home run off the bat of Mickey Mantle. The Saturday event was also notable in that it was the last game of Dominic DiMaggio's eleven-year playing career. (He appeared as a pinch hitter and popped out to second base.)

For this game, the Yankees sent a lineup that contained future Hall of Famers Phil Rizzuto at shortstop and Mickey Mantle in center field. Johnny Mize, another future Hall of Famer (at the tail end of his career) sat on the bench awaiting the moment when he might pinch hit. The Yankees manager was another eventual Hall of Famer, Casey Stengel. The Red Sox had George Kell, who would also be enshrined in Cooperstown, at third base. At this time, Ted Williams, their greatest player, was serving with the military fighting the war in Korea.

Frank Verdi's Major League opportunity came in the bottom of the sixth inning. On this day, the Yankees and the Red Sox were really battling. In the top of the sixth, with the Yankees trailing 3-2, Stengel sent Joe Collins in to pinch hit for Rizzuto. While Rizzuto was a star, Casey Stengel was known to pinch hit for him in close games. After Collins grounded out, Frank Verdi was sent into the game to replace Rizzuto at shortstop.

As he took the field for the bottom of the sixth inning, the players accompanying Verdi on the infield were Billy Martin at second base, Gil McDougald at third base, and Don Bollweg (a Yankee for 70 games) was across the infield at first base. Vic Raschi, in relief of Allie Reynolds, was pitching.

The first Red Sox batter in the sixth inning was, Jimmy Piersall. He grounded out to McDougald at third. George Kell then flew out to Mickey Mantle in center field. Finally, Dick Gernert struck out to end the inning.

In the top of the seventh inning, the Yankees staged a rally. With two outs, Mantle singled. Gene Woodling followed Mantle's hit with a single. Gil McDougald then singled home Mantle to tie the game at three. Following McDougald was Billy Martin who promptly hit a two-run double to give the Yankees the lead. The Yankees' catcher, Charlie Silvera, was then intentionally walked. Vic Raschi also walked to load the bases. It was just about time for Frank Verdi's first ever big league at-bat. But, just before he had this opportunity, the Red Sox manager, Hall of Famer Lou Boudreau, called for a pitching change. Stengel, not wishing to miss a chance to increase the Yankees' lead, then sent for another rookie, Bill Renna, to pinch hit for Verdi.

Renna grounded out. And with that, Frank Verdi's Major League career was over.

Frank Verdi played shortstop for just one inning for the Yankees. He handled no chances. He never had an opportunity to bat. As Verdi recalled, "About a week later, I was in Syracuse."

In 1954, Verdi became the property of the Kansas City Athletics. He soon found himself playing for numerous organizations—the Chicago Cubs, St. Louis Cardinals, Washington Senators, and the New York Mets—all at Triple-A. He remained close to the big leagues, but he was never called up again.

On July 25, 1959, Frank Verdi, while serving as a player/coach of the Rochester Red Wings as part of the Cardinals organization, was actually shot while on the field of play in a game in Havana, Cuba. 1959 marked the year that Fidel Castro's overthrow of the government took place and he assumed power. At that time, the Havana Sugar Kings were part of the International League representing the Cincinnati Reds organization. A number of future Major League players were members of the 1959 Sugar Kings squad including future Yankee relief ace Luis Arroyo.

Before the game was played, there was an exhibition game featuring Castro's supporters competing against Cuba's military police. The stadium was filled with infantrymen. Fidel Castro even pitched two innings in that game exciting the crowd and helping to make for a tumultuous atmosphere.

The regularly scheduled game between the Red Wings and the Sugar Kings was a lengthy affair that lasted well into the night. As midnight struck, the crowd began to recognize the arrival of July 26, the date celebrated as the beginning of the Cuban Revolution. There was music and cheering... and gunfire. The players did not know why this spontaneous celebration erupted. Verdi remembered taking cover under a Jeep that was used to bring in relief pitchers. Order was eventually restored, and the game continued into extra innings, albeit with the players feeling the tension from the crowd and the game. During an argument with an umpire, the Red Wings' manager Cot Deal was ejected. As he left the field, he turned over his managerial duties to Frank Verdi.

The next inning, as Frank Verdi was standing in the third base coach's box, gunfire again rang out. A stray .45-caliber bullet, hit Verdi in the head. Another bullet struck Cuban shortstop Leo Cardenas in the shoulder. As the umpires checked on Verdi and Cardenas, the game was immediately called, and the other players rushed off the field to safety.

In 1959, batting helmets were not yet in use, but some players, to offer protection to their heads, used plastic liners inside their baseball hats. Frank Verdi was one such player, having been beaned a few weeks earlier. On this fateful night, he had not removed the liner from his hat and the stray bullet glanced off that liner saving his life.

The next day, the Red Wings fled the island. During the 1960 season, the Havana team was moved to Jersey City, New Jersey. There has not been a minor league baseball team in Cuba since.

In 1961 and 1962, Frank Verdi served as a player/manager for the Syracuse Chiefs who were then affiliated with the Minnesota Twins. Verdi was transitioning from being a player to being a manager. During that 1962 season, Verdi was replaced as the manager and by the end of that 1962 season, Frank Verdi was back with the Yankees organization playing for the Double-A Amarillo Gold Sox of the Texas League. As Elvio Jimenez was working his way up for his one day in the majors, Verdi was barely holding onto his playing career from his only big league opportunity nine long years earlier. By 1963, Frank Verdi was a thirty-seven-year-old shortstop. He was assigned to the Greensboro Yankees in the Carolina League as a player/manager. Verdi was back in Single-A. After seven games in Greensboro, Verdi's playing days were over. His long and storied minor league managing career was beginning.

As a manager, Frank Verdi enjoyed a great deal of success. He managed in the minors for 24 years, including many years in the winter leagues, and had numerous first-place finishes and three minor league championships. In 1970, he was the International League's Manager of the Year.

After managing the Tidewater Tides for four years (1977-1980) for the New York Mets organization, Verdi returned to the Yankees and guided their Triple-A Columbus Clippers in 1981 and 1982 taking the Clippers to the postseason in 1981. In 1985, Frank Verdi managed 139 games for the Rochester Red Wings in the Baltimore Orioles organization. That was his final year as a manager in affiliated minor league baseball but Verdi managed into the 1990s for independent minor league baseball teams. He once said, "This is a great game and it is in my blood. I can't leave it. Baseball's been good to me."

As he reached old age, Frank Verdi received numerous honors. In 1999 he was recognized in Syracuse and added to the franchise's Wall of Fame at P & C Stadium. Later, Frank Verdi was inducted into the Binghamton Baseball Shrine (2004) and reached the International League Hall of Fame in 2008.

Extra Innings
The Story of Orlando "El Duque" Hernandez

In the 1950s and 1960s, there were a number of legendary big league players who came from Cuba. This list includes Hall of Famer Tony Perez and a host of All-Stars including Minnie Minoso, Luis Tiant, Mike Cuellar, Bert Campaneris, and Tony Oliva. But in 1962, ballplayers in Cuba were forbidden to play baseball abroad. This led to a long period when Cuban baseball stars were not able to reach Major League Baseball. The only way for a Cuban player to make it to the baseball leagues in the United States was to defect. This did not happen often. Between 1963 and 1991, only one Major Leaguer, Barbaro Garbey, was able to leave Cuba and make it to the big leagues.

By the 1990s, due to Cuba's struggling economy, more baseball players started to defect. These defections put the lives of the ballplayers and their accomplices at great risk. One player who defected from Cuba during this time was one of Cuba's greatest baseball stars, Orlando "El Duque" Hernandez.

A right-handed pitcher, El Duque was a star in Cuba who was also successful in international competitions. Hernandez pitched in the 1988, 1990, and 1994 World Cup competitions and was a member of the 1992 Cuban Olympic team. during his career in Cuba, El Duque won 126 games against only 47 losses for a winning percentage of .728, the highest of all time.

After his half-brother Livan Hernandez defected from Cuba, Orlando Hernandez was suspended and later banned for life from playing baseball in his homeland. He was reduced to living in poverty and working as laborer in a hospital.

On December 26, 1997 Orlando Hernandez and seven companions fled Cuba on a 21-foot fishing boat. They spent over ten hours at sea before landing on an uninhabited cay in the Bahamas where they lived on meager rations for three days before being rescued by the United State Coast Guard. El Duque then was granted a visa through Costa Rica, and a great bidding war occured among numerous Major League clubs for his services. The New York Yankees prevailed and signed him for $6.6 million.

Since El Duque had not pitched in over eighteen months, the Yankees sent him to the minors. Immediate positive results soon followed. El Duque went 7-1 in nine starts and he struck out 74 batters in just over 51 innings of work. By June, Orlando Hernandez was pitching in the majors. His success there was also immediate. For the 1998 Yankees, Hernandez went 12-4.

The 1998 Yankees dominated the American League with a 114-48 record. After their great regular season, though, they knew that the season would only be a success if they won the World Series. After sweeping the Texas Rangers in the American League Division Series, the Yankees found themselves on the verge of a crisis in the American League Championship Series against the Cleveland Indians.

After winning the first game, the Yankees dropped the next two to Cleveland, the same team that had defeated the Yankees in the American League Division Series the season before. History looked like it was on the verge of repeating itself.

On Saturday, October 10, 1998, Orlando "El Duque" Hernandez took the mound for the Yankees with their season basically on the line. El Duque had been a legendary "big game" pitcher in Cuba and now pitching what was considered a "must win" game for the Yankees, he did not disappoint. El Duque scattered three hits and no runs over seven innings propelling the Yankees to a 4-0

Courtesy of the Topps Company

victory that evened the series at two games. Following this victory, the Yankees won the remainder of their games, right through the World Series. In that World Series, Hernandez was the winning pitcher in Game 2.

All told, Hernandez pitched six seasons for the Yankees and had an impressive 61-40 overall record. In the postseason, he was even better. In fact, he was remarkable, winning his first eight decisions. El Duque was the MVP of the 1999 American League Championship Series.

After the 2002 season, injuries began to take a toll on El Duque. He finished his career pitching for the Chicago White Sox, Arizona Diamondbacks, and the New York Mets. He was an instrumental pitcher on the 2005 world-champion White Sox. El Duque retired with 95 Major League wins against just 65 losses. Between his Cuban career and the Major Leagues, Orlando Hernandez won 216 games with only 112 losses. His combined career, along with his dominating performances in the postseason, leaves little doubt that Orlando "El Duque" Hernandez was one of the greatest Cuban players to ever come to the Major Leagues.

NEW YORK YANKEES at BOSTON RED SOX

Sunday, May 10, 1953 (Fenway Park)

	1	2	3	4	5	6	7	8	9		R	H	E
NY	0	0	0	0	1	1	3	2	0		7	14	1
BOS	0	1	1	0	1	0	0	1	0		4	10	1

NY		AB	R	H	RBI	BOS		AB	R	H	RBI
Rizzuto	SS	2	0	0	0	Goodman	2B	2	1	1	0
Collins	PH	1	0	0	0	Lepcio	PH/2B	2	0	0	0
Verdi	SS					Piersall	RF	4	0	1	1
Renna	PH	1	0	0	0	Kell	3B	4	0	2	0
Brideweser	SS	0	0	0	0	Gernert	1B	4	0	1	0
Noren	RF	4	2	2	0	White	C	4	1	1	1
Bollweg	1B	5	1	3	1	Stephens	LF	4	0	1	0
Mantle	CF	5	1	2	2	Umphlett	CF	4	1	1	0
Woodling	LF	5	1	1	0	Bolling	SS	3	0	1	1
McDougald	3B	5	2	2	1	Hudson	P	2	0	0	0
Martin	2B	5	0	3	2	Kinder	P				
Silvera	C	3	0	0	0	Holcombe	P	0	0	0	0
Reynolds	P	2	0	1	0	Kennedy	P				
Mize	PH	1	0	0	0	Wilber	PH	1	1	1	1
Raschi	P	1	0	0	0	McDermott	P	0	0	0	0

NY	IP	H	R	BB	SO	BOS	IP	H	R	BB	SO
Reynolds	5	7	3	0	0	Hudson - L	6.2	9	4	2	2
Raschi - W	4	3	1	0	1	Kinder	0	2	1	2	0
						Holcombe	0.1	3	2	0	0
						Kennedy	1	0	0	0	1
						McDermott	1	0	0	1	0

Frank Verdi

Photo from the author's collection.

CHAPTER THREE
CHARLIE FALLON (1905)

Twelve of the *Least Among Them* Yankees played for the team before 1920. That was a different time in the world, in America, and in baseball as Major League Baseball was still in its infancy. Baseball history is replete with stories of players who came off the sandlots or out of a factory or coal mine and right into the big leagues. While some of those stories are probably apocryphal, an element of truth also surrounds them. In short, it may have been easier to have the chance to play in the majors during baseball's earliest days. To put the matter into some perspective, when most of these onetime Yankees played, Babe Ruth was still a kid in Baltimore. In addition, while today the Yankees are synonymous with success; these players arrived before the Yankees enjoyed any of their glory.

The challenge when researching these twelve players that were members of the Yankees franchise before Babe Ruth, is that much of the information about these players is unavailable or incomplete. Such is the story of Charlie Fallon.

Charlie Fallon was born in New York City in 1881 and seemed to have lived his whole life in the area, passing away at the age of 79 in Kings Park, New York. Fallon exemplifies this age of quick ascension into the Major Leagues. In his case, he may have moved from the college baseball diamond to the majors. We know, thanks to the efforts of Bill Haber, the great baseball historian, that Fallon's lone game came on June 30, 1905. That 1905 season was just the third for the Yankees franchise. The team in its infancy (and for about a decade after) was known as the Highlanders as they played atop a hill (at Hilltop Park) in upper Manhattan.

June 30, 1905 was not just the date of Charlie Fallon's first and only game in the Major Leagues it was also an important day in scientific history. It was on that date that Albert Einstein published *On the Electrodynamics of Moving Bodies*, which contained his special theory of relativity.

Charlie Fallon's Major League career didn't change the world in any way. In fact, for decades, Charlie Fallon's baseball career was all but forgotten. Box scores printed in the newspapers at baseball's beginning were not always accurate. Of all the box scores printed the following day, July 1, 1905, only one, the one that appeared in the *New York Times*, mentioned Charlie Fallon. This was overlooked or missed in the official annals of baseball and Charlie Fallon, for a time, vanished from baseball history.

Enter Bill Haber, a baseball historian and a founding member of the Society of American Baseball Research (SABR). Haber had a penchant for discovering and finding the overlooked or missing players from baseball's earliest days—players like Charlie Fallon who were omitted from *The Baseball Encyclopedia* and the official records at the Baseball Hall of Fame. Through Haber's diligent and persistent research, he was able to "find" over 300 players who were added to baseball's official register. One of those players was Charlie Fallon.

Fallon's lone appearance was as obscure as his entire career. It is not a surprise that it was missed in an era when all record-keeping was done by hand with pencil and paper. Fallon's appearance came, not as a batter or as a fielder, but as a pinch runner in the last inning of the game.

On the day of Charlie Fallon's one big league appearance, the

New York Highlanders were playing the Philadelphia Athletics. The Athletics were in third place, but they would be the eventual pennant winners. The Highlanders came into the game with a record of 23-31. They finished the season at 71-78, a thoroughly mediocre team, and the only team, as we shall see, to have three *Least Among Them* players take the field for it. The Athletics pitcher opposing the Highlanders that day was Eddie Plank. Plank was already one of the American League's great pitchers having won over twenty games each of the previous three seasons. Plank would go on to win 326 games in his Hall of Fame career.

Numerous legendary players were involved in the game. The Highlanders' 1905 team included Hall of Famers Wee Wille Keeler, Clark Griffith, and Jack Chesbro. Chesbro had pitched the previous day, defeating the Athletics 13-4. He and Griffith did not play in the game. Willie Keeler played the entire game in right field. Keeler had one hit that day. Also on the roster were Hal Chase and Kid Elberfeld, both of whom, along with Keeler and Griffith, served as captains (an honor awarded much more freely in those days) of the Highlanders. For the Athletics, in addition to Eddie Plank, such notables as Chief Bender and Rube Waddell (both future Hall of Famers) were on the squad. For Fallon's first, and only game, he was surrounded by legends.

The Athletics defeated the Highlanders 7-4. Pitcher Eddie

1, Kritchel; 2, Bronkie; 3, Wilson; 4, Crook; 5, O'Leary; 6, Fallon; 7, Moffitt; 8, Justice; 9, Gastmeyer; 10, Noyes; 11, Skelly.
HARTFORD TEAM—CONNECTICUT LEAGUE.
Photo from the author's collection.

25

Plank enjoyed an easy afternoon until he tired in the ninth inning after allowing the first two Highlander batters to reach base. It was the first of those batters, catcher Deacon McGuire, a 41-year-old veteran of baseball's earliest days, for whom Fallon pinch ran. Fallon assumed his place on the base paths. Since the Highlanders had the potential tying run at bat, the manager of the Athletics, a future Hall of Famer himself, Connie Mack, went to his bullpen and summoned Rube Waddell. Waddell faced three batters, including Wee Willie Keeler, retiring the side in order to preserve the win for the Athletics.

It was most likely that after his lone appearance with the Yankees that Charlie Fallon moved on to play professional baseball in 1905 for the Hartford Senators in the Connecticut League. Statistics for this team are limited. It is known that during that 1905 season, Charlie Fallon, a small man standing only 5 feet, 6 inches, played the outfield. He appeared in 56 games that first year banging out 65 hits in 254 at bats for a mediocre batting average of .256.

Charlie Fallon played with Hartford each season through the 1908 season. Following his stay there, he played two more seasons of minor league baseball, bouncing between numerous teams that included Montreal, Toronto, New Haven, Binghamton, and Troy. These were mostly A and B level squads. From the information that can be gathered, Fallon hit an unremarkable .249 in his minor league career. His best season may have been 1906, for Hartford, where he hit .302. In 1908, three years after his lone appearance in the Major Leagues, he hit his only home run.

After baseball, Charlie Fallon settled down and married. He had three children. To support his family, Fallon worked in a variety of occupations. He was involved in the ship-building industry, worked in real estate, and opened a tea room, The Brown Derby, a place that legend holds may have been a speakeasy. The Depression hit Charlie Fallon hard. He lost many assets including the properties he owned and at one time was reduced to peddling apples. Eventually he was able to find work. Toward the end of his life, to make ends meet, Charlie Fallon operated an ice cream truck. He died in 1960 in Kings Park, New York.

Extra Innings
A History of the NY Yankees Captains

I n his short time in the Major Leagues, Charlie Fallon brushed shoulders with four players who would be captains of the Highlanders. In their history, the Yankees have had fifteen different players earn the title "Captain." This has largely been a ceremonial title, often conferred upon the most notable star on a team.

The most recent Yankees captain was Derek Jeter who held this title longer than any other player. Derek Jeter was named captain in 2003 and he held this title for the rest of his career. He retired following the 2014 baseball season.

The player with the shortest tenure as captain of the Yankees was their greatest player, Babe Ruth. The Babe was the Yankees captain for a mere five days in 1922. Not long after being named captain, Babe Ruth had an altercation with an umpire after being called out running the bases. Ruth threw dirt into the umpire's face and was ejected from the game. Following this, as he left the field, the Babe charged into the stands to attack a fan who had been calling him names. For these actions, Babe Ruth was suspended by the American League and he also lost his title as Yankees captain.

Up until 1922, the Highlanders/Yankees had a captain every season. Their first captain was Clark Griffith an eventual member of the Hall of Fame. Griffith was one of the founding members of the American League in 1901 and had helped pitch the Chicago White Sox to the league's first pennant before coming to New York.

Kid Elberfeld, a shortstop, was the next Highlanders captain. In his era, Elberfeld was considered one of the game's greatest shortstops.

Following Elberfeld, future Hall of Famer Wee Willie Keeler

served as the Yankees captain. Known as one of baseball's best batters, Keeler was a star before playing for the Highlanders.

Following Keeler as captain was one of the most controversial baseball players of all time, Hal Chase, a first baseman. Chase is considered one the greatest defensive first basemen of all time. He was also the first true homegrown Highlanders star. Unfortunately, Chase was involved in numerous allegations of gambling and throwing games. He was traded to the White Sox during the 1913 season.

In 1913, the captain of the team (now known as the Yankees) was the player/manager Frank Chance who had secured his reputation as the first baseman on the Chicago Cubs and is immortalized in the famous poem *Baseball's Sad Lexicon* which is better known as "Tinker to Evers to Chance." Frank Chance didn't last long with the Yankees as a player or manager. By 1914, his playing and managerial careers with New York were over.

Roger Peckinpaugh, a shortstop, who had briefly replaced Chance as manager in 1914, at just 23 years old was the youngest manager ever, was the next captain. Peckinpaugh was known for his calm demeanor and his outstanding defensive play. Toward the end of his career, he helped lead the 1925 Washington Senators to their only world championship along the way earning the league's Most Valuable Player Award.

In total, four Yankees shortstops held this honor of being captain—Jeter, Peckinpaugh, Kid Elberfeld, and the captain who replaced Babe Ruth, Everett Scott who was the Yankees captain from 1922 until 1925. Scott was baseball's first "Iron Man." He played in 1,307 consecutive games setting the Major League record for consecutive games played that would eventually be broken by the man who would one day be the next Yankees captain, Lou Gehrig.

The last game that Everett Scott played as a starter was May 20, 1925. Two weeks later, on June 1, Gehrig began his amazing streak of 2,130 consecutive games played. No one at the time, of course knew that the legacies of these two players would intersect in such a way.

Gehrig, who it can be argued was the second greatest Yankee player of all time (after only Babe Ruth) was named their captain in 1935. Gehrig's consecutive games streak wasn't broken until 1995 when it was surpassed by Cal Ripken, Jr. Known as "The Pride of the Yankees," Gehrig was a hardworking and dignified player. Gehrig's career, and life, were cut short by Amyotrophic Lateral Sclerosis (ALS) which is today is better known as Lou Gehrig's Disease. In deference to his life and legacy, upon Gehrig's retirement no Yankee held the title as captain until 1976.

In 1976, the Yankees moved into a refurbished Yankee Stadium. They also took their place atop the American League standings again that year. The man who was considered the heart of that team was its catcher Thurman Munson. He was named Yankees captain in 1976 the same year that he won the American League Most Valuable Player Award. Like Gehrig, Munson's career ended tragically. Munson died in a plane crash on August 2, 1979.

In 1982, Graig Nettles, a standout third baseman who had been with the Yankees since 1973, was named their captain. Nettles did not remain captain for long. Just before the 1984 season, he was traded to the San Diego Padres.

For the 1986 through 1988 seasons, the Yankees employed co-captains for the only time in their history. The two honorees were longtime stars Willie Randolph, a second baseman, and Ron Guidry, a starting pitcher. Both Randolph and Guidry were soft-spoken All-Stars. The 1988 season was the last in New York for both players.

Don Mattingly was the Yankees captain from 1991 through the end of his career in 1995. In the 1980s, Don Mattingly was considered one of baseball's greatest players. Unfortunately, injuries took away his production and robbed him of a Hall of Fame career.

Interestingly, in their great history, there were very few times when the Yankees won a World Series while employing a captain. After appointing Lou Gehrig as the Yankees captain in 1935, the team won the World Series in 1936, 1937, and 1938. The Yankees won two World Series, 1977 and 1978, with Thurman Munson as their captain. The only other Yankees team with a captain to win a World Series was Derek Jeter's 2009 squad. In total, only 6 of the Yankees' 27 world championships came while they had a team captain.

PHILADELPHIA ATHLETICS at NEW YORK HIGHLANDERS

Friday, June 30, 1905 (Hilltop Park)

	1	2	3	4	5	6	7	8	9		R	H	E
PHI	1	0	0	0	1	1	0	2	2		7	13	1
NY	0	0	0	0	2	1	1	0	0		4	13	2

PHI		AB	R	H	RBI	NY		AB	R	H	RBI
Hartsel	LF	3	1	1	0	Dougherty	LF	4	0	0	0
Hoffman	CF	4	2	2	1	Keeler	RF	5	0	1	0
Davis	1B	5	0	1	2	Conroy	3B	4	0	0	0
Cross	3B	5	1	2	1	Williams	2B	3	1	2	0
Seybold	RF	3	1	1	0	Chase	1B	4	0	1	0
Murphy	2B	3	1	1	0	Elberfeld	SS	4	1	3	0
Knight	SS	5	0	2	2	Fultz	CF	4	0	0	0
Schrecongost	C	4	0	0	0	McGuire	C	4	1	3	1
Plank	P	4	1	3	0	Fallon	PR				
Waddell	P					Hogg	P	1	0	0	0
						Yeager	PH	1	0	1	1
						Powell	P	2	1	2	1
						Kleinow	PR				

PHI	IP	H	R	BB	SO	NY	IP	H	R	BB	SO
Plank	8	13	4	3	1	Hogg - L	5	5	2	3	0
Waddell - W	1	0	0	0	2	Powell	4	8	5	1	2

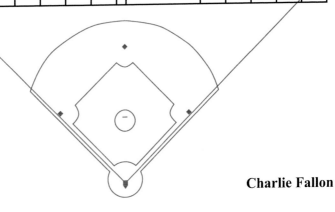

Charlie Fallon

CHAPTER FOUR
ART GOODWIN (1905)

The first pitcher to be included in this history is Art Goodwin, also a member of the 1905 Highlanders. Distance and time have left room for doubt about why the careers of Frank Verdi and Elvio Jimenez ended with their one brief game appearance as they performed admirably enough. One would have had to believe that they also exhibited their talent in other non-game situations. With Art Goodwin, the reason why he did not get another opportunity seems perfectly clear. Art Goodwin's lone opportunity was a disaster. His opportunity came on the last day of the season, he did poorly, and there was probably no reason to bring him back for a second audition.

Art Goodwin reached the Highlanders as a twenty-nine-year-old. He had been playing professional, albeit minor league, baseball since 1898. Goodwin's career began in New York State with the Bradford Pirates of the F-League and continued in 1899 with the Wilkes-Barre Coal Barons of the Single-A Atlantic League. In those early years, A-Ball was considered the highest level of the minor leagues. That year Art Goodwin appeared in 18 games, making 16 starts. It proved to be a good year for Goodwin as he enjoyed an impressive 11-4 won/loss record. He also played a few games in the outfield. Goodwin's career seemed to be heading toward success. He began the 1900 season playing again for Wilkes-Barre. While his statistics are unavailable, it is clear that by June he was no longer with Wilkes-Barre and was playing for the Utica Reds. By 1901, he was a man in motion and he began playing for a variety of teams over the next few seasons: The Schenectady Electricians, Albany Senators, Schenectady Frog Alleys, and the Memphis Egyptians. It was after his 1905 season with Memphis that Goodwin was afforded his lone Major League appearance with the New York Highlanders. He might have gotten this opportunity because of some strange occurrences that impacted the last day of the 1905 season.

Arthur Goodwin's chance as a big leaguer came, like Frank Verdi's, in Boston. He, too, did not have the opportunity to wear Yankee (Highlander) pinstripes, but, it can be assumed that this was something he did not even think or care about. The Highlanders (by then called the Yankees) did not begin wearing pinstripes until 1913.

Interestingly, the 1905 baseball season ended with twelve of the sixteen Major League teams playing doubleheaders on the last day of the season. (In the National League, the Chicago Cubs played the Pittsburgh Pirates in a single game, while in the American League the Detroit Tigers and the Cleveland Naps also played a single game.) The Highlanders played two that day in Boston.

We have already been through the list of notable Highlanders on that 1905 team. For the Red Sox of Boston, there were also a number of future Hall of Fame players. These included Jesse Burkett, Jimmy Collins, and a pitcher named Cy Young. These Red Sox had won the 1904 pennant and were the defending champions.

On the last day of the 1905 season, the Red Sox swept the Highlanders winning the two games by the scores of 7-6 and 12-9. The actual play-by-play information from those games are unavailable, but Art Goodwin's pitching numbers are recorded in the box score of the second game. It wasn't pretty. Goodwin faced five batters. He recorded one out. He gave up two hits. He walked two others. He also threw a wild pitch. All four of the runners that reached base off Goodwin, scored. For reasons now lost, only three of the runs were considered earned runs. After his lone partial inning of work, Art Goodwin left the Major Leagues with an ERA of 81.00. It doesn't get much worse.

In 1906, Goodwin returned to the minors. He played on the farm for five more seasons and never made it back to the big leagues. The teams Goodwin played for had some unique names: The Mobile Sea Gulls, Gulfport Crabs, and the Vicksburg Hill Billies of the Cotton States League, and the Syracuse Stars and the Binghamton Bingoes of the New York State League.

There was one curious situation that took place with Art Goodwin and the Troy Trojans that led to him playing for the Binghamton Bingoes in 1911. It seems that Art Goodwin was out of baseball in 1910. In late May 1911, the Troy Trojans needed some pitching help. Jim Tamsett, the player/manager of the Trojans reached out to Goodwin. Goodwin and Tamsett had been teammates in 1902 with the Albany Senators and in 1905 with the Memphis Egyptians. Via telegrams, Goodwin affirmed that he was in shape and able to play. A deal was struck and it seemed that Art Goodwin would be able to join the team. But things did not work out so smoothly. Tamsett never sent the money due to Goodwin as his would-be salary. Art Goodwin then tried, day after day, to reach Tamsett to no avail. Finally, by mid-June, Goodwin heard back. Goodwin was told that the Trojan pitchers were in good shape and his services were no longer needed. Goodwin, who had been working out, then reached out to Harry Lumley, the manager of the Binghamton Bingoes offering his services as a pitcher. Lumley accepted and Art Goodwin pitched with them for the remainder of the year. Goodwin claims to have won "six straight games and 11 out of 14" for Binghamton. (It must be noted that Baseball-Reference lists Art Goodwin's record as 7-6, although many of these early records are incomplete.)

That 1911 season was Art Goodwin's last in professional baseball.

While his career Minor League statistics are incomplete, Art Goodwin seems to have been a decent Minor League pitcher. His records indicate that he won 65 games and lost 41.

There are many players that were outstanding Minor League baseball players and just not talented (or lucky) enough for success in the Major Leagues. Art Goodwin played professional baseball for thirteen seasons. For one brief moment, he was a Major Leaguer. That experience did not go as well as he had hoped. Still, he made it and left his name, forever, in the record books.

Extra Innings
The Top Yankees' Minor League Affiliates

At the start of his career, Art Goodwin pitched for the Wilkes-Barre Coal Barons, a Single-A franchise. Today the International League's franchise in that area is the Scranton/Wilkes-Barre RailRiders. Since 2007, the Scranton/Wilkes-Barre franchise has been the Yankees' highest-level minor league team. As currently constructed, the highest minor league teams play at the Triple-A level. It hasn't always been this way.

At the turn of the century, and in fact, through most of the first half of the 20th century, the teams in the minor leagues were not affiliated with Major League ball clubs. The first team to employ a minor league "farm" system was the St. Louis Cardinals in 1921. This idea was the brainchild of Branch Rickey, one of baseball's great innovators and thinkers. In addition to developing the idea of the minor leagues, it was Branch Rickey who helped baseball break the color barrier by signing Jackie Robinson to a contract with the Brooklyn Dodgers.

The Yankees began employing a minor league system in 1932. That year they had five teams. The highest-level team was the Newark Bears who played in the International League which was then considered Double-A. In 1932, the Yankees had a Single-A team, the Springfield Rifles, who played in Massachusetts. Finally, that year, there were three "Rookie Level" teams in the Yankees organization, the Binghamton Triplets, the Cumberland Colts, and the Erie Sailors. The Sailors were managed by former Philadelphia Athletics pitching great Chief Bender. Remarkably, thirty players from that 1932 Newark Bears team reached the Major Leagues including such future Yankee stars as Red Rolfe, George Selkirk, and Johnny Murphy.

Throughout the 1930s and into the 1940s the highest-level

Yankees minor league teams played at the Double-A level. The Newark Bears were a constant through 1945, but, at certain times, the Yankees also franchised other Double-A level teams. These included the Oakland Oaks (1935-1937) and the Kansas City Blues (1937-1945). The manager of the 1945 Kansas City squad was the future Hall of Fame manager of the Yankees, Casey Stengel.

Throughout those years, minor league baseball proliferated through the country. Big league clubs employed a host of minor league franchises. Between 1937 and 1941, the Yankees never had fewer than eleven minor league teams. The high point for the minor leagues occurred right after World War II. In 1948, there were 24 teams affiliated with the Yankees. Franchises soon came to realize that having such a vast minor league system was unsustainable. By 1960, the Yankees employed fewer than ten teams. Since that time, the numbers of teams in the Yankees organization has fluctuated from a low of four (in 1975, 1977, and 1978) to as many as nine. Major League Baseball reformatted the minor leagues for the 2021 season and the Yankees again have just four affiliates.

Beginning in 1946, Triple-A became the highest level of the minor leagues. Between 1946 and 1949, Kansas City, in the American Association, and Newark, in the International League, were the Yankees' two Triple-A franchises. The Yankees broke with Newark after the 1949 season. Kansas City remained the Yankees highest minor league team until 1956. In 1951, Mickey Mantle passed through Kansas City on his way to the Major Leagues. The Yankees affiliation with Kansas City ended in 1956 when the city became the new home for the Major League Athletics who moved to Kansas City from Philadelphia. During this time period, the Yankees sporadically employed Triple-A franchises with the San Francisco Seals (1951) and the Syracuse Chiefs (1953).

In 1955, the Denver Bears became the Yankees lone Triple-A franchise. In 1956, the Yankees again had two Triple-A squads. These included Denver and a new team, the Richmond Virginians of the International League. Denver stayed affiliated with the Yankees through 1958 and Richmond through 1964.

For two years, 1965 and 1966, the Toledo Mud Huns were

the Yankees Triple-A affiliate. The 1965 Mud Hens team was managed by Frank Verdi and featured a twenty-five-year-old out-fielder named Elvio Jimenez two *Least Among Them* Yankees.

Beginning in 1967, the Yankees began a long affiliation with the Syracuse Chiefs. They were the Yankees top minor league franchise through 1977. Frank Verdi managed the Syracuse squad from midway through the 1968 season through 1970, and again in 1972. In 1969, Verdi's squad that included future Yankee great Thurman Munson. That team won the International League championship.

For one year, 1978, Tacoma, Washington was the Yankees' highest-level minor league club. Interestingly, this team finished in first place and was considered the league's co-champions when the entire championship series was cancelled due to rain.

In 1979, the Yankees franchise returned to the International League with the Columbus Clippers. That franchise remained the Yankees' Triple-A representative through the 2006 season. Numerous notable future Yankees passed through Columbus on their way to making their mark in the majors. This list includes Dave Righetti, Don Mattingly, Bernie Williams, Derek Jeter, Andy Pettitte, Jorge Posada, and Mariano Rivera. Frank Verdi managed the Clippers in 1981 and 1982.

Since 2007, Scranton/Wilkes-Barre has been the home of the Yankees' top minor league squad. In 2012, the Scranton/Wilkes-Barre stadium needed extensive renovations. The team vacated its park and played the entire season on the road utilizing six different locations as home ballparks: Rochester, New York; Batavia, New York; Syracuse, New York; Buffalo, New York; Allentown, Pennsylvania; and Pawtucket, Rhode Island. Their new state-of-the-art stadium, PNC Park, opened in 2013. Starting in 2021, the Scranton/Wilkes-Barre Rail Riders became part of the six team Triple A-Northeast Division of the Triple A-East.

NEW YORK HIGHLANDERS at BOSTON AMERICANS

Saturday, October 7, 1905 (Huntington Avenue Baseball Grounds)

	1	2	3	4	5		R	H	E
NY	0	3	1	4	1		9	8	3
BOS	3	1	2	6	0		12	12	6

NY		AB	R	H	RBI	BOS		AB	R	H	RBI
Hahn	CF	4	1	0	0	Parent	SS	4	1	3	1
Keeler	RF	3	1	0	0	Stahl	CF	4	2	1	0
Dougherty	LF	3	2	1	0	Freeman	3B	3	1	0	0
LaPorte	2B	3	1	3	1	Burkett	LF	3	3	3	2
Chase	1B	3	1	0	0	Grimshaw	1B	2	3	1	3
Oldring	SS	3	0	1	1	Godwin	2B	2	0	2	4
Connor	C	3	2	1	2	Ambruster	C	3	1	1	0
Cockman	3B	2	1	1	1	Hughes	P	2	0	0	0
Newton	P	1	0	0	0	Dinneen	PH/P	1	0	1	1
Puttmann	PH	1	0	1	1						
Goodwin	P										
Hogg	P	0	0	0	1						
Kleinow	PH	1	0	0	0						
Griffith	P	0	0	0	0						

NY	IP	H	R	BB	SO	BOS	IP	H	R	BB	SO
Newton - L	3	6	6	2	2	Hughes - W	4	8	8	0	1
Goodwin	0.1	2	4	2	0	Dinneen	1	0	1	1	1
Hogg	0.2	3	2	1	1						
Griffith	1	1	0	0	0						

Art Goodwin

Credit Jewish Major Leaguers, Inc.

CHAPTER FIVE
PHIL COONEY (1905)

Third baseman Phil Cooney is the third, and final, player who had his sole Major League experience as a Highlander in 1905. Born in New York, this player was named Philip Clarence Cohen. He changed his name to Cooney during this period because of blatant anti-Semitism in society.

Phil Cooney's baseball story is similar to the story of Charlie Fallon. Cooney was only in his second year of professional baseball, playing in New Jersey for the Paterson Intruders of the C-Level Hudson River League when he was called to play for the Highlanders. While his 1905 statistics are not available, we know that Cooney was probably not much of a hitter. For example, in 1904, for Paterson, he batted .237 in 426 at-bats. The year after his one game Major League career, in 1906, Cooney batted .191 in 314 at bats for Paterson.

An interesting incident occurred during the 1905 season that involved the Paterson team that both Phil Cooney and Art Goodwin played for. On June 12, 1905, the Paterson squad was scheduled to play a game against the Poughkeepsie Colts, however, there were no umpires. Knowing that as a man of the cloth his judgment would be deemed honest, the Reverend C.S. Rahm of the Evangelical Lutheran Church of Poughkeepsie went down to the field and offered to umpire the game. The teams agreed and the game proceded with the pastor ministering to the duties as umpire. By the accounts of day, Reverend Rahm gave a satisfactory performance.

So it was on a fateful September day, late in the 1905 season, that Phil Cooney played Major League Baseball for the New York Highlanders on loan from the Paterson team. Like many of the players previously mentioned, Phil Cooney's game came in a loss as the Highlanders were defeated by the St. Louis Browns 7-2. This was a St. Louis team that would lose 99 games in 1905. Shortstop Bobby Wallace, who would be elected to Baseball's Hall of Fame in 1953, was the one standout from that Browns team.

By September 27, 1905, it was apparent that the Highlanders and the Browns were playing out the string. The Highlanders that day might have needed a third baseman. Cooney, a native New Yorker playing across the Hudson River in Paterson, New Jersey may have been the perfect player to hold down the position. Unfortunately, he did not do much more than that. In the field, we know that Cooney handled two balls cleanly. He made one putout and had one assist. Cooney was not charged with any errors. At the plate, the left-handed hitting third baseman had three at-bats. He went hitless, striking out once. When he left Hilltop Park in Manhattan after the game, Phil Cooney's Major League career was over.

Like so many others, though, Phil Cooney continued to play professional ball. In fact, through baseball he toured much of the continental United States in a day when the coasts seemed much more distant than today. Considering that Major League Baseball did not reach the West coast until 1958, the variety of teams that Cooney played for is somewhat amazing.

Phil Cooney played 17 seasons in the minors and in such di-

COONEY, SPOKANE, N. W. L
Courtesy of TCMA Ltd.

verse locations as Paterson, New Jersey; Johnstown, Pennsylvania; Portland, Oregon; Spokane, Washington; Sioux City, Iowa; and Omaha, Nebraska. After all that travel, he returned to New Jersey in 1918 to play for the Jersey City Skeeters. In 1920, Phil Cooney then returned to the West coast and ended his career (after a stop to play again for Sioux City) with the Portland Beavers of the Pacific Coast League. Cooney's incomplete lifetime minor league batting average is recorded as a pedestrian .247.

During those travels through the bush leagues, Phil Cooney was involved in a play rarely seen on the baseball diamond—he turned an unassisted triple play. It occurred in 1917 while Cooney was playing for the Omaha Rourkes in a game against the Denver Bears. Cooney accomplished his feat during the sixth inning when Denver had runners on first and second with no outs. The runners must have been running with the pitch as the batter hit a line drive that Phil Cooney, playing first base, caught. Cooney then tagged the runner who had taken off from first and raced to the second-base bag ahead of the returning runner finishing this unassisted triple play.

After his career, Phil Cooney stayed in Paterson, New Jersey. His minor league career must have been impressive enough because in 1967, Phil Cooney was elected to the Greater Paterson National Sport Hall of Fame. In fact, Phil Cooney, who had passed away ten years prior to this election, was in the inaugural class elected to this organization. Other baseball players or related personnel elected to the Paterson Sports Hall of Fame were Hall of Famers Honus Wagner and Larry Doby, and Johnny Vander Meer, who was the only Major League pitcher to throw back-to-back no-hitters. Long-time Yankees executive Ed Barrow is also enshrined in this Hall of Fame.

The 1905 Highlanders rank as the only team with three *Least Among Them* Yankees. Each player put on the Highlander uniform for one single game. None of the three had established any type of minor league dominance before reaching baseball's highest level, yet were offered a chance to play in the big leagues. All three continued to play and chase the dream of returning after they returned to the minors. Of course, for each, those dreams would remain unfulfilled.

Extra Innings
The Unassisted Triple Play

T he unassisted triple play is one of the rarest occurrences in Major League Baseball and has only happened fifteen times. Interestingly, the first three times it occurred in a big league game, the Cleveland franchise (known as the Naps or the Indians) was involved. In 1909 Neal Ball, the Cleveland shortstop, turned an unassisted triple play against the Boston Red Sox. Eleven years later, in 1920, Bill Wambsganss, the Cleveland second baseman, turned the feat against the Brooklyn Robins (Dodgers) in the World Series, the only time this play has occurred in the fall classic. Finally, in 1923, Red Sox first baseman George Burns turned the feat against the Cleveland Indians.

Future Yankees manager Johnny Neun (who managed the team for just 14 games) turned the first ever game-ending unassisted triple play while playing for the Detroit Tigers in 1927. Playing first base, Nuenn caught a line drive off the bat of the wonderfully named Homer Summa. That was the first out. He then promptly tagged the runner from first (Charlie Jamieson) and then trotted all the way to second base to tag that bag for the third out as the base runner there, Glenn Myatt, had taken off on the pitch and was already rounding third base.

There has been only one triple play in baseball history that involved the Yankees. This was in a game that occurred at Yankee Stadium on May 29, 2000. In that game, the Yankees were leading 1-0 over the Oakland A's heading into the bottom of the sixth inning. The inning began well for the Yankees. Following a walk to Paul O'Neill, Bernie Williams hit a long triple giving the Yankees a two-run lead. Tino Martinez was then hit by a pitch. The next batter, Jorge Posada reached base on an error that scored Williams, increasing the Yankees lead to three runs. The player making the error was the A's second baseman Randy Velarde, a former Yankee. He would soon make amends for his error.

With Martinez at second base and Posada at first, Shane Spencer came to bat. With the runners moving on the pitch, Spencer hit a line drive at Velarde. In an instant he recorded the out and tagged Posada who had almost reached second base. Velarde then took two quick steps to his right and tagged second base for the unassisted triple play, the only time this play has occurred at Yankee Stadium.

ST. LOUIS BROWNS at NEW YORK HIGHLANDERS

Wednesday, September 27, 1905 (Hilltop Park)

	1	2	3	4	5	6	7	8	9		R	H	E
STL	2	0	0	1	1	1	0	0	2		7	11	0
NY	0	0	0	0	0	0	0	0	2		2	5	5

STL		AB	R	H	RBI	NY		AB	R	H	RBI
Stone	LF	4	1	1	0	Hahn	LF	3	0	0	0
Rockenfield	2B	5	2	4	1	Keeler	RF	4	0	1	0
Frisk	RF	5	1	2	3	Elberfeld	SS	4	1	0	0
Wallace	SS	5	1	1	0	Chase	1B	4	1	1	0
Jones	1B	3	1	2	1	Williams	2B	3	0	1	0
Gleason	3B	4	0	0	0	Fultz	CF	3	0	0	1
Koehler	CF	2	0	0	0	**Cooney**	3B	3	0	0	0
Spencer	C	4	0	0	1	Dougherty	PH	0	0	0	1
Howell	P	4	1	1	0	Kleinow	C	1	0	0	0
						McCarthy	C	2	0	0	0
						Puttmann	P	1	0	0	0
						Good	P	2	0	2	0

STL	IP	H	R	BB	SO	NY	IP	H	R	BB	SO
Howell - W	9	5	2	5	4	Puttmann - L	5	7	4	0	2
						Good	4	4	3	3	2

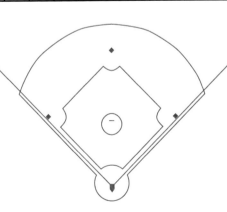

Phil Cooney

Columbus Clippers
RH Pitcher
ROGER SLAGLE—18

Card from the author's collection.

CHAPTER SIX
ROGER SLAGLE (1979)

Roger Slagle was drafted by three Major League Baseball clubs, the Philadelphia Phillies, the San Diego Padres, and the New York Yankees, during and following his college career at the University of Kansas, where he set the school's career ERA record (1.81) that still stands.

After his successful college career, the Yankees signed Slagle in 1976 and assigned him to Single-A Fort Lauderdale to begin his professional career. Slagle did well in his first minor league season earning a 6-3 record with a 2.25 ERA. In 1977, Slagle was promoted to the Double-A West Haven Yankees where he again met success winning ten games against nine losses over 24 games with an impressive 2.81 ERA. By 1978, Roger Slagle was starring for the Tacoma Yankees, the team's Triple-A franchise in the Pacific Coast League. Slagle's 13-8 record earned him recognition as the Yankees' Triple-A Pitcher of the Year. He seemed primed for success in the majors.

The winter between the 1978 and 1979 seasons though wasn't a good one for Slagle. While working a factory job, he tore a tendon in his pitching elbow. For most of the 1979 season, Roger Slagle went through rehabilitation to come back from this injury. He pitched for Fort Lauderdale and the Yankees new Triple-A franchise, the Columbus Clippers. Slagle's progress was slow, as he recorded a 9-12, 4.41 combined record at those two stops, but when the Major League rosters expanded on September 1, 1979, Roger Slagle was brought up to the Major Leagues with the Yankees. In spite of the fact that his minor league season was not impressive, the Yankees still had high hopes for Roger Slagle.

The Yankees of the late 1970s and early 1980s were extremely successful. In 1976, they were the American League champions. In both 1977 and 1978, the Yankees were World Series winners. The Yankees won the American League East in 1980. In 1981, they were, again, American League champions. The lone year between 1976 and 1981 when the Yankees did not reach the postseason was Slagle's season, 1979.

1979 was a difficult year for the Yankees. In April, designated hitter and sometimes catcher Cliff Johnson, and Yankees closer Rich Gossage had an argument and fought in the showers. As a result, Gossage severely injured his thumb and was disabled for two months. As a team, the Yankees were never able to put together any consistent winning streaks. They stayed mired in the middle of the pack through July. On August 1, the Yankees sat in fourth place with a 58-48 record, but they were 14 games behind the league-leading Baltimore Orioles. The next day, the history of the Yankees would forever change.

August 2, 1979 was one of the worst days in franchise history. On that day, Thurman Munson, the captain of the Yankees, crashed his personal airplane and died. The team never recovered. The sadness and grief that comes with sudden loss cast a pall over this team for the remainder of the year.

As the 1979 season was winding down, the Yankees also knew that that they would have to begin to plan for the 1980 season. The pitching staff seemed to be a particular concern. Star pitcher Jim "Catfish" Hunter was retiring and they did not know how much veteran Luis Tiant had left to offer the team. Youngsters Jim Beattie and Ken Clay were erratic. The only constants in the starting rotation were veteran All-Stars Ron Guidry and Tommy John. An opening seemed possible for a young pitcher of Roger Slagle's ability.

Unfortunately, though, even with everything lined up for Slagle, things do not always work out as planned. Sometimes even perfect just isn't good enough. That was the case for Roger Slagle in his one Yankees moment that came on September 7, 1979, when he took the mound for the Yankees as a relief pitcher against the Tigers in Detroit.

The 1979 Tigers were a solid squad, an up-and-coming team with a strong nucleus that would eventually form the backbone of their 1984 team that would win the World Series. Two of the players on that team, shortstop Alan Trammell and pitcher Jack Morris, are now enshrined in the Hall of Fame. Many baseball experts feel that their second baseman, Lou Whitaker, also belongs in Cooperstown.

While the Yankees, the reigning world champs at the time, had a roster filled with All-Stars, the only future Hall of Famer in the lineup on September 7 was right fielder Reggie Jackson. (Rich Gossage would also earn enshrinement, but he would not pitch in that game.)

The game didn't go as the Yankees hoped from the start. Clay was their starting pitcher. He lasted but two innings. Jim Kaat then pitched four innings in relief. With the Yankees down 6-0, Roger Slagle was called by Yankees manager Billy Martin to replace Kaat and work the bottom of the seventh inning for the Yankees.

Slagle was not offered an easy task. His debut would be against the heart of the Tigers batting order. The first batter Slagle faced was their All-Star left fielder Steve Kemp who entered the game with a .323 batting average. Slagle coaxed Kemp into hitting a soft grounder between first and second base that was fielded by Yankees second baseman Willie Randolph. Slagle rushed to first ahead of the speedy Kemp, caught the toss from Randolph, and recorded his first putout. It was a great beginning. Champ

Summers followed Kemp and struck out. Jason Thompson, an excellent power hitter, then grounded out to third baseman Fred Stanley. A better start could not be imagined, Slagle retired all three batters he faced.

The Yankees went down quickly in the top of the eighth inning and Roger Slagle returned to the mound to pitch the bottom of the frame. He first faced Jerry Morales who grounded out to third. Next, Slagle struck out Lance Parrish. Aurelio Rodriguez then lined out to Reggie Jackson in right field. Once again, it was three batters up, and three batters down. Inning over.

In the top of the ninth inning, the Yankees went down quietly. Jack Billingham, the Tigers pitcher, closed out the relatively easy 6-0 victory for Detroit.

As Roger Slagle entered the postgame clubhouse, he must have felt full of pride. He came into the game, faced six batters, and retired them all; two by strikeout. No batter had reached base. He fielded his position well. In short, his Major League debut was perfect. Sadly, it was the last Major League game he would ever play.

Days after this game, in an ironic twist, the Yankees sent Slagle back to the Columbus Clippers and recalled another pitcher, Rick Anderson, who happened to be Slagle's closest friend in the game. A few weeks later, Anderson pitched his only game as a Yankee facing ten batters over slightly more than two innings. Anderson allowed one run on one hit, but he walked four batters. The Yankees lost that game 16-3 to the Cleveland Indians. (Anderson does not qualify as a *Least Among Them* Yankee because he had another Major League opportunity. After the 1979 season, he was traded to the Seattle Mariners as part of a package of players in exchange for outfielder Ruppert Jones. Anderson may have had only one appearance as a Yankee, but made five big league appearances for the Mariners in 1980.)

One reason that Roger Slagle may have been sent down was that he was not fully recovered from the various arm injuries that had sidelined him. At the time, Slagle himself admitted, "The first 10 or 15 minutes that I warm up the pain is agonizing, but after that everything is OK." If the Yankees were considering using Slagle as a relief pitcher, this continued pain would have impacted

ROGER SLAGLE
Pitcher

Courtesy of TCMA Ltd.

on their ability to use him quickly in a game, something necessary for a relief pitcher.

Roger Slagle began the 1980 season with Columbus Clippers. It was there, while they moved him from the bullpen to the starting rotation, that he developed more serious arm trouble. Because of the setback, the Yankees moved Slagle down to the Nashville Sounds, their Double-A affiliate in the Southern League. Things were about to get worse—while with Nashville, Slagle contracted conjunctivitis (pink eye) after using a teammate's towel to rub his face. Pitching with blurred vision, Slagle was unable to stop a line drive hit back at him. The ball hit him squarely in the face breaking his nose and ending his season.

Slagle came back in 1981 to Nashville and pitched well enough, but arm troubles, including a torn rotator cuff, ended his professional career in 1982 while still pitching for the Sounds. With that injury, Roger Slagle left baseball forever.

Extra Innings
The Longest-Tenured Yankees Teammates

T wo stars from the Detroit Tigers teams of the late 1970s and throughout the 1980s were shortstop Alan Trammell and second baseman Lou Whitaker. Amazingly, they both began their big league careers on the same day, September 9, 1977. These two players starred together for Detroit from 1978 through 1995 comprising an excellent double-play combination, a pairing some consider one of the best of all time. Their partnership was the longest of any two teammates in the history of baseball. In total, they played 1,918 games together over eighteen consecutive years—a remarkable accomplishment.

In comparison, the Yankees have never had two players (non-pitchers) spend that many seasons together on the field. The two players that had the longest consecutive streak of years played together were two of the more recent Yankees—Derek Jeter and Jorge Posada. Jeter, a shortstop, and Posada, a catcher, were Major League teammates for fifteen consecutive seasons from 1997 through 2011.

As remarkable as that is, if one were to count their minor league careers, Jeter and Posada actually were actually together longer. Drafted two years apart, Posada (1990) and Jeter (1992) crossed paths numerous times during their minor league trek to the big leagues. They were first teammates for the Single-A Greensboro Hornets at the tail end of the 1992 season. While Posada played in 101 games that season, Derek Jeter, who began the year with the Gulf Coast League Yankees, a Rookie Level team, was a late promotion to Greensboro and only played eleven games there. Their paths crossed again toward the end of the 1994 minor league season. Jeter again earned a late-season promotion to the Triple-A Columbus Clippers where Posada was already playing. In 1995, both Derek Jeter and Jorge Posada played the majority of the season together for the Clippers. They both also earned brief stays with the Major League club that year and witnessed the Yankees capturing the first ever American League wild-card entry to the postseason. The next year, 1996, Jeter was promoted to the Yankees. Posada had three brief cups of coffee with the big league club that year and he also played with the team in late September. Posada earned his permanent promotion to the Major Leagues for the 1997 season. Jeter was Posada's teammate for the entirety of his fifteen-year career.

For Derek Jeter and Jorge Posada, their years together were remarkable because of the tremendous success the Yankees enjoyed. During Jeter's and Posada's fifteen years together, the Yankees earned a trip to the postseason fourteen times. The only year they were not involved in playoff baseball was 2008. In that time, the Yankees appeared in fourteen American League Division Series, eight American League Championship Series, and six World Series, winning the World Series four times (1998, 1999, 2000, and 2009). Derek Jeter is the all-time leader in games played in the postseason with 158. In second place on that remarkable list is Jorge Posada with 125 games played.

Courtesy of the Topps Company

There were two other non-pitching Yankee teammates who enjoyed lengthy tenure together. The second longest teammate partnership in the Yankees annals belongs to catcher Yogi Berra and center fielder Mickey Mantle. Berra and Mantle were teammates for thirteen seasons from 1951 through 1963. In 1964, Berra wasn't Mantle's teammate. Instead, he was the Yankees' manager. During their years together on the field, the Yankees went through a period of extended success. During those thirteen seasons, the Yankees appeared in eleven World Series winning seven (1951, 1952, 1953, 1956, 1958, 1961, and 1962). The only two times the Yankees did not appear in the World Series, they still finished near the top of the division. In 1954, they ended the season in second place despite winning 103 games and in 1959, they finished in third place.

The third longest tenured Yankees teammates were first baseman Lou Gehrig and second baseman Tony Lazzeri who formed the right side of the Yankees infield from 1926 through 1937. During Gehrig's and Lazzeri's twelve years together, the Yankees appeared in six World Series, winning five (1927, 1928, 1932, 1936, and 1937). Just as impressive, those teams finished in second place every other season except 1930 when the Yankees finished in third place.

NEW YORK YANKEES at DETROIT TIGERS

Friday, September 7, 1979 (Tiger Stadium)

	1	2	3	4	5	6	7	8	9		R	H	E
NY	0	0	0	0	0	0	0	0	0		0	6	1
DET	2	1	0	0	1	2	0	0	X		6	9	0

NY		AB	R	H	RBI	DET		AB	R	H	RBI
Randolph	2B	3	0	0	0	LeFlore	CF	4	1	2	2
Murcer	CF	4	0	1	0	Whitaker	2B	3	2	2	2
Piniella	LF	4	0	0	0	Kemp	LF	4	0	0	0
Jackson	RF	3	0	0	0	Summers	DH	3	1	2	1
Scott	DH	2	0	0	0	Thompson	1B	4	0	1	1
Gamble	PH/DH	2	0	1	0	Morales	RF	4	0	1	0
Chambliss	1B	4	0	1	0	Parrish	C	3	1	0	0
Stanley	3B	3	0	0	0	Rodriguez	3B	4	1	1	0
Dent	SS	3	0	2	0	Trammell	SS	3	0	0	0
Gulden	C	2	0	0	0						
Narron	C	1	0	1	0						

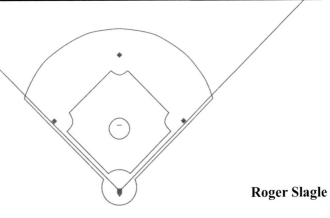

NY	IP	H	R	BB	SO	DET	IP	H	R	BB	SO
Clay - L	2	5	3	1	1	Robbins	2.2	2	0	2	0
Kaat	4	4	3	2	2	Billingham - W	6.1	4	0	0	3
Slagle	2	0	0	0	2						

Roger Slagle

Photo from the author's collection.

CHAPTER SEVEN
FLOYD NEWKIRK (1934)

Mordecai Brown was the ace pitcher for the Chicago Cubs teams that dominated baseball in the earliest days of the Twentieth Century. Brown won twenty or more games in six consecutive seasons from 1906-11. Over the span of his illustrious career, Mordecai Brown won 239 games. One of baseball's all-time greats, he was elected to the Hall of Fame in 1949. As a youngster, Brown lost one finger and damaged another during childhood accidents. Because of these injuries, he was known throughout baseball as "Three Finger" Brown. Many believed that the unique grip he had on a baseball because of the injuries to his hand contributed to his success. The same was said for one-time Yankee Floyd Newkirk although his Major League success was much shorter than Mordecai Brown's.

Floyd Newkirk also had only three fingers on his pitching hand. Like Brown, he lost the other two in a childhood accident.

Known as "Three Finger" Newkirk, Floyd followed a somewhat traditional path to the Major Leagues. He began by playing unaffiliated minor league baseball in 1930 and enjoyed a steady progression through the minors beginning with his assignment at Single-A Albany of the Eastern League. Newkirk appeared in fifteen games that summer, winning five and losing six with an ERA of 4.93. He again played for Albany in 1931 where he won twelve games (while losing twelve) with a respectable 3.10 ERA. Newkirk then began playing with the newly formed Yankees minor league organization and split the 1932 season between B-Level Binghamton of the New York Penn League and the Double-A Newark Bears of the International League. Double-A baseball at that time was the highest level of the minor leagues.

During his early days in baseball, Floyd Newkirk also attended college. In 1933, while still progressing through the minors, Newkirk graduated from Illinois College where he was a star in baseball and basketball in addition to running track. Newkirk's abilities in college sports were such that, he was posthumously enshrined in the Illinois College Hall of Fame for his baseball and basketball prowess.

While Floyd Newkirk's Major League playing career was less than notable, he was directly involved in a transaction that had a monumental impact on Yankees history, but that story actually comes later.

It was in 1933 that Newkirk had his greatest minor league season. By then a graduate of Illinois College, he pitched for the St. Paul Saints of the American Association. During that season Newkirk logged 219 innings while winning twelve games, including a no-hitter against the Kansas City Blues, against nine losses. His return to the Yankees organization and the Newark Bears in 1934 indicated that he was knocking on Major League Baseball's front door. Twenty-one of the twenty-seven players from that 1934 Newark squad eventually played in the big leagues, including future American League Most Valuable Player Spud Chandler and the man who replaced Babe Ruth as the Yankees' right fielder, George Selkirk.

It was during that 1934 season that Newkirk earned his promotion to the majors. His one and only Major League appearance came on August 21, 1934 at Yankee Stadium. On that day, the second-place Yankees, managed by future Hall of Famer Joe McCarthy, were playing the sixth-place St. Louis Browns. That Browns team was an uninspired group that would win only 67 games. They were managed by legendary player, and future Hall of Famer, Rogers Hornsby.

As he put on the Yankees pinstripes, and observed the clubhouse, Floyd Newkirk, must have been in awe. Standing in that room were some of the greatest of the great Yankees. These included Tony Lazzeri, Bill Dickey, Earle Combs, Red Ruffing, and Lefty Gomez. All would, someday, be honored with plaques in the Hall of Fame. While those players were an impressive bunch, also present in that locker room were two of baseball most legendary players, Lou Gehrig and Babe Ruth. Newkirk may have been put at ease by also seeing some of his former minor league teammates, among them Jack Saltzgaver and the aforementioned Selkirk.

Ed Wells, a former Yankee, playing in his final Major League season took the mound for the Browns that day against the Yankees' Russ Van Atta. Neither pitcher lasted through the third inning. It was Jack Knott, with six innings for St. Louis, and Danny MacFayden, with 4.2 innings for New York, who did the heavy lifting.

By the time Newkirk was called into the game, it was the top of the ninth inning, and the Yankees were trailing 8-3. The first batter he faced was second baseman Ski Melillo, a solid veteran in the ninth season of his twelve-year Major League career. Melillo hit a double to center field. Another long-time veteran, catcher Rollie Hemsley, flew out to center for the first out of the inning. Rookie shortstop Alan Strange then walked putting runners on first and second with only one out. The Browns pitcher, Jack Knott, then sacrificed both runners. On this play, Newkirk earned the assist as he fielded the bunt cleanly and threw to first baseman Lou Gehrig to record the out. This brought up the Browns' leadoff hitter Ollie Bejma, whom Newkirk retired on a ground out to shortstop Frank Crosetti to end the inning and the scoring threat.

In the bottom of the ninth, the Yankees staged a comeback. Leadoff hitter Jack Saltzgaver, the third baseman, singled. That brought up the right fielder Sammy Byrd who had entered the game in bottom of the seventh inning as a pinch runner for Babe Ruth. Byrd reached on an error by left fielder Ray Pepper. This brought up Gehrig. In the first inning, Gehrig had homered following a walk to Ruth. In the ninth inning, he again blasted a home run that narrowed the score to 8-6. It was at this point that Browns manager Rogers Hornsby removed Knott and brought in George Blaeholder. Fortunately for the Browns, Blaeholder was perfect as he retired Ben Chapman and the future Hall of Famers Bill Dickey and Tony Lazzeri. None of the three got the ball out of the infield as the Browns held on for the 8-6 victory.

Floyd Newkirk's day was finished. He acquitted himself well. In his lone Major League appearance, he faced five batters. Newkirk allowed one hit and one walk while striking out none. By allowing no runs, he gave the Yankees a chance to win, although in the end, their efforts came up short. Records indicate that Newkirk earned two assists in his one inning of work, but the play-by-play data does not seem to indicate that that was the case.

Soon Floyd Newkirk would be once again pitching for Newark unaware that his Major League career had ended and that his future included an unanticipated trade to the West Coast and a season playing alongside the player he was traded for.

Throughout the 1934 baseball season, the Yankees were keeping an eye on a tremendously talented baseball player starring for the San Francisco Seals of the highly competitive Pacific Coast League (whose level of play was compared by some to the Major Leagues). The previous season, this player had compiled a 61-game hitting streak along with an overall .340 batting average as an eighteen-year-old rookie. In 1934, the kid just kept on hitting racking up an impressive .341 batting average. Yet, a concern arose in August of that year as a knee injury kept him out of the lineup. Numerous teams that had been scouting this young star became leery and backed away. Not the Yankees.

After the 1934 season, the Yankees and San Francisco Seals agreed on a significant trade. To acquire this player, the Yankees sent $25,000 along with players Doc Farrell, Jimmy Densmore, Ted Norbert, and Floyd Newkirk to the Seals for the rights to a certain Joseph Paul DiMaggio. Since DiMaggio was still nursing the torn ligament in his left knee, Yankees owner Jacob Ruppert stipulated in the deal that DiMaggio remain with the Seals for the 1935 season to prove he was healthy.

As such, in spite of the fact that he was traded for him, in 1935 Floyd Newkirk appeared in 25 games as Joe DiMaggio's teammate winning eight games and losing five with a 5.22 ERA. During the season, DiMaggio proved that his knee was indeed healthy. He hit a robust .398 with an equally impressive 34 home runs. For Joe DiMaggio, the Bronx was calling.

Floyd Newkirk hung around for a few more seasons in the minors playing for the Tulsa Oilers and Oklahoma City Indians of the Texas League in 1936, and, after taking off the 1937 season, enjoying one last hurrah in 1938 with the New Orleans Pelicans and the Oakland Oaks.

After his baseball career, Newkirk served with the United States Army as a Private First Class in World War II. He lived until 1976 and is buried in the Jefferson Barracks National Cemetery in Missouri.

Extra Innings
Yankees in Combat in World War II

Over five hundred Major League baseball players enlisted or were drafted into the United States Armed Forces during World War II. Of course, not all of these players saw combat or dangerous action. In fact, during the war years there was some criticism that star players, being very athletic, were not more involved in combat. This certainly wasn't true of all big league players. Former (and future) professional baseball players were present at many of the important engagements of the war. This includes numerous players who wore the Yankee pinstripes.

Ralph Houk played in the Yankees (and Tigers) minor league systems before the war. During World War II, Houk served with the 9th Armored Division. He was present in numerous combat situations including The Battle of the Bulge. (Jack Knott, the pitcher who was so prominent in Floyd Newkirk's one Major League game also served at the Battle of the Bulge.) In the war, Houk was a decorated soldier earning the Bronze Star, the Silver Star, and a Purple Heart. Houk eventually rose to the rank of Major which became the nickname that followed him throughout the remainder of his life. After the war, Houk was a backup catcher on the Yankees from 1947 through 1954. After his playing days, he managed the Yankees to World Series championships in 1961 and 1962 and the American League pennant in 1963. After the season, Houk was promoted to general manager of the Yankees. Houk returned to manage the Yankees from 1966 through 1973. Later, he also managed the Detroit Tigers and the Boston Red Sox.

Buddy Hassett spent the first six years of his seven Major League seasons playing in the National League for the Brooklyn Dodgers and the Boston Braves. He spent 1942, his final season, as the Yankees' starting first baseman. His solid play and .282

batting average helped the Yankees win the pennant that year. By 1943, he was serving in the Navy. Hassett served on the aircraft carrier *USS Bennington* during the Battles of Iwo Jima and Okinawa.

Hank Bauer didn't arrive in the majors until 1948. He began his minor league career in 1941, but his ball playing was put on hold until after the war. During the war, Bauer served with the United States Marine Corps in Guam and was a platoon Sergeant during the landing at Okinawa. Of the 64 men who landed with Bauer, only six left the island alive. In his service, Bauer earned eleven campaign ribbons, two Bronze Stars, and two Purple Hearts. After the war, Hank Bauer became an All-Star for the Yankees. He played in their outfield from 1948 through 1959 and was on seven world championship teams. After his playing days, Hank Bauer managed the Kansas City Athletics, the Baltimore Orioles, and the Oakland A's. In 1966, his Orioles team won the World Series.

Yogi Berra is, of course, known for being one of the greatest catchers in baseball history. A three-time Most Valuable Player and a star player on ten world championship teams, Berra was elected to the Hall of Fame in 1972. He also managed the Yankees to the 1964 American League pennant and the 1973 New York Mets to the National League pennant. During the war, before he was a star, Yogi Berra served with the Navy during the D-Day invasion, landing on Omaha Beach.

Jerry Coleman did not reach the Yankees until 1949, well after the war. Like so many others, his minor league career was interrupted by World War II. During the war, he served as a dive bomber pilot. Coleman flew 57 missions against the Japanese and earned the Distinguished Flying Cross. Later, Jerry Coleman's Major League career was interrupted by the Korean War. In that war, he flew 63 successful missions and was again presented with the Distinguished Flying Cross. Coleman also earned thirteen air medals. Coleman played on the Yankees from 1949 through 1957 primarily as the team's second baseman. He was the 1949 American League Rookie of the Year and the World Series Most Valuable Player in 1950. All told, Coleman was on six world championship teams. He later served as a television play-by-play announcer. For seven years, Coleman called Yankees games. He is best remembered for being the voice of the San Diego Padres for 42 years from 1972 until his death in 2014. In 2005, Coleman was elected to the Hall of Fame with the Ford C. Frick Award as a baseball announcer.

ST. LOUIS BROWNS at NEW YORK YANKEES

Tuesday, August 21, 1934 (Yankee Stadium)

	1	2	3	4	5	6	7	8	9		R	H	E
STL	2	1	0	3	0	0	1	1	0		8	11	3
NY	2	0	1	0	0	0	0	0	3		6	9	2

STL		AB	R	H	RBI	NY		AB	R	H	RBI
Bejma	3B	5	2	1	0	Crosetti	SS	5	0	0	0
West	CF	3	1	1	0	Saltzgaver	3B	4	2	2	0
Burns	1B	5	2	2	3	Ruth	RF	1	1	0	0
Pepper	LF	5	1	4	3	Byrd	PR/RF	1	1	0	0
Campbell	RF	4	0	0	0	Gehrig	1B	5	2	2	5
Meillo	2B	4	0	1	1	Chapman	CF	5	0	0	0
Hemsley	C	5	0	1	1	Dickey	C	5	0	2	0
Strange	SS	4	1	1	0	Lazzeri	2B	5	0	2	0
Wells	P	1	0	0	0	Hoag	LF	2	0	0	0
Knott	P	2	1	0	0	Selkirk	PH/LF	1	0	0	0
Blaeholder	P	0	0	0	0	Van Atta	P	1	0	0	0
						MacFayden	P	2	0	0	0
						Rolfe	PH	1	0	1	0
						Newkirk	P				

STL	IP	H	R	BB	SO	NY	IP	H	R	BB	SO
Wells	2	2	2	1	0	Van Atta - L	3.1	7	6	3	2
Knott - W	6	7	4	4	3	MacFayden	4.2	3	2	2	4
Blaeholder	1	0	0	0	0	**Newkirk**	1	1	0	1	0

Floyd Newkirk

CHAPTER EIGHT
HONEY BARNES (1926)

John Francis "Honey" Barnes began his professional baseball career after graduating from Colgate University in 1925. During his last two seasons at Colgate, Barnes displayed outstanding hitting skills, batting .385 as a junior and .350 as a senior. Barnes was usually the cleanup batter in the Colgate lineup and was also the team's captain. After college, Barnes was signed by baseball scout Paul Krichell who certainly left his mark on Yankees history.

Krichell was an integral part of the early success of the Yankees franchise. A host of legendary Yankees came to the team through Krichell's efforts. For example, three out of the four members of the starting infield on the 1927 Yankees (Lou Gehrig, Tony Lazzeri, and Mark Koenig) were signed by Krichell. During his many years as a Yankees scout, Krichell also discovered or signed a host of legendary players that included Hinkey Haines, Leo Durocher, Charlie Keller, and future Hall of Famers Phil Rizzuto and Whitey Ford. Krichell also attempted to sign the great Hank Greenberg to the Yankees. However, Greenberg signed with the Detroit Tigers because, as a first baseman, his path to the Major Leagues was blocked by Gehrig. Honey Barnes was talented enough to be brought to the Yankees organization by one of its most legendary scouts.

In 1926, Honey Barnes began playing for the Buffalo Bisons of the International League. It wouldn't be long before he was called to the Yankees.

Barnes got his big chance on April 20, 1926 in a game at Griffith Stadium against the Washington Senators. The Senators had long been known as a poor baseball club. The standard phrase, "First in war, first in peace, last in the American League" typified most of the Senators' history, but the Senators of this era were different. The Senators team that faced the Yankees on that April day entered the game as the two-time American League champions having won the AL pennant in 1925 and the World Series the previous year. This Washington team was a powerhouse.

If Honey Barnes' Major League experience lasted but one game, he was fortunate in that he was able to experience that game alongside a large collection of baseball legends. In the starting lineup for Washington that day were a host of future Hall of Famers. In fact, they batted one after the next at the top of the order with Sam Rice (center field) batting leadoff, Bucky Harris (second base) batting second, and Goose Goslin (left field) batting third. The Senators' starting pitcher that day was Walter Johnson, one of greatest pitchers in the history of baseball.

The Yankees, the eventual 1926, 1927, and 1928 pennant winners, were just beginning their Murderers' Row era. There was no shortage of stars on the Yankees' side of the diamond. From manager Miller Huggins down through Earle Combs, Tony Lazzeri, Lou Gehrig, and Babe Ruth, the Yankees also had their share of future Hall of Fame enshrinees. Although they did not pitch in this particular game, the pitching staff included eventual Hall of Famers Herb Pennock and Waite "Schoolboy" Hoyt.

There is no doubt that Walter Johnson, the Washington hurler, was one of baseball's greatest pitchers, but on this day, he did not seem to bring his best stuff. The Yankees scored early and often against him. The great Babe Ruth homered in the first inning. By the time Johnson was removed, after just the third inning, the Yankees had scored seven runs. The assault continued as the Yankees scored three runs in the fourth inning, four runs in the fifth inning, and one more run in the sixth. In the eighth inning, they scored three more times. Each of the top seven batters in the Yankees lineup had a multiple-hit game. Mark Koenig, the shortstop, had three hits. Earle Combs, the center fielder, had four. Babe Ruth, the right fielder, totaled five hits with five runs scored and six runs batted in.

With the Yankees leading 18-3 heading into the top of the ninth inning, it seemed a perfect time to allow Honey Barnes to get his first taste of the big leagues. He was sent to the plate to lead off the inning (replacing the catcher Pat Collins who had gone 1-for-4 that day). In his only plate appearance, Barnes walked. He also didn't get past first base as the batters behind him went down in order. Honey Barnes then served as the catcher in the bottom of the ninth inning receiving the offerings from Yankees reliever Hank Johnson who surrendered two runs. Barnes did not record a putout nor make an assist. His lone inning behind the plate was memorable for him, but unremarkable in the record books. The Yankees won the game 18-5.

Honey Barnes was soon returned to the minors where he played for the next five seasons, all but one for Buffalo. The 1930 season, Barnes' last, was played with the Louisville Colonels. His incomplete minor league batting average stands at .300 proving that he was an adept hitter. As a Major Leaguer, Honey Barnes was perfect as a batter. In the history of Major League Baseball no one was able to get him out. Since he walked, he didn't have a batting average, but his on-base percentage is an even 1.000. One cannot do better than that!

After his playing days, Honey Barnes became an investigator for the Niagara County Welfare Department. He passed away on June 18, 1981.

Extra Innings
Mark Koenig and The Babe's Called Shot

The Yankees shortstop on the April day that marked the totality of Honey Barnes' big-league career was Mark Koenig. Koenig was the Yankees' starting shortstop throughout the late 1920s. He usually served as the number two batter in the lineup, hitting right in front of Babe Ruth. But, in 1930, Koenig got off to a slow start. By the end of May, he was batting only .230 and he was traded, along with Waite Hoyt, to the Detroit Tigers. This began Koenig's new life as a nomad. He eventually bounced between four teams over the remaining six years of his career, but in that time he influenced one pennant race and, in an indirect way, one of the most legendary moments in the history of baseball.

In 1932, Mark Koenig was starring in the minor leagues when his contract was purchased in early August by the Chicago Cubs who were looking for infield depth because of a shooting incident that involved one of their players.

The Cubs' shortstop in 1932 was Billy Jurges. In a situation that most likely influenced author Bernard Malamud when he wrote *The Natural*, Jurges was shot by a showgirl, Violet Valli after she entered Jurges' hotel room and was rebuffed by him. Valli brandished a .25-caliber pistol and as Jurges struggled for the gun, Valli fired three shots, injuring herself and Jurges who sustained injuries to his left hand, ribs, and right shoulder. Interestingly, Jurges never pressed charges and Valli went on to some fame in Chicago as this incident brought her celebrity status. As it relates to baseball, the Cubs, in the heat of a pennant race, needed a shortstop and called upon Koenig to fill that position.

Koenig appeared in his first game for Chicago, on August 14. On that day, the Cubs sat atop the National League by the tiniest of margins. Within days, Koenig's great play cemented him as the team's shortstop. Overall, he batted .353 and was instrumental in the Cubs winning the NL pennant. But, when it came time for the Cubs players to vote on player shares for the 1932 World Series, they elected to offer Mark Koenig only a half-share of their earnings.

This outraged the Yankees players who felt that the Cubs wouldn't have even won the pennant if not for their former teammate. When the World Series began, the Yankees, most notably Babe Ruth, taunted the Cubs by calling them, among other things, cheapskates. The Cubs gave the taunts right back, especially targeting Ruth. The name-calling continued through the first two games which were won by the Yankees.

The third game of the World Series was played in Chicago. Wrigley Field was packed. The fans were eager to see a victory. Their beloved team had not won a World Series since 1908. Chicago was thirsting for a world championship.

In the top of the first inning, Ruth hit a three-run home run to give the Yankees a convincing lead just as the game was getting underway. The resilient Cubs battled back, even after Lou Gehrig later hit a home run. Aiding the Cubs comeback was a ball misplayed by Ruth in the outfield. By the end of the fourth inning, the game was knotted at four.

During the game, fans and the Cubs players screamed and yelled pejoratives at Ruth. Lemons flew out of the stands at him when Ruth was in the outfield. By the time he came to bat with one out in the top of the fifth inning, the tumult was rising even more.

Charlie Root was pitching for the Cubs. He got off to a fast start by throwing a called strike on Ruth. This brought louder screaming. Root missed the strike zone on his next two offerings but was able to even the count at two balls and two strikes after another called strike. By this point the ballpark was in a frenzy. The Cubs players were relentless in their attacks on Ruth, some even leaving the dugout to hurl their verbal attacks at the baseball legend.

And then Babe Ruth pointed. Later some would swear he pointed to the mound as if to say, "You have only two strikes on me, I get one more." But many others swear that he pointed to center field and indicated that he would hit the next pitched ball over the fence. Had Babe Ruth just called his next hit?

What happened next is clear. Ruth hit Root's pitch into the seats for a home run giving the Yankees a 5-4 lead. The blast was one of the longest ever hit at Wrigley Field. It was majestic and considering the moment, absolutely amazing. This was the legendary "Called Shot."

Debate may rage about whether Ruth actually called his shot, but the results were obvious. He rose above the bench jockeying and slammed a home run.

While the blast is still debated even today, there is contemporary evidence that Babe Ruth called his shot. That evening's edition of the New York World Telegram had a headline that read, "RUTH CALLS SHOT AS HE PUTS HOMER NO.2 SIDE POCKET."

After Ruth's long home run, Lou Gehrig batted and hit a home run. These homers propelled the Yankees to victory. The next day, the Yankees finished off their World Series sweep.

And thus, a legend was born, in part because some Cubs players didn't vote a full World Series share to former Yankee Mark Koenig.

NEW YORK YANKEES at WASHINGTON SENATORS

Tuesday, April 20, 1926 (Griffith Stadium)

	1	2	3	4	5	6	7	8	9		R	H	E
NY	2	0	5	3	4	1	0	3	0		18	22	0
WASH	1	1	0	0	0	0	0	1	2		5	9	4

NY		AB	R	H	RBI	WASH		AB	R	H	RBI
Koenig	SS	7	3	3	0	Rice	CF/RF	4	0	1	1
Combs	CF	7	4	4	1	Harris	2B	2	0	0	1
Gehrig	1B	4	4	2	2	Stewart	2B	1	0	0	0
Ruth	RF	6	5	5	6	Goslin	LF	3	1	1	0
Meusel	LF	4	0	2	3	Jeanes	LF	2	1	1	0
Lazzeri	2B	4	0	2	2	Harris	RF	2	0	1	1
Dugan	3B	5	1	2	2	McNeely	CF	3	0	1	1
Collins	C	4	1	1	0	Judge	1B	5	0	1	0
Barnes	C	0	0	0	0	Bluege	3B	4	0	1	0
Shocker	P	4	0	1	1	Myer	SS	3	1	1	0
Cullop	PH	1	0	0	0	Ruel	C	0	0	0	0
Johnson	P					Severeid	PH/C	3	1	1	0
						Johnson	P	1	0	0	0
						Kelley	P				
						Tobin	PH	1	0	0	0
						Hadley	P				
						Ruether	PH	1	0	0	0
						Morrell	P				
						Thomas	P				
						Tate	PH	0	1	0	0

NY	IP	H	R	BB	SO	WASH	IP	H	R	BB	SO
Shocker - W	8	7	3	4	2	Johnson - L	3	8	7	2	3
Johnson	1	2	2	2	0	Kelley	1	4	3	1	1
						Hadley	3	6	5	2	0
						Morrell	1	4	3	1	2
						Thomas	1	0	0	1	1

Honey Barnes

Courtesy of The Topps Company.

CHAPTER NINE
STEVE GARRISON (2011)

After graduating high school in 2005, Steve Garrison, a pitcher, began his professional baseball career. He was drafted by the Milwaukee Brewers and began that year in rookie league ball with the Arizona Brewers. In that first season, Garrison made eleven appearances. He won two games, lost two games, saved two games, and pitched to a 2.86 ERA. This solid season, pitching as both a starter and reliever, earned him a promotion the following season to the Single-A West Virginia Power of the South Atlantic League. Primarily a starting pitcher, Garrison continued his slow climb to the big leagues. Pitching for West Virginia, Garrison won seven games against six losses with a 3.45 ERA. His progress may have been slow, but it was steady.

2007 looked to be a breakout year for Garrison, now pitching for the Brevard County Manatees of the Advanced-A Florida State League. Garrison had already won eight games (against four losses) as July was winding down. At that time, the Major League

Brewers were in the midst of the pennant race. On July 25, 2007, the Brewers made a trade deadline deal with the San Diego Padres to acquire veteran relief pitcher Scott Linebrink. Steve Garrison was one of the three minor league players sent to the Padres organization in the deal. Garrison was immediately sent to a California League (A) team to finish out the season where he won two games and lost three.

Garrison's slow climb continued in 2008 which brought him his first taste of Double-A baseball. In his third start of the year, Garrison pitched seven innings of no-hit baseball. Later, in June, Garrison struck out eleven batters in one game. His stock was rising, but in late August he suffered a shoulder injury that ended his season. In spite of a 7-7 record, Garrison's 3.82 ERA was seventh best in the league. The question was how he would respond following rotator cuff surgery.

The 2009 season saw Garrison appear in only thirteen games spaced out over three levels of the minors. The results were mixed. To continue his growth, Garrison was assigned to the Arizona Fall League where he suffered the second major injury of his career, this time to his right knee.

As he did with the previous injury, Steve Garrison battled back. In 2010, he was able to make seventeen minor league appearances in the Padres system. This included his first trip to Triple-A where, pitching for the Portland Beavers of the Pacific Coast League, Garrison went 1-3, with an 8.87 ERA in five starts. In early September, he was designated for assignment by the Padres. Seeing a potential diamond in the rough, he was claimed off waivers by the Yankees.

In 2011, Steve Garrison went to spring training with the big league club. He acquitted himself well enough to be on the verge of making the Major League squad, but as spring training wound down, he was assigned to the Double-A Trenton Thunder. For Steve Garrison, a native of Ewing, New Jersey, who attended the Hun School in Princeton, this was a bit of a homecoming.

After a strong start at Trenton, Steve Garrison was summoned to the big league club on July 19, 2011. Following a minor league career that included just five uninspired games above Double-A, Steve Garrison was on his way to The Show. Garrison had to wait a number of days for his Major League appearance.

On a personal note, the author of this book happened to be in attendance at Yankee Stadium with two of his sons on July 25, 2011, the day of Steve Garrison's lone Major League opportunity—a game in which the Yankees defeated the Seattle Mariners 10-3.

Like so many other players chronicled in this text, Garrison may have been one of the least among them, but he sure played alongside some of the game's biggest stars that day, including Mariano Rivera, Derek Jeter, Alex Rodriguez, Jorge Posada, and Robinson Cano of the Yankees and Ichiro Suzuki and Felix Hernandez of the Mariners.

In the game, the Yankees scored ten times with the big blows home runs from Mark Teixeira and Derek Jeter. The Yankees led from the bottom of the first to the end. It was in the ninth inning of this blowout that Steve Garrison got his shot. With one out in the inning, Yankees' manager Joe Girardi visited the mound and called for Garrison.

Wearing uniform number 61, Steve Garrison ran in from the bullpen. This seemed like a low-pressure situation to get his feet wet and taste big league ball. Garrison's first challenge was against the Mariners' first baseman Justin Smoak, a powerful switch hitter. Smoak hit a towering fly ball to deep left field that was eventually run down by Brett Gardner. It was a loud out, but it was, for Garrison and the Yankees, an out. The next batter was Franklin Gutierrez, Seattle's center fielder. He, too, hit a bomb—a deep blast to right-center field. Curtis Granderson, the Yankees' center fielder, ran the ball down and caught it to end the game. For Garrison, it was two batters faced, two batters retired. Garrison closed out the only game in which he would appear in the Major Leagues.

Baseball is a unique game in that the playing field, or at least the distance of the outfield fences differs from one stadium to the next. No two fields have identical dimensions. Every ballpark has a unique atmosphere. The fences in Yankees Stadium are deeper than in many other parks. It is possible that had Garrison pitched in a smaller ballpark that day, the results would have been vastly different. Rather than retiring the two batters he faced, he might have been on the receiving end of back-to-back home runs. Due, possibly in part, to the vast expanses of the Yankees outfield, Garrison, though, was perfect. He allowed no base runners. He allowed no runs. Steve Garrison's pitching statistics, like Roger Slagle's, are perfect.

Five days after his big-league debut, the Yankees activated pitcher Rafael Soriano from the disabled list and Garrison was returned to Trenton.

Garrison was released by the Yankees franchise after that season. He was picked up by the Seattle Mariners organization where he spent the 2012 season pitching mostly for the Jackson Generals of the Double-A Southern League. Garrison also made seven Triple-A appearances that season. He was then released by the Mariners and picked up by the Arizona Diamondbacks. Garrison spent the 2013 season pitching entirely at Double-A for the Mobile BayBears. He made 47 appearances, all as a reliever, but was again released following the season.

The Baltimore Orioles then took a flier on Garrison, but he wasn't able to stick with the organization. With no Major League or affiliated minor league prospects, Steve Garrison began pitching in the independent minor leagues, hoping, eventually, for a return ticket to the big leagues. It never came.

Garrison has returned to his roots and is the associate director of admissions and assistant baseball coach at The Hun School of Princeton, N.J.

Extra Innings
Yankees Who Came from Japan

One of the players on the field on July 25, 2011 was Ichiro Suzuki of the Mariners. After starring in Japan, Ichiro came to America and became one of the game's greatest hitters. Suzuki was a ten-time All-Star who twice led the American League in batting. Along the way he won the American League Rookie of the Year and Most Valuable Player awards. In 2004, Ichiro set baseball's all-time single-season record with 262 hits. In total, Ichiro Suzuki banged out 3,089 hits in his Major League career.

On July 23, 2012, Ichiro Suzuki was traded to the New York Yankees for two minor league pitchers. Ichiro would spend two-and-a-half seasons as a Yankee appearing in 360 games, batting .281.

In addition to Ichiro, six other Japanese players have appeared in uniform as a Yankee.

The first player to don Yankees pinstripes after a successful career in Japan was Hideki Irabu, a hard-throwing right-hander who began his Yankees career in 1997. Irabu was called by some "The Japanese Nolan Ryan." A superstar pitcher, Irabu was coming off his three best seasons. In 1994, he led the Japanese league in wins. In 1995, he struck out 239 batters in 203 innings while leading the league in earned run average (2.53). In 1996, he again led the league with a 2.40 ERA.

Hideki Irabu's path to the majors in the United States came with some controversy. Following the 1996 Japanese baseball season, Irabu expressed his desire to play in America. Acquiescing, his team, the Chiba Lotte Marines, sold him to the San Diego Padres. This was not acceptable to Irabu who only wanted to play for the Yankees. The Yankees were eventually able to acquire the negotiating rights to Irabu for a package of players.

Irabu made his Major League debut on July 10, 1997 against the Detroit Tigers in a game that captured international attention. Over 51,000 fans and an army of media were in attendance at Yankee Stadium and Irabu did not disappoint. He struck out nine of the first nineteen batters he faced and pitched into the seventh inning, allowing just two runs on five hits. Irabu then won his next start, but his big league star would never shine brighter. He lost his next two games and was eventually removed from the starting rotation.

Irabu bounced back to pitch to a 24-16 record over the next two seasons. Yet, throughout these years, he struggled with his consistency. Following the 1999 season, the Yankees traded Hideki Irabu to the Montreal Expos.

The next Yankee who came from Japan was also named Hideki. This Hideki also came with a larger-than-life image and larger-than-life expectations.

In his ten-year career in Japan, Hideki Matsui hit .304 with 332 home runs. Along the way, Matsui won three MVP awards and led the league in home runs and RBIs three times each. Matsui helped lead his team, the Yomiuri Giants of Tokyo, to four Japanese World Series and three championships. He signed with the Yankees for the 2003 season.

Hideki Matsui, like Godzilla, the fictional character from which he drew his nickname, took New York by storm. On Opening Day 2003, in Toronto, Hideki Matsui drove in the first run of the game in his first ever Major League at-bat. Eight days later, in his first game in Yankee Stadium, Matsui hit a grand slam to propel the Yankees to victory.

That first season, Matsui was a steady presence on the team and in the field. He played in every game, mostly as the Yankees left fielder. (He wouldn't miss a game until the 2006 season when he broke his wrist diving for a sinking line drive in a game against the Red Sox.)

In 2003, Hideki Matsui was a clutch presence in the Yankees lineup that won the American League pennant and reached the World Series. On October 19, 2003, Hideki Matsui became the first Japanese player to hit a home run in the World Series.

In each of his first four full Major League seasons with the

Yankees, Hideki Matsui drove in 100 or more runs. Year after year, he was a star.

Matsui's greatest moments as a Yankee came in 2009. On July 20 of that year, he hit a walk-off game-winning home run that propelled the Yankees into first place. They remained there for the reminder of the season. After a successful American League Division Series and American League Championship Series, Matsui had an amazing World Series in which he batted a remarkable .615 with three home runs and eight runs batted in. For his efforts, Hideki Matsui was awarded

Hideki Matsui Topps Card
Courtesy of the Topps Company

World Series MVP honors—the second of his career on two continents as he had also won the Japan Series MVP in 2000.

After later playing for three other teams, Hideki Matsui signed a one-day contract with the Yankees so that he could retire as a member of baseball's greatest team.

Kei Igawa was a left-handed pitcher who had success in Japan, but was a bust in New York. He began the 2007 season as a member of the Yankees starting rotation, but success never came. Igawa ended his career with a 2-4 record and a 6.66 ERA in just 16 total games. Most of Igawa's career in America was spent pitching for the Yankees' Triple-A team in Scranton/Wilkes-Barre. In five minor league seasons, Igawa appeared in 107 games.

A right-handed pitcher, Hiroki Kuroda enjoyed three very successful seasons in the Bronx after pitching for the Los Angeles Dodgers, his first team in America. In Japan, Kuroda led the league in wins in 2005 and in ERA in 2006. Kuroda pitched three very successful seasons in pinstripes, each season throwing 199 or more innings. His lifetime record as a Yankee was 38-33, with a 3.44 ERA. After the 2015 season, Kuroda returned to the Hiro-shima Carp for the final season of his career.

Ryota Igarashi, a hard-throwing right-handed pitcher who had been a six-time All-Star in Japan pitched in two games for the Yankees in 2012. Previously he had pitched for the New York Mets and the Toronto Blue Jays.

Masahiro Tanaka, a hard-throwing right-handed pitcher, signed a huge seven-year $155 million contract with the Yankees before the 2014 season. In seven seasons pitching for the Tohoku Golden Eagles, Tanaka established himself as one of Japan's great pitchers. He won the Pacific League Rookie of the Year and the MVP in 2013. A six-time All-Star, Tanaka led his league in wins and ERA twice and strikeouts once.

Masahiro Tanaka pitched with the Yankees from 2014 through 2020. In that time, he pitched in 174 games, accumulating an impressive 78-46 record with a 3.74 ERA. Tanaka's star shined brightest in the postseason where, for many years, he seemed almost unbeatable. After his first eight postseason starts, Tanaka had a miniscule 1.76 ERA. Like Kuroda, Tanaka also returned to pitch in Japan following his career with the Yankees.

SEATTLE MARINERS at NEW YORK YANKEES

Monday, July 25, 2011 (Yankee Stadium)

	1	2	3	4	5	6	7	8	9		R	H	E
SEA	0	0	1	0	0	0	1	1	0		3	8	2
NY	2	0	1	5	0	1	0	1	X		10	11	0

SEA		AB	R	H	RBI	NY		AB	R	H	RBI
Ichiro	RF	3	1	1	1	Jeter	SS	5	2	2	3
Ryan	SS	4	0	1	1	Granderson	CF	2	1	1	2
Ackley	2B	3	0	1	0	Teixeira	1B	4	1	2	3
Olivo	C	4	0	0	0	Cano	2B	4	0	0	0
Kennedy	3B	4	1	1	0	Laird	3B				
Carp	DH	4	0	1	0	Swisher	DH	4	0	1	0
Smoak	1B	4	1	2	1	Martin	C	4	1	0	0
Gutierrez	CF	4	0	1	0	Jones	RF	3	1	1	0
Halman	LF	3	0	0	0	Dickerson	RF				
						Nunez	3B/2B	4	2	2	1
						Gardner	LF	4	2	2	1

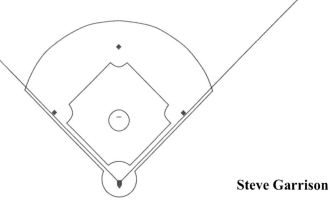

SEA	IP	H	R	BB	SO	NY	IP	H	R	BB	SO
Vargas - L	4	7	8	1	2	Garcia - W	7.2	8	3	1	5
Ray	2	2	1	1	0	Logan	0.2	0	0	0	2
Pauley	2	2	1	0	1	**Garrison**	0.2	0	0	0	0

Steve Garrison

EDDIE S. QUICK
From SABR website.

CHAPTER TEN
EDDIE QUICK (1903)

In the first year of the Yankees franchise, 1903, a pitcher named Eddie Quick had his one day of glory. If you plan to be a Major League pitcher, it helps to have a name like Quick. A name like that might help people take notice of you. Quick is probably a better surname for a ballplayer than Slow, or Still, or even Stillwell. One can only wonder today if baseball was the reason that Eddie Stillwell of Baltimore, Maryland changed his last name to Quick.

Eddie Quick began his professional baseball career far from home in the Pacific Northwest League in 1902, pitching for the Smoke Eaters of Spokane, Washington. That first year Quick appeared in twenty-four games, twenty of them as a pitcher. His pitching records are lost to history, but as a batter he compiled a somewhat less-than-terrific .227 batting average. The next year, 1903, Quick played for the Portland Green Gages and the Salt

Lake City Elders of the Pacific National League. He appeared in a combined thirty-one games as a right-handed pitcher winning only 14 games and losing 21. From these numbers, it does not seem that Eddie Quick was on the fast path to the big leagues, yet, newspaper accounts told a different story.

The *Topeka State Journal* identified Eddie Quick as "the star pitcher of the Salt Lake Pacific national team" when it reported that he signed to play with the American League team in New York. The *Star-Gazette* of Elmira, New York indicated that Eddie Quick was known as the "Iron Man of the Coast" by Salt Lake fans after he pitched, and won, both ends of a doubleheader earlier that season.

It was on September 29, 1903, in the penultimate game of the season, that Quick was called on to be the New York Highlanders' starting pitcher against the Detroit Tigers in a game the Yankees eventually won 7-6.

1903 was not a standout year for the Highlanders or the Tigers. New York finished the season in fourth place with Detroit in fifth. There were not any legendary players on that Tigers team, but the names of a few players, among them Deacon McGuire, Sport McAllister, Fritz Buelow, Paddy Greene, and Rube Kisinger, have names that hearken back to a long-lost time. On those Tigers teams were two pitchers, Wild Bill Donovan and George Mullin, who would anchor their pennant-winning teams of 1907, 1908, and 1909. In 1915 and 1916, Wild Bill Donovan would pitch for the Yankees. The Highlanders employed a shortstop named Kid Elberfeld who early that season was traded to them from the Tigers. That trade was, in fact, the first trade in the history of the New York Yankees. Also on the Highlanders were future Hall of Famers Clark Griffith, Jack Chesbro, and Wee Willie Keeler.

Eddie Quick's Major League career was over... quickly. It ended after two brief innings. In those two innings, he faced twelve batters. Six were retired. Of the other six batters, Quick walked one and surrendered hits to the five others. Of the six batters that reached base, five scored. The good news for Eddie Quick was that only two of the runs were earned. His lifetime earned run average stands at 9.00. We know from the game (although no play-by-play data exists) that Eddie Quick batted once and was retired and that he also made an assist. In the end, the Highlanders won the game 7-6.

Following the season, Eddie Quick was involved in a bit of a contract fight between the Salt Lake team and the Highlanders. There was an ownership dispute in Salt Lake and there was a question whether Quick was released by the team and purchased by the Highlanders or just loaned to the New York team. Quick himself, an article in the *Salt Lake Herald* explained, was attempting to get his released from New York to return to Salt Lake to resume his career and promote the career of his "kid" brother.

As one searches newspapers of that time, it seems that as he headed east to play baseball in New York, it was reported numerous times, incorrectly, that Eddie Quick had signed to pitch for the New York Giants, not the Highlanders. There were stories told that the famous manager of the Giants, the great John McGraw, who was also from Baltimore (he had played and managed there as recently as 1902) had seen Quick pitch, expressed interested in him, and urged him to sign with a minor league team to get experience. Quick's lone big league game came, though, with the Highlanders, not the Giants.

For the next few seasons, Eddie Quick returned to the farm leagues playing mostly on the West Coast. Quick's career statistics on baseball-reference.com show him bouncing around, playing for eight teams over a five-year span before his professional career ended after the 1908 season. It seems that he continued playing, possibly for semi-professional teams, for years. A local paper, *The Butte Daily Post* reported that he was lined up to be the Opening Day starting pitcher for a team in Butte, Montana to begin the 1911 season.

Alas, it was not just his Major League Baseball career that passed too suddenly. In 1913, Eddie Quick died from pneumonia in Rocky Ford, Colorado. He was just 31 years old.

Extra Innings
Some Yankees Who Changed Their Names

In Yankees' history, Eddie Quick was not the only player to change his given name. Phil Cooney, another *Least Among Them* player, changed his name from Phil Cohen. At times, name changes were made to make players seem less ethnic or associated with a particular religion as, at certain times, racism and anti-Semitism were a reality of life. At other times, some players changed their names to monikers that were easier to pronounce or that may have possibly seemed more "ballplayer like."

It would probably take volumes to examine all of the Yankees whose given names were changed at one time or another in their lives. Some of the changes just involved spellings. For example, Roger Maris was actually born Roger Maras. Other players were better known by their middle names rather than their given first names with a certain Henry Louis Gehrig coming to mind as an obvious example.

It is worth noting the following four players in the history of the Yankees franchise who were better known by names other than those they were born with. All four of these players had a direct impact on Yankees history in one way or another.

Between 1918 and 1921, the Yankees had an outfielder named Francesco Pezzolo who was better known as Ping Bodie. Bodie played in 385 games in pinstripes batting .272. In the days just before the birth of the "live-ball era," Bodie clubbed 16 home runs, a not insignificant total. As a minor league ballplayer, Bodie was the first player in the Pacific Coast League to slug 30 or more home runs in a season. It is said that "Ping" earned this unique name because that was the sound the ball made when it came off his extremely heavy 52-ounce bat. It is assumed that "Bodie" was the name of a town he may have lived in as a child. As with many tales from long ago, some of this may be apocryphal.

In his career, Ping Bodie might best be remembered as Babe Ruth's first roommate on the Yankees. It was Bodie who made the quip, "I don't room with Babe, I room with his suitcase." Ping Bodie was also one of the first Italian-Americans from the San Francisco Bay Area to reach the Major Leagues. He was an early trailblazer whom other players followed—among these were Tony Lazzeri, and, of course, Joe DiMaggio.

Following Ping Bodie, from 1922 through 1925, the Yankees had another outfielder who did not play under his given name. Ladislaw Waldemar Wittkowski was better known as Whitey Witt. Originally signed to play for the Philadelphia A's, the legend goes that Connie Mack began writing "Witt" in the lineup because Wittkowski was too long of a name. The "Whitey" part came because of Witt's blond hair.

Witt was the leadoff batter on the 1922 American League champion Yankees and the 1923 world champion Yankees. He was the first Yankee to bat in Yankee Stadium. While his name is no longer well-known, Witt was an excellent baseball player. Over the course of his ten-year Major League career, Whitey Witt batted .287 with a .362 on-base percentage. Witt was often found among the league leaders in singles and walks. Witt was also a fine defensive center fielder.

Edmund Walter Lopatynski was a pitcher who shortened his last name to Lopat and as "The Junkman" enjoyed a very successful career as a Yankee. Eddie Lopat was a soft-tossing, but extremely effective left-handed pitcher who helped anchor the Yankees teams that won five consecutive World Series between 1949 and 1953. Year after year his winning percentage was .600 or better. These yearly totals deserve attention: 15-10 3.26 (1949), 18-8 3.47 (1950), 21-9 2.91 (1951), 10-5 2.53 (1952), 16-4 2.42 (1953). In those five years, Lopat won 80 games and lost only 36. He was a rock of consistency who teamed with Allie Reynolds and Vic Raschi to anchor the Yankees' pitching staff.

In the history of the Yankees, there have been many famous home runs hit in crucial and important times. For example, Chris Chambliss (whose given first name was Carroll) hit a famous walk-off home run that secured the 1976 American League championship in the bottom of the ninth inning against the Kansas City

Royals. That blast ended a long drought for the Yankees as it was their first trip to the World Series since 1964. As Chambliss circled the bases, a new winning era was beginning for the Yankees. It was during this period that another Yankee hit an even more famous home run. That player's birth name was Russell Earl O'Dey.

After a yearlong struggle in 1978, the Yankees and the Red Sox ended up tied atop the American League East Division. Since a champion needed to be crowned, the Yankees and the Red Sox were required to play a one-game playoff to determine the winner of the division. This game was played in Fenway Park on October 2, 1978. Former Yankee Mike Torrez took the mound for the Red Sox against the eventual 1978 Cy Young winner Ron Guidry. Through much of the game, the Red Sox held a slim lead, but in the top of the seventh inning, the game suddenly changed. With two outs and two runners on base, the Yankees shortstop, originally named Russell O'Dey came to bat and hit a three-run home run to propel the Yankees into the lead they would never relinquish. The Yankees were on their way winning the game, the American League East title, and eventually, the World Series. That player, better known as Bucky Dent, also won MVP honors in the World Series after batting .417 against the Los Angeles Dodgers.

Russell Earl O'Dey was born to Denise O'Dey, a single parent who gave her baby to her sister and brother-in-law, Sarah and James Dent, to raise. In the process, Russell's birth certificate was also changed. The nickname "Bucky" came during his childhood.

DETROIT TIGERS at NEW YORK HIGHLANDERS

Monday, September 28, 1903 (Hilltop Park)

	1	2	3	4	5	6	7	8	9		R	H	E
DET	1	3	1	0	0	0	1	0	0		6	9	3
NY	0	0	1	0	3	1	1	1	X		7	13	4

DET		AB	R	H	RBI	NY		AB	R	H	RBI
Barrett	CF	4	1	1	1	Conroy	SS				
Lush	LF	5	1	1	0	Davis	LF	4	2	1	0
Crawford	RF	5	1	0	1	Fultz	CF/3B	5	1	3	0
Carr	RF	5	1	0	1	Keller	RF	5	0	1	0
McAllister	SS	4	1	2	1	Williams	2B	5	1	2	2
Yeager	3B	3	0	1	0	Ganzel	1B	5	0	1	1
Burns	2B	4	1	1	1	McFarland	LF/CF	4	2	1	2
Buelow	C	4	1	1	1	Zalusky	C	4	0	3	0
Kitson	P	4	0	0	0	Howell	3B/SS	4	1	1	0
						Quick	P	1	0	0	0
						Bliss	P	3	0	0	0

DET	IP	H	R	BB	SO	NY	IP	H	R	BB	SO
Kitson - L	8	13	7	1	4	**Quick**	2	5	5	1	0
						Bliss - W	7	4	1	0	3

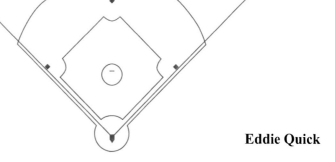

Eddie Quick

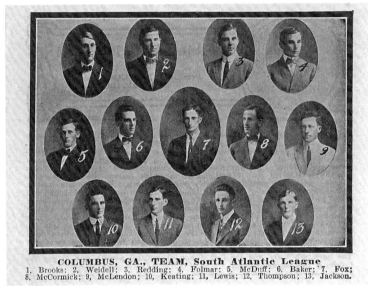

COLUMBUS, GA., TEAM, South Atlantic League
1, Brooks; 2, Weidell; 3, Redding; 4, Folmar; 5, McDuff; 6, Baker; 7, Fox; 8, McCormick; 9, McLendon; 10, Keating; 11, Lewis; 12, Thompson; 13, Jackson.

Photo from the author's collection.

CHAPTER ELEVEN
HOMER THOMPSON (1912)

Eddie Stillwell changed his last name to a much better sounding moniker for baseball—Quick. Homer Thompson did not have to do any name changing—he was named Homer Thomas Thompson from the start. If you want your child to grow up to play professional baseball, a good place to begin is by naming him "Homer."

Homer's opportunity to play for the New York Highlanders came on October 5, the very last day of the 1912 season. Historians often cite 1913 as the year that the Highlanders officially became known as the Yankees. With that being the case, Homer's first, and last, game was also the last game for the Highlanders. On that Highlander squad that day was an important person in Homer's life, his older brother Tommy. Tommy Thompson's career was also not lengthy. He played but one Major League season, appearing in only eight games. Tommy Thompson's introduction to professional baseball was as a big leaguer. He started at the top. After the season, older brother Tommy spent three years in the minor leagues.

This, though, is Homer's story. Unfortunately, there is not much to tell. Before joining the Yankees for his one Major League opportunity, Homer had been out of organized baseball for three years. In 1909, Homer played for the Denver Grizzlies of the Single-A Western League. He acquitted himself well in that first season batting .318 in 68 games. After that season, though, Homer seems to have stopped playing professional ball. There are no recorded instances of Homer Thompson playing organized baseball in 1910, 1911, or 1912, the three years prior to his one day in the big leagues.

Sometimes an author is forced to make guesses or assumptions based upon the information and data he can find. Based upon the fact that the very-soon-to-be Yankees were completing a last-place season, finishing an almost unheard of fifty-five games behind the first-place Boston Red Sox, it seems likely that Homer's brother, Tommy, a pitcher, played a role in Homer's sudden appearance on A Major League diamond. It seems likely that as the Highlanders played out the string, they offered these brothers the opportunity to play ball together on that last day of the 1912 season. Homer Thompson was the Highlander's catcher for one half inning. In that inning, Homer had two chances. On one, he made an error. On the other, he recorded a putout. Homer never had a chance to bat. Tommy also appeared in that game, as a pinch runner. While they didn't appear on the field at the same time, they had both dressed and appeared in the same Major League Baseball game for the same team. This was the first time that occurred in the history of the Yankees franchise.

While the 1912 season was a forgettable one for the Highlanders, in the game in which Homer appeared, they defeated the Washington Senators 8-6. Washington was a strong team that finished in second place with a 91-61 record and was managed by former Highlander and future Hall of Famer Clark Griffith, who also, seemingly for the fun of it, appeared in the game as a pitcher to face one batter. That Washington squad was led by ace pitcher Walter Johnson who won 33 games that year against

12 loses. Also on that Washington club was first baseman Chick Gandil. A few years later, Gandil became involved in the infamous 1919 Black Sox Scandal.

The 1912 Highlander squad was one of the few in Yankees franchise history to possess no future Hall of Famers. One player of note on that team, though, was first baseman Hal Chase, whose own career was marked with inappropriate gambling accusations and strong speculation that he was also a behind-the-scenes figure in that same Black Sox scandal.

Homer Thompson played baseball during the game's dead ball era, a time before Babe Ruth and before the sudden explosion and fascination with the home run. During his day, singles, doubles, and triples were more important than the home run. The 1912 league leaders in hits were Ty Cobb and Joe Jackson each with 226. Tris Speaker led the league in doubles with 53. Joe Jackson led the league with 26 triples. It was, obviously, a different time. Two players tied for the league lead in home runs in 1912, both hitting but ten homers. One of these home run leaders was the aforementioned Tris Speaker. The other (it's almost too perfect for this story) was John Franklin "Home Run" Baker.

After his single appearance with the Yankees, Homer Thompson played two seasons of C-Level minor league baseball with the Columbus (Georgia) Foxes of the Sally League before leaving the game. During those seasons his brother Tommy played for the Birmingham Barons and the Atlanta Crackers of the Single-A Southern Association. While they played on the same team and in the same game as Major Leaguers, they were not able to replicate that feat in the minors.

Extra Innings
Yankee Brothers

In the history of baseball, there have been a host of brothers who played Major League Baseball. The largest sibling contingent were the five Delahanty brothers (Ed, Frank, Jim, Joe, and Tom). In the twenty-four years between 1888 when Ed Delahanty played his first big league game, and 1912, when Jim Delahanty played his last game, there was always at least one member of this family playing Major League Baseball.

Ed Delahanty was the most famous of the brothers. He was one of baseball's earliest superstars and possibly the greatest player of the 1890s. "Big" Ed Delahanty batted over .400 three times and led the league many times in various batting categories.

In 1903, Ed Delahanty's season, career, and his life, were cut short when he died tragically at Niagara Falls. The circumstances surrounding this death remain one of baseball's great mysteries. In the middle of the night, he either fell or jumped into the raging Niagara River and was swept over the falls.

Of the five baseball playing Delahanty brothers, Frank was the only one to play for the Yankees franchise. In the early days of baseball, Frank Delahanty played for the New York Highlanders in 1905, 1906, and 1908. In 138 games as a Highlander, Frank's lifetime batting average was .242.

Many players in Yankees history have had at least one sibling who also played in the Major Leagues. The most famous of these are probably the DiMaggio brothers. The three brothers to play were the great Joe DiMaggio, a Yankee from 1936 through 1951; Dominic DiMaggio, a member of the Red Sox from 1940-1953; and Vincent DiMaggio, who played for five National League clubs between 1937 and 1946.

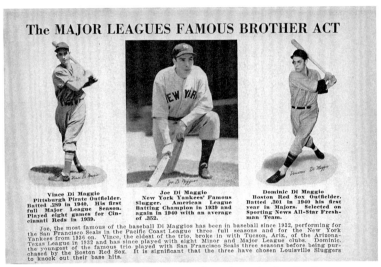

The DiMaggio Brothers. Image from the author's collection

Bob Meusel (Yankees) and Irish Meusel (New York Giants) were brothers who battled against each other in the 1921, 1922, and 1923 World Series.

Other Yankee Hall of Famers who had big league siblings include Bill Dickey, Stan Covelski, Joe Sewell, Paul Waner (a Yankee for only one day in his storied career), and Gaylord Perry. Ken Brett and Wes Ferrell were two Yankees whose brothers (George Brett and Rick Ferrell) have been enshrined in the Hall of Fame.

There were even a few brothers who both played for the Yankees at points in their careers.

Marcus Lawton and Matt Lawton both played for the Yankees, but not together. Marcus Lawton made his Major League debut with the Yankees in 1989. Sixteen years later, in 2005, brother Matt played briefly for the Yankees.

In the late 1980s, one of the Yankees' prized pitching prospects was a left-hander named Al Leiter. After some injuries, Al Leiter was traded to the Toronto Blue Jays where he began a solid 19-year career pitching for the Blue Jays, Florida Marlins, and the New York Mets. Leiter appeared in two All-Star Games (1996, 2000) and was a member of two World Series champion pitching staffs in Toronto and Florida. In 2000, Al Leiter pitched against the Yankees in the World Series. It was Al Leiter who took the loss for the Mets in the decisive Game 5 that earned the Yankees their

26th world championship. In 2005, Al Leiter returned to the Yankees to close out his Major League career. In 1990, Al's brother, Mark Leiter, also pitched briefly for the Yankees.

Then there were Donzell and Darnell McDonald. The McDonald brothers both had very brief Yankee careers. Donzell, an outfielder, appeared in five games in 2001. His brother, Darnell, appeared in four games with the Yankees in 2012.

The Perez brothers, Pascual and Melido, just missed being teammates. Pascual Perez was a flamboyant right-handed pitcher who enjoyed an eleven-year career spent mostly in the National League. Unfortunately, his promise was cut short by injuries and drug problems. After seemingly returning to health in 1989, Perez was signed to a lucrative free-agent contract with the Yankees who had high hopes for his rebirth. It wasn't to be. Pascual Perez pitched as a Yankee between 1990 and 1991 winning only three games and losing six. The next season Melido Perez joined the Yankees. While he wasn't a star, Melido Perez pitched four seasons (1992-1995) in pinstripes. Interestingly, in their careers, both Pascual Perez and Melido Perez pitched rain-shortened no-hitters. Melido's no-hitter came on July 12, 1990 against the Yankees.

In addition to Homer and Tommy Thompson, there were three other brother combinations who were teammates on the Yankees at the same time, some, if only briefly.

The brother teammate combination (other than the Thompsons) who played together for the shortest amount of time as Yankees were Bobby and Billy Shantz. Bobby Shantz was a solid left-handed pitcher who enjoyed a successful sixteen-year career in the Major Leagues. In 1952, while pitching for the Philadelphia Athletics, Shantz won 24 games against only 7 losses and was named the American League Most Valuable Player. He was also an All-Star in 1951 and 1952. Just before the 1957 season, Shantz was traded to the Yankees.

Bobby Shantz would spend four seasons in pinstripes appearing in 138 games, mostly as a relief pitcher. He was a member of the 1958 world championship team.

Brother Billy Shantz did not have as distinguished of a Major League career. A catcher, Billy Shantz arrived in the majors in

1954. With his brother, he was also a member of the Philadelphia A's.

In thirteen games during the 1955 season, Bobby and Billy Shantz formed the pitcher and catcher battery. Their best game together came on April 29, 1955. On that day, Bobby hurled a complete game 6-0 shutout, scattering only three hits against the Yankees.

During the 1955 season, Billy Shantz returned to the minor leagues where, except for one brief game in 1960, he spent the remainder of his career. The Yankees organization acquired Billy Shantz in 1959. In 1960, the Yankees brought Billy Shantz to the Major Leagues. He appeared in one game and while Bobby was also a member of the 1960 Yankees, he did not pitch in that game.

At the tail end of the 1985 season, two brothers who both happened to both be knuckleball pitchers, served as members of the Yankees' starting rotation. Future Hall of Famer Phil Niekro came to the Yankees after pitching for the Milwaukee and Atlanta Braves. Phil Niekro was a five-time All-Star. After the 1983 season, the forty-four-year-old pitcher signed a free-agent contract with the Yankees.

During the last few weeks of the 1985 season, the Yankees swung a trade with the Houston Astros for the other knuckleball-throwing Niekro brother—Joe. While his career was not quite at the level of his brother, Joe Niekro had won 195 games at the time of the trade.

On October 6, 1985, Phil Niekro pitched a four-hit shutout of the Toronto Blue Jays, but neither the complete game, nor the shutout was the big story. This accomplishment, Niekro became only the eighteenth pitcher in baseball history to win 300 games.

This story also has human interest side. At the time of the game, Phil and Joe Niekro's father was sick in the hospital. In the bottom of the ninth inning, just before the final out was recorded, Joe Niekro went to the mound with the news that their father had just been taken out of intensive care. Phil and Joe Niekro are the only brothers to be in uniform together on the same team for a pitcher's 300th win.

There was one other set of brothers who were Yankees teammates. Outfielders, Felipe and Matty Alou played together on the

Yankees in 1973. There was also a third big league brother, Jesus Alou, but he never donned pinstripes. As remarkable as it might be that the Yankees had two brothers patrolling in the outfield at the same time. The San Francisco Giants actually did the the Yankees one better. During Jesus' rookie season, the three Alou brothers played in the outfield at the same time in the same game three times.

For most of 1973 season, Felipe and Matty Alou played together on the Yankees. During that season, Felipe had an ancillary role in baseball history. That was the season the designated-hitter position was born. On that day, Ron Blomberg was penciled into the lineup as the designated hitter, becoming the first DH in baseball history, partially because Felipe Alou got the nod as the Yankees first baseman a position Blomberg also played.

In 1973, the Yankees spent much of the season battling for the division lead. They were in first place through August 2. Yet, the team could not maintain its winning. After a difficult August, winning only nine games while losing eighteen, the team dropped to fourth place. On September 6, 1973, both of the Alou brothers were sold by the Yankees. Felipe was sold to the Expos, Matty to the Cardinals.

In discussing baseball-playing brothers, it must be noted that there were two *Least Among Them Yankees* who had big league siblings. Elvio Jiminez's brother Manny played 429 games for the Kansas City A's, Pittsburgh Pirates, and Chicago Cubs. Floyd Newkirk's brother Joel pitched in a total of three games for the 1919 and 1920 Chicago Cubs.

WASHINGTON SENATORS at NEW YORK HIGHLANDERS

Saturday, October 5, 1912 (Hilltop Park)

	1	2	3	4	5	6	7	8	9		R	H	E
WASH	0	1	3	1	0	0	1	0	0		6	11	4
NY	1	0	0	1	2	1	0	3	X		8	9	3

WASH		AB	R	H	RBI	NY		AB	R	H	RBI
Moeller	RF	5	1	1	0	Midkiff	3B	5	2	3	0
Foster	3B	3	1	3	1	Chase	1B	3	1	1	4
Ryan	3B	1	0	0	0	Daniels	LF	5	1	1	0
Milan	CF	4	1	1	0	Lelivelt	RF	4	2	3	3
Gandil	1B	4	1	1	1	Stumpf	2B	2	0	0	1
Agler	1B					Smith	CF	4	0	0	0
Griffith	P/2B	1	0	0	0	McMillan	SS	4	0	0	0
LaPorte	2B	3	1	1	1	Williams	C	1	0	0	0
Schaefer	2B/P	1	0	1	0	Thompson	PR				
Shanks	LF	4	0	2	0	Schulz	P	1	1	0	0
McBride	SS	3	1	0	0	Keating	P	1	0	0	0
Morgan	SS					Fisher	P				
Williams	C	2	0	1	2	Sterrett	PH/C	3	1	1	0
Henry	C					**Thompson**	C				
Hughes	P	1	0	0	0						
Cashion	P	0	0	0	0						
Alltrock	P/1B	1	0	0	0						

WASH	IP	H	R	BB	SO	NY	IP	H	R	BB	SO
Hughes	4.1	4	4	1	1	Keating	3	6	4	3	2
Cashion	1.2	2	1	2	0	Fisher	1	2	1	0	1
Altrock - L	1.1	1	2	2	0	Schulz - W	5	3	1	4	3
Griffith	0	1	1	0	0						
Schaefer	0.2	1	0	0	0						

Homer Thompson

CHAPTER TWELVE
GEORGE BATTEN (1912)

There is one other player from that forgettable 1912 Highlanders roster that was a *Least Among Them* player—George Batten, a twenty-year-old second baseman from New Jersey who had his cup of coffee with the Yankees a few days before Homer Thompson. If Thompson's rise to the Major Leagues was improbable, Batten's was, well, seemingly impossible.

George Batten's minor league career wasn't just unmemorable—it didn't exist. It seems that George Batten never played professional baseball before, or even after, his appearance with the Highlanders. During this period of baseball history, professional franchises sometimes took players from collegiate teams to have a taste of big league ball, but even that was not the case with Batten. He never even finished high school!

George Batten's lone appearance in professional baseball came on September 28, 1912 during a doubleheader against the Philadelphia A's. He was just twenty years old. We have previously met the 1912 Highlanders, a last-place team that seemed to be literally taking players off the street to play for them at the end of the season. The 1912 Philadelphia Athletics were an altogether different squad. The Athletics were in the midst of one of their dynasties. Between 1909 and 1914, the Athletics won four American League pennants and three World Series. This 1912 squad was the weakest of the bunch as they finished in third place. That finish should not belie the fact that this was a talented squad. The 1912 Athletics finished with a very impressive 96-57 record. Note, also, that the 1912 A's season was bookended by world championships in 1911 and 1913. As the saying goes, "You can't win them all."

There were a host of future Hall of Famers and legendary players on the 1912 Philadelphia Athletics beginning with manager Connie Mack. Also on the squad were Chief Bender, Eddie Collins, Eddie Plank (who retired after being traded to the Yankees in 1918), and three future Yankees: Home Run Baker, Herb Pennock, and Stan Coveleski. Another player on that team, Jack Coombs, was a standout pitcher for a number of years before retiring. He coached collegiate baseball at Williams College, Princeton University, and Duke University. Coombs authored *Baseball: Individual Play and Team Strategy*, in 1938. This text became one of the most influential instruction baseball books of its time—one that influenced countless coaches and players for decades. The baseball field at Duke University is named for Jack Coombs.

As noted, the Highlanders and the Athletics played a double-header on the day of George Batten's big league debut. As can be guessed by the strength of these two squads, the Philadelphia team won both games. Batten seems to have had his fair share of playing time in one of the games. Unlike many of the players whose careers lasted but one game, it seems that he played eight innings in his lone game. Batten batted three times without a hit. He struck out once. In the ninth inning, with the Highlanders trailing 4-2, Del Paddock, a Highlander only in 1912 (although he played in 46 games), pinch hit for Batten and did not reach base.

In the field, Batten played second base. According to Baseball-Reference, he handled two chances without an error recording a putout and an assist. This writer's research shows that he committed an error in this game. In fact, it was George Batten's error that led to the Athletics' first run of the game as it allowed leadoff hitter Harl Maggert to reach base. The September 29, 1912 edition of the Philadelphia Inquirer reads, "The home folks got this run... by some fast work on the bases. Maggert getting a life on Batten's boot of his grounder..." The box score printed in that day's paper also shows an error credited to George Batten.

After George Batten left baseball, he returned to his home in New Jersey. Within two years, he was married. He lived most of his adult life in Cape May. Batten had a number of jobs including as a clerk for the Pennsylvania Rail Road Company. In 1917 or

1918 as a twenty-five-year-old man, he completed his registration for the draft for World War I, but his number was not called. He registered for World War II in 1942 as a fifty-year-old man, but again wasn't called. George Batten died in Florida in 1972. It seems that after his one day in baseball, George Batten went about living a typical American life.

Extra Innings
A Void in Monument Park

The Yankees have a tradition of honoring the greatest players in their history with monuments or plaques in Monument Park located within Yankee Stadium. The Yankees have honored players from every position on the diamond except for third base. There are no Yankee third basemen in Monument Park.

That absence might make the casual fan assume the Yankees have never had great third basemen. This is certainly not the case. Yankees' history is replete with third basemen who have been an important part of their success.

The first great Yankee to play third base for the Yankees was Frank "Home Run" Baker, who, in George Batten's one game in 1912, was still a member of the Philadelphia A's. An eventual member of the Hall of Fame, Baker became a Yankee in 1916. In four years as their starting third baseman Frank Baker hit .289 with 32 home runs.

Frank Baker left baseball after the 1919 season to care for his family which had been devastated by Scarlet Fever. During that epidemic, Baker lost his wife and had to care for his two young daughters who eventually recovered. He returned to the Yankees in 1921 and was the starting third baseman on their first ever American League championship team. Baker also contributed as a part-time player in 1922, a season when the Yankees again won the American League title.

The next Yankees third baseman of note was the one who replaced Home Run Baker at the position. This player was a minor star in his own right—"Jumping" Joe Dugan. A fourteen-year Major Leaguer, Joe Dugan's best years were the seven (1922-1928) he played third base for the Yankees. Dugan was the third baseman on the Yankees first ever world championship team in 1923 and was on the legendary Murderers' Row Yankees world champion in 1927 and 1928.

While future Hall of Famer Joe Sewell manned third base for three seasons (1931-1933), third base did not have a long-term permanent resident until Red Rolfe took over the position beginning in 1935. Rolfe patrolled this spot on the diamond as a starter through 1941. Rolfe was a Yankee for his entire big league career. He played a total of ten seasons in pinstripes and was a four-time American League All-Star. For seven consecutive years, he scored 100 or more runs. Rolfe's best season was 1939 when he led the American League in hits (213), runs (139), and doubles (46). The Yankees appeared in six World Series during his tenure, winning five.

After his playing days, Rolfe was the head baseball coach at Yale University. He also managed the Detroit Tigers for three-and-a-half seasons from 1949 to 1952. Finally, he served as the director of athletics at Dartmouth College from 1954 through 1967. The baseball field at Dartmouth is named for Red Rolfe.

Following Rolfe, a series of third basemen came and went. It wasn't until 1954 that Andy Carey brought some stability to the position. Carey would man third base for five seasons. His best season was 1955 when he led the league in putouts, assists, and double plays at third base. Carey's Yankees appeared in five World Series winning three. Andy Carey's greatest World Series moment may have been in 1956 when he made two strong defensive plays that helped preserve Don Larsen's perfect game.

From 1960 through 1966, Clete Boyer held down the third-base position. Although he wasn't much of a hitter, with a .241 lifetime batting average as a Yankee, he was renowned for his defense and he still is considered one of baseball's greatest defensive third basemen. In the years 1960-1964, Boyer played in five consecutive World Series, winning two.

Graig Nettles was the next great Yankees' third baseman. Nettles played eleven years as a Yankee. He was a powerful hitter, a stellar defender, and a team leader. In 1982, Nettles was named the team's captain, an honor that had been given only to Lou Gehrig and Thurman Munson in the previous 47 years. During Nettles' years in New York, the Yankees won five division titles,

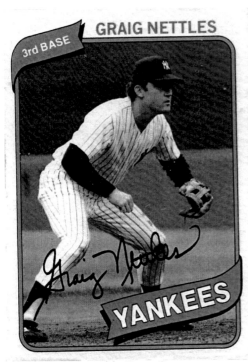

GRAIG NETTLES
3rd BASE
YANKEES

Courtesy of the Topps Company

four American League championships, and two World Series.

Nettles hit twenty or more home runs in each of his first seven seasons in pinstripes and in 1976, he led the American League in home runs with 32. In the decade of the 1970s only Hall of Famer Reggie Jackson hit more home runs as an American League player. In addition, Nettles is the all-time leader in home runs by an AL third baseman.

Although he was considered a clutch hitter, Nettles was known even more for his defensive abilities, winning the Gold Glove in 1977 and 1978 and was named an American League All-Star on five separate occasions. Nettles is also firmly entrenched as the Yankees all-time leader in games played at third base. During his Yankees career, Graig Nettles played 1,508 games at the hot corner.

Based on his longevity, his power hitting, his exemplary fielding, and the championships won during his time in New York, many consider Graig Nettles to be the greatest third baseman in Yankees history. Many also believe that Nettles belongs in the Hall of Fame.

Following Nettles, third base became a weak position again for the Yankees. For a brief time in the mid-1980s, a scrappy player named Mike Pagliarulo manned the position. He enjoyed some success with the long ball. Between 1985 and 1987, Pagliarulo hit 79 home runs, but his flame burned out rather quickly.

The next truly great Yankee third baseman was former Red Sox star Wade Boggs who came to the Yankees in 1993. In five seasons, Wade Boggs hit .313 including a high of .342 in 1994. Boggs' strong bat, better-than-advertised defense (Boggs won the Gold Glove in 1994 and 1995), and leadership helped bring the Yankees back to respectability and championship form. Boggs was the Yankees' starting third baseman on their 1996 world championship team.

Between 1998 and 2000, the Yankees won three consecutive world championships. Their third baseman during those years was Scott Brosius. Brosius was an American League All-Star in 1998 and he won the Gold Glove in 1999.

Finally, any discussion about Yankees third basemen would be incomplete without mentioning Alex Rodriquez. He was one of the greatest all-around player the Yankees ever had, along with being one of their most controversial.

From 2004 through 2012, Rodriguez was the Yankees starting third baseman. In that time, Rodriguez played more games at that position (1,193) than any player in Yankees history other than Graig Nettles (1,508).

When he arrived to the Yankees in February 2004, Alex Rodriguez already was widely hailed as one of the greatest players of his generation. He was baseball's premier shortstop—a seven-time All-Star who had led the American League in home runs each of the three seasons before arriving in New York. Rodriguez won the Gold Glove at shortstop in 2002 and 2003. He was also the American League's Most Valuable Player in 2003. Rodriguez was a superstar in every sense of the word. Yet the Yankees at that time had a great shortstop of their own, the legendary Derek Jeter. Upon his arrival in New York, Alex Rodriguez deferred to Jeter and voluntarily moved from shortstop to third base where he would star for many seasons.

As a Yankee third baseman, Alex Rodriguez put up numbers that had never been seen by a Yankee at that position. From 2004 through 2010, Rodriguez enjoyed seven consecutive 30+ home run seasons. In each of those seasons, Alex Rodriguez also drove in at least 100 runs. A-Rod was the American League MVP in 2005 and again in 2007.

Alex Rodriguez's statistics through 2009, and then beyond, would have been enough, judging by the numbers, to easily rank him as the premier Yankees third baseman of all time. But, just as he seemingly had won over the Yankee faithful, his career started to unravel when his name became associated with steroids.

The steroid talk actually began in 2009 with the release of a positive test and then articles and a book that claimed Rodriguez had used steroids throughout his career. For the sake of brevity, the allegations, dishonesty, lawsuits, and such that played a major role in this story greatly tarnished Alex Rodriguez's legacy as a Yankee and as one of baseball's premier players. His close association with performance-enhancing drugs puts Rodriguez's body of work in question. His numbers alone would rank him as an all-time great, but the controversies that surround his career leave much of his legacy in doubt.

What is clear is that throughout the Yankees' impressive history many great players patrolled third base and contributed to the team's glory. The absence of a third baseman in Monument Park is an oversight that should be immediately corrected. It is time to begin honoring these legendary Yankees. The Yankees should begin by honoring their former captain, a two-time world champion, and the player who played more games at third base than any other Yankee, Graig Nettles.

NEW YORK HIGHLANDERS at PHILADELPHIA ATHLETICS

Saturday, September 28, 1912 (Shibe Park)

	1	2	3	4	5	6	7	8	9		R	H	E
NY	1	0	0	0	0	0	0	0	1		2	6	2
PHI	1	3	0	0	0	0	0	0	X		4	8	1

NY		AB	R	H	RBI	PHI		AB	R	H	RBI
Midkiff	3B	4	1	2	0	Maggert	RF	4	1	0	0
Chase	1B	3	1	0	0	Oldring	CF	4	0	0	0
Daniels	LF	4	0	0	0	Collins	2B	4	0	1	0
Lelivelt	RF	4	0	1	1	Baker	3B	4	0	1	0
Batten	2B	3	0	0	0	McInnis	1B	3	1	2	0
Paddock	PH	1	0	0	0	Walsh	LF	3	1	1	0
Smith	CF	3	0	1	0	Barry	SS	2	1	1	1
McMillan	SS	3	0	1	0	Egan	C	3	0	1	1
Sweeney	C	3	0	0	0	Houck	P	3	0	1	1
Ford	P	3	0	1	0						

NY	IP	H	R	BB	SO	PHI	IP	H	R	BB	SO
Ford - L	8	8	4	1	3	Houck - W	9	6	2	0	9

George Batten

CHAPTER THIRTEEN
HARRY HANSON (1913)

The 1912 Highlanders were not a very impressive squad. In 1913, the team became known as the Yankees, but the results on the field did not change dramatically. They were still not very good. In 1912, the Highlanders won 50 games and finished in last place in the eight-team American League. This squad, the 1913 New York Yankees, fared only slightly better, earning 57 wins and a seventh-place finish.

There were two *Least Among Them* Yankees who played for the 1913 squad and they played within eleven days of one another. Let us first look at a man who set a Major League record that still stands today, a catcher by the name of Harry Hanson.

Harry Hanson had his one opportunity to play Major League Baseball as a seventeen-year-old on July 14, 1913. Hanson was signed by the Yankees because the team was suffering through a period when it lacked depth at the catcher position. It was said that manager Frank Chance took Hanson, a Chicago schoolboy, so that his "backstopping staff" could get back on its feet. It is assumed that Hanson was signed while the team was in Chicago during its three-game series from July 9 through 11. It was just three days after they left Chicago, on July 14, that Harry Hanson enjoyed his only professional baseball game. When he appeared in the game, Hanson, at 17 years and 178 days old, became the youngest player to ever appear in an American League game as a catcher. (The second youngest catcher to appear in an American League game was eventual Hall of Famer Jimmy Foxx who appeared as a catcher for the Philadelphia Athletics on May 26, 1925. Foxx was 17 years, 216 days old at the time.)

Hanson's opportunity did not come in New York at the Polo Grounds, rather his game came in St. Louis against the lowly

Browns. In 1913, there was only one team that finished below the Yankees in the standings. That was the Browns. That unremarkable team finished in last place winning 57 games against 96 losses. (The 1913 Yankees also won only 57 games, but they ended with two fewer losses, and, as a result, finished above the Browns.)

There were not many players of note on the 1913 Browns. The only future Hall of Famer was Bobby Wallace who, by this point in his career was a reserve player who hit only .211 for the season. One of the Browns' most proficient batters was Del Pratt a sophomore second baseman. Pratt hit .296 in 1914 while leading the league in games played for the first of four consecutive years. Pratt would soon impact the history of the Yankees.

Pratt was traded to the Yankees in January 1918 along with legendary pitcher Eddie Plank in exchange for five players including Urban Shocker who would win 20 or more games in four consecutive seasons for the Brownies before returning to the Yankees in 1925. Plank never suited up for the Yankees and instead retired from baseball to his home in Gettysburg, Pennsylvania. But it was Pratt who brought some legitimacy to the pre-Babe Ruth Yankees. In fact, sportswriter Fred Lieb first called the Yankees lineup "Murderers' Row" after they had acquired Pratt. He was an able batsman who was an important part of what Lieb called "the greatest collection of pitcher thumpers today." Pratt helped take the Yankees franchise from league doormats to a team that began contending, if eventually falling short, for the American League title. Pratt remained a Yankee until after the 1920 season when he was traded to the Red Sox, in general manager Ed Barrow's first trade. In the trade, the Yankees received Wally Schang and Waite Hoyt, two key contributors to the dynasty of the 1920s.

The 1913 Yankees also were not an overly talented squad, but there were some players of note. Roger Peckinpaugh was playing in his first of nine years as the Yankees' shortstop. Peckinpaugh would be named Yankees captain, and, a year later, would manage the team for 20 games.

In 1914, a part-time third baseman on that squad, Fritz Maisel, would set the long-standing Yankees single season record for most stolen bases with 74. This record lasted until 1985 when it was eclipsed by Rickey Henderson. Henderson remains the only Yankee to ever steal more bases in a single season than Maisel. Henderson bettered Maisel's mark three times—in 1985 with 80 stolen bases; in 1986 with 87 stolen bases; and in 1988 with 93 stolen bases. Each of these totals, in succession, became the Yankees' all-time record.

Also on the 1913 Yankees was pitcher Russ Ford, playing in his final season with New York. Earlier in his career Ford had some brilliant seasons, winning more than twenty games in both 1910 and 1911.

Yankees manager Frank Chance, was also a part-time player. Chance, the first baseman of the legendary poem, *Baseball's Sad Lexicon* (better known as "Tinker to Evers to Chance") was in the first of his two seasons managing the Yankees. The team's lack of success under Chance, a four-time pennant winner and two-time World Series manager with the Chicago Cubs, helped to prematurely end his managerial career. After being fired by the Yankees in 1914, Chance had only one other Major League managing opportunity. In 1923, he managed the Boston Red Sox who finished in last place. Chance died just a year later. He had been hit by pitched balls 137 times in his career, often in the head. Blood clots from these beanings contributed to his early demise at just 48 years old.

The ballgame between the visiting Yankees and the Browns on July 14, 1913 was actually not much of a game. The Browns had their way, winning 11-1. As noted, when Harry Hanson went into the game as catcher, he set the Major League record for the being youngest player ever to appear in a big league game as a catcher. That unique record still stands. Hanson played for three innings. He recorded one assist and one putout against no errors. The assist came when he threw a runner out who was trying to steal a base. *Sporting Life* recorded his game in this manner:

> "While the New Yorks were in Chicago manager (Frank) Chance picked up a young catcher named Harry Hanson. He played with the Washington Heights team. He is a sturdy lad... and seems to have a good whip. He made his first appearance

with the New Yorks on July 14, when he caught three innings, got a putout and an assist, and in two times at bat hit hard though not safely."

Unfortunately, after the loss, Hanson's Major League career was over.

Sports fans often call their favorite players heroes. Ordinary men can become regarded as larger than life based upon their exploits on a playing field. Harry Hanson was a hero, but his heroics came away from the baseball diamond when he served his country in the United States Army. Based on this author's research, Harry F. Hanson served in the U.S. Army from 1915 until 1954. During his many years of military service, Harry Hanson served with distinction. He was a member of the Third Infantry Division in the early days of World War I, from 1916 to 1918, but was discharged honorably from that division in April 1918 before that unit went to Europe to fight in the war.

In the years between the wars, Harry Hanson rose through the ranks. He attended Officers School, Infantry School, and Tank School. For a time, he was stationed under Commander Douglas MacArthur in the Philippines. Hanson became a colonel in December 1941 and served in World War II with the 6th Armored Division (the "Super Sixth") that fought at The Battle For Brest and in the Battle of the Bulge.

Colonel Harry Hanson died on October 5, 1966. He passed away while enjoying a round of golf at the Savannah Golf Club. He was 70 years old. Hanson may not have had a long baseball career, and he might not have ever played a game in New York, but his most notable exploits came in service to his country.

Extra Innings
A Watershed Year

I913 was a watershed year for the franchise as three changes took place that, in their own ways, defined the organization going forward. The impact of those changes still resonates today.

First, the Highlanders moved out of Hilltop Park. By 1912, this team began playing some home games at the Polo Grounds, the home of the National League's New York Giants. In 1913 the move became permanent. Since the team was no longer playing atop a small rise in upper Manhattan, Highlanders no longer seemed an appropriate name. Almost since the team's inception, the Highlanders had been known by various other names including the New York Americans and the New York Yankees. With the move out of Hilltop Park, the team became known, forever more, as the Yankees. Within a year, Hilltop Park was demolished. The eventual path to the construction of Yankee Stadium had begun.

In addition, the Yankees made a modification in their uniform design for 1913 that remains today. Interestingly, the long-lasting change was not the advent of pinstripes on the home uniform. In fact, the 1912 Yankees home uniform, with pinstripes and the interlocking NY on the right breast was almost identical to the uniform the team still wears today. For 1913, the Yankees actually eliminated the pinstripes. (The pinstripes returned in 1915 and have remained a staple of the Yankees home uniform ever since.) The uniform change that lasts today and that started in 1913 was in regard to the away threads. It was in 1913 that the Yankees, for all intents and purposes, initiated the grey road uniform with the words "NEW YORK" in capital letters across the front. This idea had been used on occasion in 1911, but from 1913 forward it has—except for a four-year period from 1927-1930—remained, the standard Yankees "away" uniform design.

Thus, while the 1913 Yankees were not a successful team, it was this squad that brought them their name, their away uniform, and began the process, because of their move from Manhattan, of having their own stadium.

One might say that in a number of important ways, the Yankees of today were truly born during that 1913 season.

1913 Yankees Team Photo
Library of Congress, Prints and Photographs Division, [LC-DIG-bbc-2079f]

NEW YORK YANKEES at ST. LOUIS BROWNS

Monday, July 14, 1913 (Sportsman's Park)

	1	2	3	4	5	6	7	8	9		R	H	E
NY	0	0	0	0	0	0	0	0	1		1	6	0
STL	3	2	2	4	0	0	0	0	X		11	12	0

NY		AB	R	H	RBI	STL		AB	R	H	RBI
Daniels	RF	4	0	0	0	Shotton	CF	5	1	3	2
Wolter	CF	3	0	0	0	Brief	1B	5	1	1	1
Cree	LF	4	0	2	0	Pratt	2B	3	2	1	0
Hartzell	2B	4	0	0	0	Williams	RF	4	2	2	3
Peckinpaugh	SS	3	1	0	0	Johnston	LF	0	1	0	1
Knight	1B	4	0	2	0	Flanagan	LF	1	0	0	0
Midkiff	3B	3	0	0	0	Wallace	3B	2	1	1	2
Smith	C	2	0	0	0	Lavan	SS	4	0	0	0
Hanson	C	2	0	0	0	Agnew	C	3	1	1	0
Warhop	P					McAllester	C	1	0	0	0
Schulz	P	1	0	0	0	Baumgardner	P	4	2	3	2
Clark	P					Schmidt	P				
Caldwell	P	3	0	2	1						

NY	IP	H	R	BB	SO	STL	IP	H	R	BB	SO
Warhop - L	0.2	4	3	0	0	Baumgardner - W	7	3	0	1	2
Schulz	2.1	6	4	2	0	Schmidt	2	3	1	2	0
Clark	0	0	4	4	0						
Caldwell	5	2	0	2	3						

Harry Hanson

Manhattan College 1913 Varsity Basesball Team, Photo Courtesy of Manhattan College

CHAPTER FOURTEEN
JIM HANLEY (1913)

I913 was the year the Yankees, in name at least, were born. It was also the year that left-handed pitcher James Patrick Hanley enjoyed his one game in the Major Leagues. That day was July 3, 1913, eleven days prior to Harry Hanson's solitary Yankees appearance.

Like Hanson, Jim Hanley seemingly arrived in the Major Leagues with no minor league experience, although he did play semiprofessional baseball in North Adams, Massachusetts in 1909, the summer after his freshman year of college.

An engineering major, Jim Hanley pitched for the Manhattan College Jaspers from 1909 through 1913. He was the captain and the team's Most Valuable Player in each of his final two seasons of college ball. There is a 1972 letter from Manhattan College that indicates that Jim Hanley was the top college pitcher in the nation in 1913. That he went straight from his college graduation to the Yankees is not a great surprise.

Hanley signing with New York's American League baseball team was newsworthy enough to be reported in numerous newspapers including *The North Adams Transcript, The Berkshire Eagle* (Pittsfield, MA), Brooklyn, New York's *Times Eagle,* and *The Boston Globe* among others. One newspaper account, from Connecticut's *Bridgeport Times and Evening Farmer* (June 13, 1913) highlights, in clear print, how in 1913 the team name for this ball club was changing. This team wasn't the Highlanders one day and the Yankees the next. The change in names was gradual and for a time the names were used interchangeably as indicated in the text of the article that reads:

> HANLEY SIGNED BY N.Y. YANKEES
> Jim Hanley captain and star pitcher of the Manhattan College baseball team, was signed yesterday to pitch for the New York Highlanders.

That article goes on to state that Hanley, along with a pitcher at Seton Hall, are "considered by followers of college games to be the two best bets in the college ranks."

Jim Hanley's lone big league game was played at home at the Polo Grounds against the eventual world champion Philadelphia Athletics. The 1913 Athletics were a powerhouse team. Future Hall of Famers abounded. On that A's team were Home Run Baker, Chief Bender, Eddie Collins, Herb Pennock (who would one day be a Yankee), and Eddie Plank. Also on that squad were two rookies who would later play significant roles on the Yankees, catcher Wally Schang and pitcher Bob Shawkey.

Wally Schang was a standout catcher who made an immediate impact during his rookie year. In his time, Schang was considered one of the great defensive catchers in the game. While his 1913 statistics don't look overly impressive today (he batted just .266 in 79 games), his overall play was notable enough to earn him enough votes to place eighth for the Chalmers Award which was given to the league's Most Valuable Player. Schang's three home runs that year led all catchers and, combined with his defensive abilities, helped make him one of the most well-rounded players in the game. The next season Schang again appeared among the leaders in the Chalmers Award voting, though he fell well short of earning the award. In 1915, Schang set a record by throwing out six potential base stealers in one game. In 1916, he became the first switch hitter to hit home runs from both sides of the plate in the same game. In total, Wally Schang played five years with the Athletics before being traded to the Red Sox for the 1918 season when the A's dismantled their roster. After three successful years in Boston (one that included the 1918 world championship), Wally Schang was traded to the Yankees. His solid play as catcher helped make the position a strength for the Yankees. It is no coincidence that the Yankees won pennants (and one World Series) in each of Schang's first three seasons in New York. During his career, Wally Schang played on seven teams that reached the World Series.

Bob Shawkey was also a rookie on that 1913 Philadelphia squad. He pitched for the Athletics from 1913 through 1915 amassing a 27-19 record in two-and-a-half seasons before being sold to the Yankees in June 1915. It was as a Yankee, for whom he pitched 13 seasons, that Shawkey made his mark. He won twenty or more games four times as a Yankee. Shawkey helped to anchor the pitching staff that brought the first pennants and World Series championship to the Yankees in the early 1920s. Shawkey started the first game at Yankee Stadium in 1923. After the stadium was remodeled in 1976, Bob Shawkey threw out the ceremonial first pitch to open that new era in Yankees history.

The 1913 Yankees were not a strong squad, destined to finish the year in seventh place with only 57 wins. As such, it is no surprise that Jim Hanley's game was one the Yankees lost. Unlike many of the players in this history, though, Hanley actually played a relatively large role in the game, pitching the final four innings. One might wonder if he gave much thought during the game to the seventh-inning stretch, but as will be seen, the history of that time-honored tradition was something Jim Hanley probably knew all about.

In his four innings, Hanley allowed five hits, four walks, and three runs (all earned). He also struck out two batters. Hanley also had one plate appearance. He made an out, although no data exists that tells how he was retired although it is known that he did not strike out. It is also known that a Yankee rookie, Dashing Dan Costello, pinch hit for Hanley in the ninth inning. Costello was also retired. Dan Costello appeared in only two games as a Yankee in 1913 before heading to the Pittsburgh Pirates for three seasons where he was a part-time outfielder.

This one outing seemed to be enough for Yankees' manager Frank Chance who announced that Hanley was being released a few days later. According to *The North Adams Transcript*, "It did not require much time for the Highlander manager to discover that Hanley was not big league stock." The article went on to note that Hanley "had a fairly good breaking curve but nothing else and Chance decided that he could not use him."

There is a story on the internet, widely reported in the few articles there even are about Jim Hanley, that in this game he was hit in the head by a line drive that left him partially blind. This author disputes that account on a number of grounds. First, the box score indicates that Hanley finished the ninth inning on the mound. If he had been hit by a line drive that left him blind, he surely couldn't have finished the inning. There also seems to be no accounts of this happening in any newspapers of the day, including the July 3, 1913 edition of the *Evening World* and the July 4, 1913 editions of three other New York City newspapers: *The Sun, New-York Tribune,* and *The New York Times*. Further, on October 22, 1913, *The Brattleboro Daily Reformer* noted that while pitching for a team known as the Montcalms of Manville, "Jim Hanley the old Manhattan College twirler who was with the Highlanders... allowed three hits, fanned 17 and lost his game, 1-0." That would be some feat for a partially blind pitcher to accomplish. Finally, when noting that Jim Hanley was released, *The North Adams Transcript* did not mention a line drive or an injury.

Like Harry Hanson, outside of this lone Major League appearance, there are no records of Jim Hanley playing professional baseball at any level ever again, although, he stayed active in the game with some local clubs in New England.

Hanley used his engineering degree from Manhattan College to secure a job as an engineer for the Atlas Powder Company where he worked until his death in 1961.

Extra Innings
The Seventh-Inning Stretch

Before his moment on the big league diamond, Jim Hanley attended and was a graduate of Manhattan College. To date, thirty-two Manhattan alumni have participated in a Major League Baseball game. The most notable player to come off the Manhattan College campus was probably Buddy Hassett, primarily a first baseman and outfielder who played seven Major League seasons between 1936 and 1942 before his career was cut short by World War II. Hassett played primarily in the National League for the Brooklyn Dodgers and the Boston Bees/Braves. In 1942, his last season, Hassett played for the Yankees.

Hassett was an excellent ballplayer batting over .300 in three of his first four seasons. In his rookie season, 1936, Buddy Hassett tied for the league lead in games played (with Arky Vaughan and Gus Suhr) with 156. He also set the Major League record for the fewest strikeouts in a full season by a rookie. He struck out just 17 times in 635 at bats. Hassett did more than just play ball. While he was with the Dodgers, Hassett utilized his other talent, singing tenor; a skill for which he had no formal training. Known as "The Bronx Thrush," during his semi-pro career, he sometimes entertained crowds by singing into a megaphone during rain delays. Hassett also sang stage shows between movies at the Brooklyn Strand, sometimes appearing with sportswriter Stan Lomax.

During World War II, Hassett served as a lieutenant in the Pacific Theater aboard the aircraft carrier USS Bennington (CV-20). This carrier earned three battle stars and, most notably, was involved in the invasions of Iwo Jima and Okinawa. Hassett was the ship's athletic director. The USS Bennington was also the recovery ship for the unmanned Apollo 4 space mission.

After World War II, Hassett served as the manager for the Yankees Triple-A club in Newark in 1949, the last season that the famous franchise was affiliated with the Yankees.

Yet, there was another person affiliated with Manhattan College who made a much larger impact on the game of baseball. That man was Brother Jasper of Mary, F.S.C., Manhattan's prefect of students, among other titles including athletic director and baseball coach. A strong disciplinarian, Brother Jasper required the students attending the game and watching from the stands to sit straight up during the games. As relayed on the Manhattan College website:

> "During one particularly hot day, Br. Jasper noticed the students were becoming restless during the seventh inning of a close game. To relieve the tension, Br. Jasper called time-out and told the students to stand up and stretch for a few minutes until the game resumed.
>
> Since Manhattan College annually played the New York Giants baseball team in the late 1880's and into the 1950's at the Polo Grounds, the Manhattan College practice of the "seventh-inning stretch" spread into the Major Leagues where it has now become a time-honored custom practiced by millions of fans annually."

In 2014, The Wall Street Journal confirmed this story adding that the legend that President William Howard Taft created the tradition in 1910 is a falsehood.

In honor of Brother Jasper, the Manhattan College sports teams are still known as the Jaspers.

Today every Major League Baseball team recognizes the "Seventh-Inning Stretch." At certain times, various teams employ activities during this break in the action. Most often, the song *Take Me Out To The Ball Game* is sung. At various times at Yankee Stadium a popular country line dance song *"Cotton-Eye Joe"* has also been played. But, since September 11, 2001, the Yankees added the tradition of playing *"God Bless America"* during the seventh-inning Stretch.

PHILADELPHIA ATHLETICS at NEW YORK YANKEES

Thursday, July 3, 1913 (Polo Grounds)

		1	2	3	4	5	6	7	8	9			R	H	E
PHI		1	1	3	0	0	0	1	0	2			8	11	2
NY		0	0	0	0	2	0	0	0	2			4	5	2

PHI		AB	R	H	RBI*	NY		AB	R	H	RBI
Murphy	RF	2	1	1		Daniels	RF	3	0	1	2
Walsh	RF	1	1	0		Wolter	CF	4	0	0	0
Oldring	LF	5	2	4		Cree	LF	3	0	0	0
Collins	2B	5	1	1		Sweeney	C	3	1	0	0
Baker	3B	5	1	1		Hartzell	2B	4	1	2	0
McInnis	1B	4	1	2		Peckinpaugh	SS	4	0	2	1
Strunk	CF	4	0	1		Borton	1B	1	1	0	1
Barry	SS	3	0	0		Midkiff	3B	4	1	0	0
Lapp	C	3	1	1		Keating	P	1	0	0	0
Brown	P	4	0	0		McConnell	P	1	0	0	0
						Caldwell	PH	1	0	0	0
						Hanley	P	1	0	0	0
						Costello	PH	1	0	0	0

* No official record on Philadelphia's RBIs for this game.

PHI	IP	H	R	BB	SO	NY	IP	H	R	BB	SO
Brown - W	9	5	4	5	2	Keating - L	2.1	5	5	2	0
						McConnell	2.2	1	0	1	1
						Hanley	4	5	3	4	2

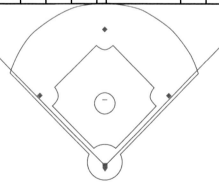

Jim Hanley

Photo from the author's collection.

CHAPTER FIFTEEN
RUGGER ARDIZOIA (1947)

Rinaldo Joseph "Rugger" Ardizoia was born in Italy in 1919 and is one of three *Least Among Them* Yankees to have been born in Europe along with Stefan Wever and Bob Davidson. (Wever and Davidson were both born in Germany.)

Ardizoia followed the traditional path to the Major Leagues participating in a long journey through the minors before arriving in The Show. Like so many baseball players in the 1940s, the long trail was extended by three years of military service during World War II. The story of Ardizoia's World War II experience deserves to be told along with his baseball exploits.

Ardizoia's trek to the majors began in 1937 almost as soon

as he graduated from Commerce High School in San Francisco, California. Rugger had been a standout pitcher in high school throwing two no-hitters. In one of those games, neither team had a hit and the game eventually was stopped because it ran too long. Because of his high school success, Rugger signed a contract with the Mission Reds of the Pacific Coast League six months before graduation. Since he was considered a professional athlete, he had to turn down a scholarship from Stanford University.

His professional career began with a game against the 1937 San Diego Padres of the Pacific Coast League. That team was filled with a host of former Major Leaguers, including Cedric Durst, a member of the 1927 Yankees, and Jimmy Reese, once Babe Ruth's roommate. The youngest player on that San Diego squad was an eighteen-year-old slugger named Ted Williams. Ardizoia pitched five innings that day, allowing only one hit.

After two additional seasons on the west coast, Ardizoia was acquired by the Yankees in December, 1939. In the trade with Hollywood, they acquired former Major Leaguer Ivy Andrews and Hiram Bithorn. Bithorn's name may not be familiar to many baseball fans today, but his impact on the game was tremendous. Bithorn eventually made it to the Majors in 1942 with the Chicago Cubs to become the first player from Puerto Rico to play Major League Baseball. Bithorn, a light-skinned man, confronted racial stereotyping and harassment from managers, players, and fans not unlike the trials that Jackie Robinson would go through five seasons later. Hiram Bithorn truly was a baseball pioneer. The baseball stadium in San Juan, Puerto Rico, built in 1962, is named for Hiram Bithorn. Between 2003 and 2004, the Montreal Expos played 42 home games at Bithorn Stadium. In June 2010, the Florida Marlins hosted a three-game series at the stadium against the New York Mets.

In an arrangement similar to the trade for Joe DiMaggio, even though he was with the Yankees, Ardizoia spent the 1940 season in the Pacific Coast League with the Hollywood Stars playing alongside Bithorn.

Before the 1941 season, Rugger Ardizoia trained with the Yankees. He was sent to the Newark Bears of the International League at the end of Spring Training. Rugger's own Italian na-

RENALDO (Rugger) ARDIZOIA
Ooks Pitcher   20
Courtesy of TCMA Ltd.

tionality soon became a problem forcing the Yankees to send him to their Kansas City franchise. Ardizoia played for Kansas City for the 1941 and 1942 seasons before heading off to war.

Rugger Ardizoia's path to serving his country in World War II is worth looking into. In 1941, Ardizoia was transferred from the Yankees' Newark team to their Kansas City squad. This happened early in the season before a series in Canada. There were two Canadian franchises (Toronto and Montreal) in the International League that year. Before the team's first trip to Canada, it was discovered that Ardizoia was not a citizen of the United States. Since Canada was at war with Italy, and he was technically an enemy alien, he was not allowed into the country. Kansas City, which was placed in the American Association had no such problems, since all eight of the franchises in that league were in the United States.

After the war, Rugger Ardizoia began his slow, steady climb to the majors. In 1946, he played for the Oakland Oaks in the Pacific Coast League. Under soon-to-be legendary Yankees manager Casey Stengel, the Oaks won 111 games. There were three pitchers on that squad who each won fifteen games—future Major Leaguers Gene Bearden (15-4) and Spec Shea (15-5) along with Ardizoia (15-7).

Six years and a war later, in 1947, Rugger Ardizoia, returned to spring training with the Yankees. In the Yankees' twelfth game of the season, Ardizoia was afforded his one big league opportunity. It came in St. Louis against the Browns. The Yankees would win 97 games against only 59 losses that year, but on this day the St. Louis squad bested the New Yorkers. For Ardizoia, his opportunity to pitch came in the mop-up role as the Browns rolled 15-5.

Ardizioa pitched the seventh and the eighth innings, facing ten batters allowing two runs on four hits and one walk. He allowed a home run to Walter Judnich. Late in life, Ardizoia admitted to grooving the ball to Judnich who had been a teammate of his when the two soldiers were stationed on Iwo Jima. Judnich also had played in the Pacific Coast League and had once been in the Yankees' system.

In the top of the ninth inning, Johnny Lindell pinch hit for Ardizoia and with that his Major League career was over. Soon he was returned to the Hollywood Stars. He played for the Stars, the Seattle Rainiers, and the Dallas Eagles before calling it a career in 1951.

By 1943, Ardizoia was inducted into the U.S. Army. He served in the Army Air Force from 1943 through 1945. While stationed in Honolulu, he joined the baseball team—a move that may have saved his life. On one particular night, he was relieved of flying duties because he was scheduled to pitch the next day. The plane he would have been on crashed. During his enlistment he served and played baseball in Tinian, Saipan, and Iwo Jima. After returning from the war, he visited a judge who, upon learning that he faithfully served the United States in the war, declared him a citizen.

Rugger Ardizoia went home to his wife and two children after his playing days. He worked as a seller for a linen company for over thirty years and was a founder of the San Francisco Old Timer's Baseball Association.

His Major League career may have lasted for a brief two innings, but Ardizoia was a Yankee until he passed away in 2015 at the age of 95. At that time, he was the oldest living Yankee.

Extra Innings
Yankees Born in Europe

To date, nineteen players in the history of the Yankees, including Rugger Ardizoia, were born in Europe. The first to appear as a New York Highlander was "Honest" John Anderson. Born in Norway, Anderson emigrated to the United States when he was eight years old and was one of baseball's earliest switch hitters. In the 1890s, playing in the National League, Anderson was a power hitter who also batted over .300 on four separate occasions. He earned the nickname "Honest John" because he rarely argued any calls made by the umpires.

Anderson became a Highlander in 1904, the first season in which the team enjoyed success and a pennant race. That year he played 143 games in the outfield and at first base and led the team with 82 runs batted in. The Highlanders lost the pennant on the last day of that season to the Boston Red Sox.

"Dirty" Jack Doyle, who was born in Ireland, became a star in the 1890s. In 1905, he became a Highlander for one game. It was his hard-nosed style of play that earned him the nickname "Dirty Jack" as did his propensity to battle opponents, umpires, and fans.

In 1908 and 1909, Henry Cooke "Irish" McIveen, who hailed from Belfast, Ireland played for the Highlanders. He appeared in just 48 games batting only. 209.

The 1909 Highlanders saw two European born players arrive as rookies, Jack Quinn, a pitcher, and Jimmy Austin, who was an infielder. Both of these players enjoyed long careers which were spent on teams other than the New York Highlanders/Yankees.

Throughout his life, and even into recent years, it was assumed that Jack Quinn was born in Pennsylvania. Recent research has uncovered that he was actually born in Europe in what today is known as the Republic of Slovakia but in 1883 was part of

Austria-Hungry. Quinn's family emigrated to America before his first birthday and settled in Northeastern Pennsylvania. There is also debate about Jack Quinn's given name. It has been recorded that he believed his given name was John Pajkos or Paykosh which was further Americanized to Picus. While he was never considered a top pitcher, he amassed 247 career victories over a 23-year career that saw him pitch until the age of fifty. Quinn was one of the last pitchers to legally throw the spitball.

Jimmy Austin was born in Wales and did not emigrate to the United States until he was seven or eight years old. He began playing minor league baseball in 1904 with a team in Dayton, Ohio. A slight player, Austin was known for his aggressive style and energetic personality, both on and off the field. He amassed a great number of stolen bases in the minors which brought him to the attention of the Highlanders who signed him. Austin played for the Highlanders in 1909 and 1910. Jimmy Austin was playing third base when the famous baseball photographer Charles M. Conlon snapped one of his legendary photographs of Ty Cobb. In that famous photo, Austin is the player Ty Cobb is sliding into.

Jack Lelivelt, who was born in the Netherlands, joined the Highlanders in 1912. Lelivelt enjoyed a long professional playing and managerial career, although most of HIS success came in the minor leagues. Lelivelt excelled on the farm, amassing 2,658 hits in his minor league career that lasted through 1925. Combined with his 347 Major League hits, Jack Lelivelt collected over 3,000 hits as a professional baseball player.

Klondike Smith who hailed from London, England appeared as an outfielder in seven games for the 1912 Highlanders.

In 1914, Jimmy Walsh, a native of Ireland came to the Yankees after playing two seasons with the Philadelphia A's. Walsh spent 43 games with the Yankees, batting .191, before being returned to the A's. Walsh was a renowned minor league ballplayer who collected 2,699 minor league hits to go along with his 410 more in the majors, making him another player who reached 3,000 or more hits in professional baseball.

Paddy O'Connor, a catcher, also from Ireland, was a Yankee for one game in 1918 after playing for the Pittsburgh Pirates and the St. Louis Cardinals (as well as in the Federal League) and then served as a Yankees coach in 1918 and 1919.

The native European who enjoyed the longest tenure with the Yankees was Arndt Jorgens who hailed from Norway. Jorgens was a Yankee from 1929 to 1939. A reserve catcher, he played behind Hall of Famer Bill Dickey, appearing in only 307 games over that time. Such was playing behind Dickey that although Jorgens was on the roster for five world championship teams (1932 and 1936-39), he never appeared in a World Series game. No player appeared on more World Series rosters without an appearance in a game.

Elmer Valo who was born and spent the first six years of his life in Czechoslovakia, was a Yankee, briefly, in 1960. Valo began his Major League career as an outfielder in 1940 with the Philadelphia Athletics. He remained with the A's as they moved to Kansas City in 1955. This was the first of three franchises Valo played for that moved while he was in uniform (the others were the Brooklyn/Los Angeles Dodgers and the Washington Senators/Minnesota Twins). In 1960, Valo appeared in eight games with the Yankees.

Third baseman Mike Blowers, who was born in Germany, came to the Yankees from the Montreal Expos as a highly touted prospect, but he never lived up to his promise. In parts of three seasons with the Yankees (1989-91), Blowers appeared in 76 games and compiled a .203 batting average.

In 1994, the Yankees promoted a highly touted minor league infielder Robert Eenhoorn, who hailed from the Netherlands. Eenhoorn was a member of the Netherlands team that won the 1987 European Championship. He also appeared in the 1988 Olympics in Seoul, Korea and in the 1988 Baseball World Cup for the Netherlands. After coming to the United States and attending Davidson College, Eenhoorn was drafted by the Yankees. A gifted defensive shortstop, he was soon eclipsed by another rising shortstop in the Yankees' system—Derek Jeter. Eenhorn reached the Major Leagues in 1994 but did not last. He returned to the Netherlands as a player and coach where he found great success in national and international competitions. These included winning the 1999 European Championship, the 2000 Holland Series title (where he was also the team's manager), and appearing in the 2000 Olympics. When he managed the Dutch team in the 2008 Olympics, Robert Eenhoorn became the only person to play for two Olympic baseball teams and manage two others. After the Netherlands won the 2011 Baseball World Cup, Eenhoorn was knighted by the Netherland's Queen Beatrix.

Pitcher Dave Pavlas, from Germany, pitched briefly for the 1995 and 1996 Yankees.

Danny Rios was born in Spain but spent most of his life in the United States after his family moved to America when he was two years old. After a stellar minor league career, Danny Rios reached the majors in 1997 but he only pitched in two games for the Yankees.

The most recent Yankee of European descent, Didi Gregorius, might have been the best of them all. Gregorius was acquired by the Yankees in December 2014 as the cornerstone piece of a three-team trade with the Arizona Diamondbacks and the Detroit Tigers. Gregorius was acquired to replace Derek Jeter as the Yankees shortstop following Jeter's retirement. Gregorius, also knighted, was an outstanding shortstop for the Yankees from 2015 through 2019. In his five seasons in New York, he became a fan favorite who played exceptional defense and hit numerous home runs including some postseason blasts that remain on the highlight reels.

NEW YORK YANKEES at ST. LOUIS BROWNS

Wednesday, April 30, 1947 (Sportsman's Park)

	1	2	3	4	5	6	7	8	9		R	H	E
NY	0	0	4	0	0	0	0	1	0		5	5	0
STL	4	0	3	0	6	0	0	2	X		15	14	1

NY		AB	R	H	RBI	STL		AB	R	H	RBI
Rizzuto	SS	4	1	1	2	Dillinger	3B	4	2	3	2
Brown	3B	2	1	0	1	Zarilla	RF	4	2	1	2
McQuinn	1B	4	1	2	1	Stephens	SS	5	3	4	2
BiMaggio	CF	4	0	0	1	Heath	LF	3	3	2	4
Keller	LF	4	0	0	0	Witte	1B	4	0	0	0
Berra	RF	4	0	0	0	Judnich	CF	4	2	2	3
Silvestri	C	4	0	1	0	Berardino	2B	3	1	1	0
Stirnweiss	2B	2	1	0	0	Early	C	4	1	1	0
Reynolds	P	1	1	0	0	Galehouse	P	2	1	0	1
Gumpert	P					Sanford	P	0	0	0	0
Lucadello	PH	1	0	1	0						
Page	P	0	0	0	0						
Queen	P										
Drews	P										
Colman	PH	1	0	0	0						
Ardizoia	P										
Lindell	PH	1	0	0	0						

NY	IP	H	R	BB	SO	STL	IP	H	R	BB	SO
Reynolds - L	3	7	7	1	1	Galehouse - W	8	4	5	4	3
Gumpert	1	0	0	1	1	Sanford	1	1	0	0	0
Page	0.2	0	4	4	0						
Queen	0.1	3	2	0	0						
Drews	1	0	0	1	0						
Ardizoia	2	4	2	1	0						

Rugger Ardizoia

Courtesy of TCMA Ltd.

CHAPTER SIXTEEN
STEFAN WEVER (1982)

Sometimes, it is said, life imitates art. In the 1980s, there was a very popular television series titled *Cheers.* The show focused, primarily, on the tale of Sam Malone, a retired Major League pitcher who overcame alcoholism and opened a bar. In the show's eleven-year run, it won 28 Emmy Awards. In 2013, TV Guide ranked *Cheers* as the eleventh greatest television series of all time. Cheers would have no problem gaining enough votes to be included in the Television Hall of Fame, if one existed.

Former Yankee Stefan Wever has lived a real-life story very similar to that of the fictional Sam Malone. Wever was a Major League pitcher who struggled with alcohol dependency. Today, Stefan Wever owns the Horseshoe Tavern in San Francisco.

If life is about overcoming obstacles, as the fictional Sam Malone on *Cheers* did, then Wever just might belong in a hall of fame for resiliency. Having a career in which one attains the highest levels in his profession would, for many, signify one of life's great accomplishments. For Wever, the success he had on the baseball diamond was too short lived, and the fact that his career ended so suddenly, after being filled with such promise, led him to despair.

One of the greatest baseball films of all time is *Field of Dreams*. In 2001, the readers of *ESPN Magazine* ranked *Field of Dreams* as the single greatest baseball film. It is also ranked number one by the Internet Movie Data Base (IMDB). The movie is centered on a man who builds a baseball diamond in an Iowa cornfield after hearing voices that say, "If you build it, they will come." The man builds the field and soon after, the 1919 Chicago White Sox arrive out of the rows of corn to play ball as they did in their youth.

Stefan Wever had a similar dream. Long after his playing days, he recalled a dream of being out in a cow pasture. There is also a baseball field there. Wever's former teammates, including Buck Showalter and Don Mattingly, are there. Somehow, though, in the dream, Wever never makes it back to the field.

Art and life...

Of all the primary players detailed in this book, our *Least Among Them* Yankees, Stefan Wever may have had the greatest promise. His path to the Major Leagues looked straight and secure. And it was.

Born in Germany but raised in Massachusetts, Stefan Weaver was a baseball fan from his earliest days. He was a diehard Red Sox fan, but it was the Yankees who drafted him in 1979 from the University of California, Santa Barbara where he starred as a pitcher. Wever was 6 feet 8 inches tall, a giant of a man, who possessed a tremendous fastball and a terrific curve. After signing with the Yankees, he began his steady climb to the big club. This path began in Oneonta, N.Y. in 1979 where he went 6-3 with a 1.77 ERA in nine starts. He was promoted to Fort Lauderdale in 1980. The next season saw Wever promoted to Nashville in Double-A. He played alongside future Major League batting champions Willie McGee and Don Mattingly. (McGee outhit Mattingly that year .322 to .316.) In 1982, Stefan Wever led the Nashville Sounds to the Southern League title. He threw over 214 innings with a record of 16-6, with a 2.78 ERA. Wever won two games in the postseason and was voted the league's Most Valuable Player.

During the Sounds' victory celebration, Wever was called into the manager's office. He was told by his pitching coach, the legendary Hoyt Wilhelm, and his manager, Johnny Oates, that his season wasn't quite over—that he was heading to the Major Leagues. Wever's success to that point had almost made this promotion seem inevitable.

One can only imagine the thrill that a player must feel when he is called to the Major Leagues. Upon joining the Yankees, Stefan Wever found that he was immediately treated as member of the team—as a true Major League ballplayer. Wever was assigned a locker next to two future Hall-of-Famers, Dave Winfield and Rich "Goose" Gossage. He was also issued uniform number 25 which had been most recently worn by All-Star Tommy John. Teams do not issue low Major League numbers to players who have little chance of sticking with the big club. This is especially true for the Yankees.

In spite of the fact that the 1982 Yankees finished in fifth place, the locker room was filled with star power. This was a team that had reached the postseason in five of the six previous seasons. The list of notable Yankees on that squad, in addition to Winfield and Gossage, is seemingly endless—Ron Guidry, Graig Nettles, Bobby Murcer, Willie Randolph, Lou Piniella... They welcomed this newest Yankee with open arms.

On his sixth day in the Major Leagues, September 17, 1982, Stefan Wever was called to start his first Major League game. The Yankees were in Milwaukee and he was chosen to start against the first-place Brewers.

The 1982 Brewers were a powerhouse team of their own. There were four eventual Hall of Famers on that team: Rollie Fingers, Don Sutton, Paul Molitor, and Robin Yount. Known as Harvey's Wall Bangers (after manager Harvey Kuenn), the team led the American League in home runs (216) on its way to 95 victories and the American League pennant.

When Wever took the mound for the Yankees, who had gone down in order in the top of the first, he immediately set a team record. Standing 6 feet, 8 inches tall, Wever became the tallest player ever to pitch for the Bombers. Unfortunately, for Wever, the Brewers struck quickly and often. Paul Molitor singled. He was then doubled home by Robin Yount. The first baseman, Cecil Cooper, then doubled home Yount. After an error, and then, finally, an out, Gorman Thomas, the American League leader in home runs, added to his total by hitting one out. In his first inning of work, Wever allowed five runs. His day, and the pain, wasn't over.

In the second inning, Wever allowed another run. But then, in the third inning, what was being held together by a thread all fell apart. With one out, Thomas walked. The next batter, Roy Howell, grounded out but not sharply enough for a double play. Wever then threw two wild pitches (he had also thrown a wild pitch in the second inning) that allowed Howell to reach third base. Charlie Moore, the Brewers catcher, then singled him home. When second baseman Jim Gantner followed with a walk, Stefan Wever's game was over.

It was during that first inning of work that Wever felt a twinge in his right shoulder. He knew something wasn't quite right, but this was during a time period in sports when players were often seen as weak when they admitted to an injury. Wever tried to battle through it. He couldn't. The results for this game demonstrated that there was something physically wrong. Still, it took years of struggle before Wever saw the renowned shoulder specialist Dr. James Andrews. The diagnosis came quickly; Wever's rotator cuff was fully torn. He needed immediate surgery. A long rehabilitation followed, but Wever never recovered his fastball and his career was soon over.

Like the fictional Sam Malone of *Cheers*, Wever's life went into a tailspin. Transitioning to a non-player, so immediately, after so much promise was devastating. Wever began to look to alcohol and drugs to ease his anguish. It was only after his third DUI arrest and the prospect of prison that Wever knew what he had to do. He quit using illegal substances and alcohol and entered Alcoholics Anonymous. Stefan Wever used the strength he originally learned as a ball player to face each day. Yet, his struggles were not over.

In 2009, Wever was diagnosed with a rare, extremely aggressive form of cancer known as anaplastic large-cell lymphoma. After an intense treatment program, he seemed to be cancer-free only to have the disease return. Another struggle ensued. By 2010, the doctors reported that he was again cancer-free. Other health problems continued to ravage Wever including a stroke, but he continues to fight these health problems. So far, he is winning. In recent years, Wever has enjoyed life as a successful high school baseball coach.

Stefan Wever may not have been able to win a Major League game, but he has defeated many of life's other (and tougher) opponents—alcoholism and cancer. His story is a testament to the fact that there is life after baseball and that while that one moment in the sun must be great, that single moment doesn't always define a life.

Extra Innings
The Tallest Yankees of All-Time

When he took the mound in 1982, Stefan Wever became, at the time, the tallest player to pitch for the
Yankees, the latest in a long line of tallest Yankees
pitchers.

In 1903, the Highlanders employed one of baseball's tallest
men, left-handed pitcher Ambrose Puttmann who stood 6 feet, 4
inches. Puttmann was also one of the youngest Highlanders at 22
years old. The only younger player to play for the 1903 Highlanders was Eddie Quick, a *Least Among Them* player who, in his one
appearance, was just 21 years old.

Ambrose Puttmann pitched in and out of the Major Leagues
for the Highlanders from 1903 to 1906 and for the St. Louis Cardinals in 1906. He appeared in 33 big league games compiling a
record of 8-9, 3.58.

Following Puttmann as the tallest Yankee pitcher was the
6-feet 7-inch lefthander Slim Love who pitched for the Yankees
from 1916 through 1918. Before examining Mr. Love, though it
is important to note that another player, Hippo Vaughn, who also
stood 6 feet 4 inches (the same height as Puttmann), is considered by some sources as the tallest big league pitcher before Slim
Love.

Vaughn, a lefty, was a Highlander in 1908 and from 1910
through 1912. He wasn't overly successful in New York owning
a lifetime 23-29 record, but he became an excellent pitcher later in his career with the Chicago Cubs. Between 1914 and 1920,
Vaughn won 20 or more games in a season five times in sev-
en years. Over that period, he had an overall record of 143-93.
Vaughn was also famous for being the losing pitcher in a 1917
duel with Fred Toney of the Cincinnati Reds. That game is famous
because it is baseball's only double no-hit game. Vaughn did not

allow a hit or a run until the 10th inning and lost the game to Toney who was able to hold the Cubs hitless in all ten innings that he pitched.

Once he came along, the wonderfully named Slim Love who stood 6 feet, 7 inches became baseball's tallest pitcher when he took the mound for the Washington Senators in 1913. Love pitched in five games that year but soon returned to the minors. He would not reach the big leagues again until 1916 with the Yankees. Love pitched three seasons for the Yankees, both as a starter and a reliever, accumulating a 21-17, 3.05 record in 91 games. Love's strength, his size and ability to throw hard, were also his undoing. He threw only fastballs, never gaining the ability to learn to throw the curve making him often too hittable. His size also led to an erratic delivery which led to bouts of wildness. In 1918, a season in which he started A career-high 29 games, Love led the league in walks. After the 1918 season, the Yankees traded him to the Red Sox, who less than a month later traded him to the Detroit Tigers. Love pitched in 23 games over two seasons for the Tigers and was out of the Major Leagues in 1920. Like so many other almost-great players, Slim Love returned to the minors where he enjoyed success until 1930, primarily in the Texas League.

Love was the tallest pitcher in Yankees history for 66 years until Stefan Wever, standing 6 feet, 8 inches, eclipsed his record while pitching in his one game.

Stefan Wever also held his claim as the tallest Yankee pitcher for many years. Although there were numerous Yankees pitchers (Lee Gutterman, Graeme Lloyd, and Jeff Nelson) over the years who also stood 6 feet 8 inches, no one stood taller in pinstripes until the Yankees brought in a future Hall of Fame pitcher at the tail end of his own legendary career.

In 2005, the tallest Yankees pitcher ever became left-hander Randy Johnson who stood 6 feet, 10 inches. By the time he became a Yankee, Randy Johnson was already a legend. In his 16-year career prior to being traded to the Yankees, Randy Johnson had won 246 games and struck out over 4,100 batters. Johnson was a ten-time All-Star and he had won the Cy Young Award five times (once in the American League and four times in the

National League). An overpowering pitcher, Johnson also threw two no-hitters including a perfect game in 2004.

In addition to his legendary regular-season success, Johnson was also a dominating presence in the postseason and was at the heart of two of the Yankees' most bitter postseason series losses. In the 1995 AL Division Series, Johnson, then with the Seattle Mariners, won two games in the hard-fought series as the Mariners defeated the Yankees in five games. Later, in the 2001 World Series, Johnson went 3-0 (securing a share of the World Series MVP Award—with fellow pitcher Curt Schilling) as he helped pitch the Arizona Diamondbacks to the series victory over the Yankees.

Johnson's career with the Yankees was short-lived. He pitched two seasons in New York, winning 17 games each year, before being traded back to Arizona. He finished his career in 2009 with the San Francisco Giants, with whom he won his 300th career game.

No New York Yankee pitcher since has stood taller than Randy Johnson. In 2011, for a brief moment, there was one Yankee pitcher, Andrew Brackman, who stood just as tall. Of the tallest pitchers in Yankees history, Brackman, who stands at 6 feet 10 inches, is the only one who threw right-handed.

Brackman was the first player selected by the Yankees in the 2007 Amateur Draft. A hard-throwing strikeout pitcher, the Yankees hoped that Brackman's powerful arm could anchor their pitching staff. Unfortunately, it wasn't to be. Before he would pitch in a professional game, Brackman needed Tommy John surgery. He finally made his minor league debut in 2009. Brackman's trip through the bush leagues was fast. Late in the 2011 season, he received his taste of Major League ball when he made three appearances for the Yankees. In just over two innings of work in the big leagues, Brackman walked three batters. He was released by the Yankees organization after the 2011 season and never made it back to the big leagues.

NEW YORK YANKEES at MILWAUKEE BREWERS

Friday, September 17, 1982 (County Stadium)

	1	2	3	4	5	6	7	8	9		R	H	E
NY	0	0	0	0	0	0	0	0	0		0	3	1
MIL	5	1	3	0	0	1	4	0	X		14	15	0

NY		AB	R	H	RBI	MIL		AB	R	H	RBI
Randolph	2B	4	0	0	0	Molitor	3B	4	4	3	1
Mumphrey	CF	4	0	0	0	Yount	SS	5	2	4	4
Griffey	RF	4	0	1	0	Cooper	1B	4	1	3	2
Winfield	LF	2	0	0	0	Simmons	C	4	1	0	1
Piniella	DH	3	0	0	0	Oglivie	LF	4	0	0	0
Balboni	1B	3	0	1	0	Thomas	CF	4	1	1	3
Evans	3B	3	0	0	0	Howell	DH	4	2	1	0
Cerone	C	3	0	1	0	Skube	PH/DH	1	0	1	0
Robertson	SS	3	0	0	0	Moore	RF	5	1	1	1
						Gantner	2B	2	2	1	0

NY	IP	H	R	BB	SO	MIL	IP	H	R	BB	SO
Wever - L	2.2	6	9	3	2	Caldwell - W	9	3	0	1	3
Frazier	0.1	1	0	1	0						
Alexander	4	7	5	1	1						
McGlothen	1	1	0	0	0						

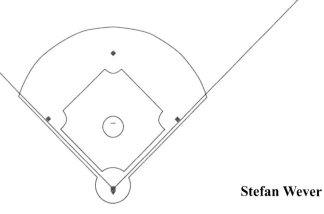

Stefan Wever

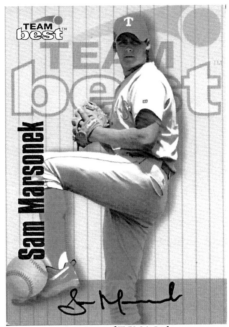

Courtesy of TCMA Ltd.

CHAPTER SEVENTEEN
SAM MARSONEK (2004)

S am Marsonek's story is one of redemption and salvation. He was once a can't-miss prospect and now he is changing lives.

Sam Marsonek was drafted by the Texas Rangers in the first round of the 1996 Amateur Draft. Marsonek was the 24th player selected that year. Interestingly, Christian Parker, a *Least Among Them* Yankee, was also taken in this draft—by the Montreal Expos, but not until the fourth round.

Marsonek's minor league career began in 1997 with the Pulaski Rangers of the Rookie League where he got off to a solid start winning seven games and losing only three. He did allow 90 hits in just over 71 innings, but flashes of his promise were apparent. He was promoted to the Port Charlotte Rangers of the

Florida State League which is considered a challenging level of Single-A baseball. 1998 did not treat Marsonek kindly as he was injured for most of the year, appearing in only four games. In 1999, back with Port Charlotte, Marsonek started 15 games with an unimpressive 3-9 record along with a 5.54 ERA. It was after the 1999 season that he was traded, along with Brandon Knight, a pitcher at Triple-A, to the Yankees organization.

It was while pitching in the Yankees' system that Marsonek began his climb to the majors. In 2000, he played for Greensboro of the South Atlantic League, a low-level Single-A team. Marsonek was able to compile a 6-7 record in 18 starts. More significantly, for the first time in his professional career, he was able to log over 100 innings pitched (114.1). In 2001, Marsonek was promoted to a higher level of Single-A ball where he toiled for Tampa of the Florida State League. Marsonek's 138.1 innings pitched led the team by a significant margin. He was developing into a work-

Courtesy of TCMA Ltd.

horse. For the next season, 2002, Marsonek was promoted to Double-A pitching for the Norwich Navigators. He again reached the 100-inning plateau. In 2003, Sam Marsonek toiled for the Columbus Clippers, the Yankees' highest minor league team. It was during that season that the Yankees decided to convert him to a full-time relief pitcher. Marsonek appeared in 54 games, closing out 34 of them with a team-leading 18 saves.

By 2004, it was apparent Marsonek was on his way to his opportunity in the Bronx. In the first half of the season pitching for Columbus, Marsonek appeared in thirty games, saving seventeen. It was on July 6 that Sam Marsonek was informed that he was heading to the Major Leagues.

Sam Marsonek's big league appearance came just a few days later in a game against the Tampa Bay Devil Rays on July 11, 2004.

This was the last game the teams would play before the All-Star break. The Yankees came into the game in first place, six games ahead of the Red Sox and 12.5 games ahead of the third-place Devil Rays who were managed by former Yankee Lou Piniella.

By the time Marsonek appeared in the game, the Yankees were comfortably in the lead. After left-hander Felix Heredia retired the first two Tampa batters in the top of the eighth inning, Marsonek was summoned to the mound by manager Joe Torre. The first batter Marsonek faced was Julio Lugo who promptly doubled. Damian Rolls followed by flying out to deep center field, with Bernie Williams tracking down the ball to record the out and close out the inning.

In the Yankees' half of the eighth, Gary Sheffield homered, increasing their lead to 10-3. Sam Marsonek came out, as he had been doing so often in the minors, to close out the game. Toby Hall singled for Tampa before Geoff Blum flew out to center field. Carl Crawford then grounded into a fielder's choice. Now with two outs and a runner on second base, Marsonek pitched to Rocco Baldelli. Baldelli swung at Marsonek's first pitch and lofted a long fly to center field. Bernie Williams tracked it down to record the game's final out.

For Sam Marsonek, it was a successful debut in the big leagues. He pitched 1.1 innings allowing two hits and no runs. Three of the four outs he recorded were putouts by Bernie Williams. Marsonek felt like he was in the majors to stay, but it was not meant to be. Back home in Florida, Sam Marsonek made the fateful decision to get behind a boat on a wake board. He fell, blew out his knee, and his career, for all intents and purposes was over. In 2005, he did pitch in 49 games for Columbus, but his 6.61 ERA told the story. Sam Marsonek was no longer the same pitcher.

That same year, during a trip to the Dominican Republic for a baseball clinic, Sam Marsonek's life was changed. He saw young boys living in poverty doing their best to play baseball. He realized that the only hope for these children, some playing without shoes and proper equipment was through the dreams that baseball provided. Marsonek found God that day and began to dedicate his life to others. In this quest, he coached three years for Cambridge Christian School in Tampa before becoming the director of player development and a head coach at SCORE International, a private Christian academy. Fellow former Yankees pitcher Ramiro Mendoza also works for SCORE International.

Occasionally, the Yankees reach out to Marsonek to assist with players in their system who encounter troubles. Highly touted minor leaguer Slade Heathcott faced the personal struggles of alcohol and a fast life—problems that Marsonek also confronted before he found his faith. Heathcott credits Marsonek for helping him find peace through the church. Although his own career was for just a little more than an inning, Sam Marsonek may be giving back to the Yankees through his ministry and service well into the future.

Extra Innings
A Forgotten Two-Sport Legend

As he made his way to the Major Leagues, one of Sam Marsonek's teammates on the 2003 Columbus Clippers was third baseman Drew Henson a multi-sport athlete who would play both Major League Baseball and in the National Football League. Henson was considered a "can't-miss" prospect. He was drafted by the Yankees out of high school in 1998. The organization thought so highly of him that they allowed him, after summers playing minor league ball, to play football at the University of Michigan where he apprenticed under future NFL legend Tom Brady before becoming the starting quarterback after Brady's graduation. As a professional baseball player, Henson spent six years in the minors never quite realizing his potential. In over 500 games, Henson hit an unremarkable .248 with 67 home runs. He did get his own short taste of Major League ball, appearing in a total of eight games over the course of two Septembers in 2002 and 2003. After giving up baseball, Henson had the opportunity to play briefly in the NFL, appearing in seven games with the Dallas Cowboys in 2004 and two games for the Detroit Lions in 2008.

Drew Henson was one of six players to have playing ties between the Yankees and the National Football League.

The most well-known two-sport Yankees player is Deion Sanders. Drafted by both the NFL's Atlanta Falcons and the Yankees, Sanders enjoyed significant time in both the Major Leagues and the NFL. He played nine seasons in the majors, appearing in 641 games while playing for the Yankees, Atlanta Braves, Cincinnati Reds, and San Francisco Giants. In 1992, while playing for Atlanta, Sanders hit .533 in the World Series against the Toronto Blue Jays. It was in the NFL, though, where Sanders true greatness was realized. He played for fourteen seasons in the

NFL, most notably for the Falcons and, like Henson, for the Dallas Cowboys. Sanders was an eight-time All-Pro defensive back and kick returner. In 2011, Deion Sanders was inducted into the Pro Football Hall of Fame.

John Elway is another Pro Football Hall of Famer who had ties to the Yankees franchise. John Elway's NFL body of work is legendary: 9 Pro-Bowls, the 1987 MVP, and two Super Bowl championships. As a quarterback, he ranks in the top ten all time in most passing categories and is considered by many to be one of the greatest quarterbacks in the history of professional football. Yet, before all of that took place, John Elway played for the Yankees in the minor leagues. For one season, 1982, John Elway was a standout outfielder for the Oneonta Yankees of the New York-Pennsylvania League. In 42 games for Oneonta, Elway hit .318 with four home runs and 25 runs batted in. He also stole 13 bases. After that initial season, though, John Elway returned to Stanford University where he led the nation in touchdown passes and was second in the Heisman Trophy balloting. The next April, John Elway was selected by the Baltimore Colts as the first player in the NFL draft. A few weeks later, he was traded to the Denver Broncos. Elway soon made the decision to focus on football, leaving baseball behind.

Probably the least known former Yankee who also played in the NFL was a right-handed pitcher named Joe Vance. Vance pitched for the White Sox in 1935 and later played five games for the Yankees over parts of the 1937 and 1938 seasons. While he was still in the minors, Joe Vance played professional football for the Brooklyn Dodgers. In 1931, he appeared in eleven games in the NFL as a running back and rushed for two touchdowns.

One of the largest legends in the history of the NFL is George "Papa Bear" Halas who was one of the co-founders of the league and one of the greatest coaches the game has ever seen. Halas was also an excellent player. In 1919, he was the MVP of the Rose Bowl while playing for the University of Illinois. He was considered one of the best ends in the game and was selected to the NFL's 1920's All-Decade Team. As a coach, his record is spectacular: 318 wins against only 148 losses (and 31 ties) for a .682 winning percentage. Halas guided the Chicago Bears to eight NFL championships. In 1963, he was an inaugural member of the Pro Football Hall of Fame (which is located on George Halas Drive in Canton, Ohio).

Yet, before he began to establish his legendary NFL career, Halas was, for twelve games in 1919, a member of the Yankees. Halas played both center field and right field. In 22 at bats, he managed only two singles for a batting average of .091. Legend states that Halas was replaced in right field the next year by Babe Ruth. While it is true that Halas patrolled that position the year before Ruth did, it would be a stretch to state that Ruth replaced Halas considering that Halas played in just five games as the Yankees right fielder. (The actual starting right fielder for the 1919 Yankees was Sammy Vick.) By 1920, George Halas was out of baseball and pursuing the path that would take him into the pantheon of NFL greats.

The final player who appeared for the Yankees and also played in the NFL holds a singular and very impressive record—he is the only player in history to have been on a World Series winning team (the 1923 Yankees) and an NFL championship team (the 1927 Giants). This player was Hinkey Haines.

The fact that Hinkey Haines is not well-known today is somewhat remarkable. In his day, he was one of the biggest sports stars in New York City. Haines was a teammate and friend of Babe Ruth and Lou Gehrig. He was also a football teammate with Jim Thorpe.

As a youth, Hinkey Haines was a star player for Lebanon Valley College where he played football, basketball, baseball, and ran track. After his sophomore year, Hinkey Haines served in the United States Army during World War I. After the war, Haines enrolled in Penn State, playing varsity basketball, football, and baseball. Hugo Bezdek, Haines' baseball and football coach, forbade him from competing in any varsity track meets, but one could speculate that he would have had success in that sport as well. During his baseball career, Babe Ruth once commented that Haines was as fast as any man in the league. Later, Giants coach Bob Folwell stated that he never saw a faster man on a football field.

Hinkey Haines' played minor league baseball most seasons

Hinkey Haines played baseball for the Yankees (left) and football for the Giants (right). Photos from the author's collection

between 1921 and 1934, but his only time in the Major Leagues was in that 1923 season. Haines played the entire season with the Yankees and was present when Yankee Stadium first opened that year. (Haines was also present at the 25th anniversary of Yankee Stadium when Babe Ruth made his final appearance and in 1976 after Yankee Stadium was remodeled. Haines was one of the six living members from that 1923 team, including Oscar Roettger, Whitey Witt, Bob Shawkey, Joe Dugan, and Waite Hoyt to be present for the dedication of the "New" Yankee Stadium.) In 1923, Haines appeared in 28 games for the Yankees. He batted only .160 and was used primarily as a defensive replacement and pinch runner.

In the 1923 World Series, Haines appeared in two games. In Game Three, he took over for Ruth in right field (with Ruth moving to first base) in a game the Yankees lost to the New York Giants 1-0. (The only run that game came on an inside-the-park home run hit by Giants outfielder and future Yankees manager Casey Stengel.) Later, in Game 6, the final game of that World Series, Haines pinch ran in the eighth inning and scored the tying run as the Yankees won to secure their very first world championship. After pinch running, Haines played center field and was on the field when the final out was recorded.

In 1925, Hinkey Haines, who had also been playing football in Pennsylvania, signed to play for the New York Football Giants. He was considered the star of the team, playing an important role in the backfield as a runner and passer. The 1927 New York Giants enjoyed an 11-1-1 record. Since there was no Super Bowl, or even a championship game at that time, the title "champion" was bestowed upon the team with the best record. Haines played a huge role in late-season games against the Chicago Bears (George Halas was a player and coach on that team) and the New York Football Yankees. (Those Yankee football teams had a star of their own—the legendary Red Grange.) Hinkey Haines has been called the first superstar of the New York Giants.

After the season, a gala event was held in Hayes' honor at the Hotel Astor in New York City. This event was attended by numerous popular sports figures of the day including Lou Gehrig and Joe Dugan of the Yankees.

It was reported that Haines, who roomed with Gehrig during spring training in 1924, was the best man at Gehrig's wedding. There is also a story that he arranged for Babe Ruth to practice on one occasion with the football Giants. It was said that Ruth played as a tackle for only two plays before deciding that football might not be his game.

TAMPA BAY DEVIL RAYS at NEW YORK YANKEES

Sunday, July 11, 2004 (Yankee Stadium)

	1	2	3	4	5	6	7	8	9		R	H	E
TBR	0	0	0	2	0	1	0	0	0		3	9	1
NY	0	1	4	0	0	2	2	1	X		10	15	0

TBR		AB	R	H	RBI	NY		AB	R	H	RBI
Crawford	LF	5	0	1	0	Williams	CF	5	0	0	0
Baldelli	CF	5	0	0	0	Jeter	SS	5	1	1	0
Huff	3B	3	1	1	1	Sheffield	RF	4	2	3	2
Martinez	1B	3	1	1	0	Crosby	RF				
Cruz	RF	4	0	0	0	Rodriguez	3B	5	1	1	0
Lugo	SS	3	1	2	0	Giambi	DH	4	1	1	1
Fick	DH	2	0	0	0	Posada	C	2	1	2	2
Rolls	PH/DH	2	0	0	0	Flaherty	PR/C	2	0	0	0
Hall	C	4	0	3	2	Matsui	LF	4	2	3	2
Blum	2B	4	0	1	0	Clark	1B	4	2	2	3
						Cairo	2B	4	0	2	0

TBR	IP	H	R	BB	SO	NY	IP	H	R	BB	SO
Hendrickson - L	3	8	5	0	1	Hernandez - W	5	5	2	3	5
Sosa	3	4	2	1	4	Heredia	2.2	2	1	0	1
Carter	1	2	2	0	1	**Marsonek**	1.1	2	0	0	0
Baez	1	1	1	0	2						

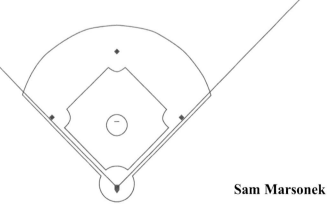

Sam Marsonek

Courtesy of TCMA Ltd.

CHAPTER EIGHTEEN
CHRISTIAN PARKER (2001)

Christian Parker's tale is one of a player who rose to the Major Leagues in a sudden burst but faded just as quickly.

Parker was originally drafted by the Montreal Expos in 1996. This was the same draft in which Sam Marsonek was taken as the 24th overall pick. Parker was drafted in the fourth round, the 100th player selected after an impressive college career pitching for Notre Dame.

Parker began playing for the Vermont Expos in the New York-Penn League (Single-A) during the 1996 season. He became the ace of the staff, going 7-1 with a 2.48 ERA over 14 starts. This performance earned him a promotion to the Cape Fear Crocs of the South Atlantic League where he was again a staff leader, starting 25 games and finishing with an 11-10 record. In 1998, Parker was promoted to Double-A Harrisburg where the Expos franchise began his conversion to a relief pitcher. Between 1998 and 1999, Christian Parker appeared in 79 games, but only 22 as a starting pitcher.

It was during spring training in 2000 that Parker was sent to the Yankees franchise as a "player to be named later" to complete the trade that sent Japanese pitcher Hideki Irabu to the Expos. That season the Yankees moved Parker back to the starting rotation where he impressed while pitching for the Double-A Norwich Navigators. Between June 28 and August 23, Parker won nine consecutive decisions while tossing forty consecutive scoreless innings. Overall Christian Parker went 14-6 with a 3.13 ERA that year. This performance would earn him an invitation to big league spring training the next season.

The 2001 Yankees were an extremely impressive squad. They were the three-time defending world champions and had won four of the five previous World Series (1996, 1998, 1999, and 2000) and is still the last team to win three consecutive World Series. The pitching staff was anchored by Roger Clemens, Andy Pettitte, Mike Mussina, and Orlando "El Duque" Hernandez. Throughout spring training Parker impressed the decision-makers as much with his poise and composure as with his ability. He arrived in camp as a depth piece, but his work and his attitude won him the coveted fifth spot in the starting rotation. What nobody knew was that Christian Parker was pitching through a sore shoulder.

Christian Parker's Major League debut came on April 6, 2001, the Yankees' fourth game of the year. This powerhouse team had won its first three games. In this contest, Parker would face the dangerous Toronto Blue Jays who came into the game with a 3-1 record. It was a chilly, 49-degree night. Following a practice that he had learned from watching the other great Yankee starting pitchers, he waited until after the national anthem was played before emerging from the dugout to begin his warm-up pitches. His poise indicated confidence and several teammates remarked that it seemed as if he already belonged in the Major Leagues. A bounced pitch, though, during the warm-ups may have indicated Parker's true emotions.

Parker's first pitch of the game was a called strike to Toronto's leadoff hitter Shannon Stewart. The next pitch though, was lined into center field for a hit. Accounts differ on what transpired next, but in short, Stewart either stole second base on a subsequent pitch or moved there on a ground out to Parker off the bat of Alex Gonzalez. Raul Mondesi then grounded out to third base, bringing up Carlos Delgado with two outs. Delgado had started the season with a hot bat, homering three times in the Blue Jays' first four games. This night was no different; he swung at Parker's first offering and sent the ball into the night—a long blast for a two-run home run to put the Blue Jays ahead. Parker then retired Brad Fullmer on a pop out to end the inning.

Christian Parker demonstrated the poise that impressed the Yankees in the second inning. He was seemingly not intimidated by Delgado's home run. He retired the Blue Jays in order on only six pitches. It was the third inning that became the start of Parker's undoing. Ryan Freel, the Blue Jays' second baseman, and ninth-place hitter, led off with a single. He promptly stole second. Stewart, now batting for his second time, was retired on a ground out to the pitcher's mound. With Gonzalez now batting, Freel quickly stole third base. Parker coaxed Gonzalez to pop out to Yankee first baseman Tino Martinez. Raul Mondesi then doubled scoring Freel. Delgado walked and Fuller then singled home Mondesi before Tony Batista struck out.

Trailing 4-0, Christian Parker came out to begin the fourth inning. His Major League career would end that inning and it didn't last long. On a 3-1 count, Darren Fletcher singled. Jose Cruz, Jr. followed with a home run. When Freel singled on the next pitch, Parker's night was over. The numbers weren't pretty: 3 innings, 8 hits, and 7 runs. He would end up the losing pitcher in the Yankees' first loss of the season, a 13-4 drubbing by the Blue Jays.

After the game Yankees manager Joe Torre said he intended for Parker to make his next start. Torre understood how the emotions of one's first game might negatively impact performance. Parker said that now that he had reached the Major Leagues, his job was to pitch well enough to stay. It wasn't to be. Before that next start ever came, Parker was placed on the disabled list. He didn't pitch again for two years. In 2003, Parker began a minor league comeback, but it didn't last. In 2005, he spent time between AA and AAA pitching for the Colorado Rockies organization before retiring from the game.

Extra Innings
How Carl Yastrzemski Almost Became a Yankee

Christian Parker is one of eighty-nine players to reach the Major Leagues after playing at The University of Notre Dame. Most of the names on that list are unexceptional, except, interestingly, the first and last names when listed alphabetically. The list begins with Hall of Famer Cap Anson and ends with another Hall of Famer, Carl Yastrzemski.

Anson was baseball's first true superstar. He set hosts of batting records. Anson was baseball's first member of the 3,000-hit club. Playing from 1876 through 1897, Anson hit over .300 twenty times. He was also a legendary manager and innovator. Anson is credited with inventing, or at least popularizing, such baseball traditions as the hit-and-run play, pitching rotations, and spring training. Anson is also believed to have been the first manager to introduce the idea of giving signals to the players. Today, though, Anson's playing greatness is greatly marred by the fact that he used his fame and role as an ambassador to the game to exclude black players—a tradition that lasted from Anson's time until Jackie Robinson broke the color barrier in 1947. Anson's racism, like all prejudice, created an ugly reflection on himself and the game.

The other Hall of Famer who also played for Notre Dame was Carl Yastrzemski who became legendary while playing for the Boston Red Sox between 1961 and 1983. Yaz, as he was affectionately known, won the Triple Crown in 1967 when he helped lead the Red Sox to the World Series. He was also a member of the Red Sox's 1975 World Series team. In his career, Yastrzemski totaled 3,419 hits to go along with 452 home runs and 1,844 runs batted in. Yaz was the first American League player to amass both 3,000 hits and 400 home runs.

Yastrzemski earned his 3,000th hit against the Yankees on September 12, 1979 at Fenway Park in Boston. The clean single to right field came off Yankees pitcher Jim Beattie. A year earlier, Yastrzemski famously popped out to third baseman Graig Nettles ending the famous one-game playoff game to determine the American League East champion in 1978.

As a member of the hated Red Sox, Yastrzemski was a true rival to the Yankees. Yet, there was a time when instead of playing for the Red Sox, Yastrzemski had the opportunity to sign with the Yankees.

This occurred while Yaz was still a high school student; a senior at Bridgehampton (N.Y.) High School on Long Island. Yastrzemski grew up a Yankees fan, and was a well-known ballplayer from a young age. He played alongside his father and other family members at the semi-pro level beginning at the young age of fourteen. His promise was so great that his father believed that he would be able to command a $100,000 signing bonus when the time came for him to be signed by a Major League franchise.

Although they were forbidden to sign Yastrzemski while he was still in high school, the Yankees sent scout Ray Garland to meet with his family to discuss the future possibility of his signing with the Yankees. During the conversation, Garland presented $60,000 as a hypothetical bonus number that the Yankees might be prepared to offer. The elder Yastrzemski countered with the aforementioned $100,000 asking price. Garland was incredulous. He said the Yankees would never pay that kind of money, and, according to the tale, flipped (or threw) his pencil in the air as he made this statement. That act of hubris caused Garland to be thrown out of the house and with that disappeared all chances of the Yankees signing the great Carl Yastrzemski. After a protracted negotiation period with many big league clubs, Yaz eventually signed with the Red Sox for $108,000. The rest, as they say, is history.

TORONTO BLUE JAYS at NEW YORK YANKEES

Friday, April 6, 2001 (Yankee Stadium)

	1	2	3	4	5	6	7	8	9		R	H	E
TOR	2	0	2	5	0	0	0	0	4		13	16	0
NY	0	0	0	0	0	1	1	2	0		4	10	0

TOR		AB	R	H	RBI	NY		AB	R	H	RBI
Stewart	LF	5	2	2	0	Knoblauch	LF	5	0	0	1
Gonalez	SS	5	2	2	0	Soriano	2B	5	1	1	0
Mondesi	RF	4	2	1	1	O'Neill	RF	4	1	2	2
Delgado	1B	2	3	2	5	Williams	CF	3	1	0	0
Fullmer	DH	5	0	1	1	Justice	DH	4	0	2	1
Batista	3B	5	1	1	2	Martinez	1B	4	0	1	0
Fletcher	C	5	1	3	1	Oliver	C	3	1	1	0
Cruz	CF	5	1	2	2	Posada	PH/C	1	0	0	0
Freel	2B	5	1	2	0	Sojo	SS	4	0	1	0
						Brosius	3B	4	0	2	0

TOR	IP	H	R	BB	SO	NY	IP	H	R	BB	SO
Loaiza - W	7	8	2	0	6	**Parker - L**	3	8	7	1	1
Painter	0.1	2	2	1	0	Almanzar	3	4	2	0	3
Quantrill	1.2	0	0	0	0	Choate	2.2	1	3	2	2
						Williams	0.1	3	1	0	0

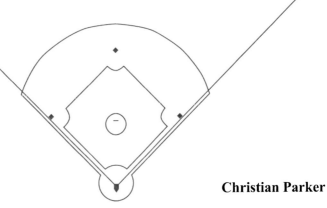

Christian Parker

Courtesy of The Topps Company.

CHAPTER NINETEEN
HAL STOWE (1960)

Throughout this text, we have seen the exploits of many players who were exceptional collegiate athletes. Left-handed pitcher Hal Stowe was no exception. As a member of the Clemson University Tigers, Stowe led the team to consecutive College World Series appearances. In 1958, Stowe was considered by some as the top starting pitcher in all of college baseball. He won 14 games and amassed 126 strikeouts that year. The next year, in a move that predated modern baseball's reliance on a standout closer to finish games, Stowe was moved to relief duty. Pitching out of the bullpen, he appeared in 18 of Clemson's 29 games with a 7-3 record to go along with a 1.78 earned run average. While the Tigers did not ultimately win college baseball's championship, Stowe's performances have been forever recognized. In 1979, Hal Stowe was elected to the Clemson Athletic Hall of Fame and today Clemson's best pitcher each year is presented with the Hal Stowe MVP Award.

After his impressive college performance, Hal Stowe was signed by the Yankees as an amateur free agent in 1959. His path to the Major Leagues was quick. In 1959, he played at the lowest levels of the minor leagues for the Greensboro Yankees (Class B), and Fargo-Moorehead Twins (Class C). In 1960, while pitching for the Amarillo Gold Sox of the Double-A Texas League, Stowe began to shine. There he went 12-12 and earned a late season call-up to the Yankees.

It was September 30, 1960 when Hal Stowe enjoyed his only inning as a Major League player. The game featured the first-place Yankees facing the seventh-place Red Sox in a three-game series to close out the regular season. The Red Sox team that appeared that day was full of also-rans. The most famous member of the team, Ted Williams, had bowed out after hitting a home run with his final swing in his final game at Fenway Park. Rather than seeing Teddy Ballgame in left field during those last games, the Yankees faithful witnessed Carroll Hardy. The Red Sox leadoff hitter and shortstop that day was Pumpsie Green, the first African American to play for the Red Sox. Green was completing the second of his five years in the big leagues. Also on that Red Sox squad was first baseman Vic Wertz who, in the 1954 World Series, hit the long fly that Willie Mays caught with his back to the infield in what is still considered one of baseball's greatest catches.

The Yankees, who would soon be in the World Series, featured a host of superstars. These included shortstop Tony Kubek, the 1957 Rookie of the Year, right fielder Roger Maris, who would win the 1960 and 1961 American League MVP awards, first baseman Bill Skowron, an eight-time All-Star, second baseman Bobby Richardson, also an eight-time All-Star, in addition to future Hall of Famers Yogi Berra and Mickey Mantle. Twelve-time All-Star Elston Howard did not play in the game. Neither did future Hall of Famer Whitey Ford. There were legends wherever one looked on the Yankee bench, including manager Casey Stengel.

Hal Stowe came into the game in the top of the eighth inning with the Yankees trailing 4-2. The first batter Stowe faced was Wertz who reached on a walk. Stowe then committed a balk

HAL STOWE

Courtesy of TCMA Ltd.

sending Wertz to second base. Russ Nixon, the Red Sox catcher, sacrificed Wertz to third for the first out of inning. Red Sox third baseman Frank Malzone then scored Wertz on a sacrifice fly to left field. Marlan Coughtry then popped out to the Yankees third baseman Clete Boyer (who, while never an All-Star, did win the 1969 Gold Glove Award) to end the inning and Hal Stowe's Major League career. The Yankees eventually scored three runs in the bottom of the ninth inning to win 6-5.

It was said that Casey Stengel had a great deal of confidence in Stowe, but as spring training rolled around in 1961, Stengel was no longer the Yankees' manager. After the Yankees lost the 1960 World Series, Stengel was replaced by Ralph Houk. Stowe helped his own cause that spring by performing with excellence and winning the team's Most Outstanding Young Pitcher Award, but Houk just did not seem enamored with him, in spite of this success. While Stowe came north with the team, he was never used in a game and was eventually sent back to the minors where he played until 1964, never again reaching the Major Leagues.

Before calling it a career, Stowe did have one especially memorable game in the minor leagues. In this game, he came in as a relief pitcher and won the game without even throwing a pitch. This was in Stowe's final season of professional ball while he was playing for the Charlotte Hornets of the Southern League, a Double-A franchise affiliated with the Minnesota Twins. In that game, Stowe was called out of the bullpen with two outs in the top of the ninth inning with the go-ahead run on first base. Stowe promptly picked the runner off before even delivering a pitch to the batter. In the bottom of the frame, Charlotte scored a run to win the game giving Stowe the easiest win of his professional career.

Extra Innings
Dave Righetti's Move to the Bullpen

When Clemson's head baseball coach Bill Wilhelm moved Hal Stowe to the bullpen, in spite of his success as a starting pitcher, he predated a similar move that a Yankees manager, Yogi Berra, would make twenty-six years later with another player who exhibited untold potential as a starting pitcher. That pitcher was Dave Righetti.

The story of Righetti being moved to the bullpen actually occurs a number of years before he was even part of the Yankees organization when he was just a kid himself. Just before the 1972 season, the Yankees acquired left-handed relief pitcher Albert "Sparky" Lyle from the Boston Red Sox. Lyle was immediately recognized as the Yankees' top reliever or "fireman." In that 1972 season, Lyle saved a league-leading 32 games. This was the beginning of a tremendous six-year span when Sparky Lyle served as the Yankees' closer. His great bullpen work served as a cornerstone of the Yankees' ascension back to the top of the division. Sparky Lyle's work in 1977 was so impressive (137 innings over 72 games with a 2.17 ERA, all out of the bullpen) that he earned the American League Cy Young Award as he provided the consistency that helped the Yankees reach and win the World Series.

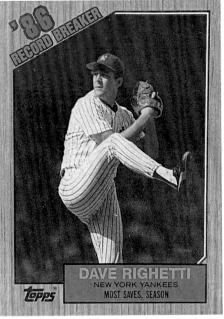

Courtesy of the Topps Company

Even with Lyle's success the Yankees signed the top available free agent relief pitcher, Rich "Goose" Gossage that offseason. There was talk that Gossage and Lyle would share the job of closing out games, but, in practice, Gossage became the Yankees new relief ace. At the end of the 1978 season, Lyle was traded to the Texas Rangers as the main component of a nine-player deal that netted the Yankees a hard-throwing left-handed starting pitcher named Dave Righetti.

By 1981, Dave Righetti was in the Major Leagues. In that strike-shortened year, Righetti made 15 starts, delivering an 8-4 record with a 2.05 earned run average and was named the American League Rookie of the Year.

The 1982 season was not as kind. Righetti suffered a bit from the sophomore jinx with an inability to consistently throw strikes and was even sent back to the minors to try to find his "stuff." By 1983, though, Righetti seemed to come into his own. He logged 217 innings, pitching to a 14-8 record with the highlight of his season (if not career) coming on July 4 when he pitched a no-hitter against the Red Sox. Righetti's no-hitter was the first pitched by a Yankee since Don Larsen had thrown a perfect game in the 1956 World Series.

After that 1983 season, Rich Gossage left the Yankees to sign with the San Diego Padres as a free agent. This left the Yankees with no late-inning closer. Yankees manager Yogi Berra made the fateful decision to move Dave Righetti from the starting rotation to become the closer. Righetti was made the Yankees relief ace using a logic similar to that one used for Hal Stowe—as a relief pitcher he would be able to be used more often.

Righetti enjoyed a great deal of success as a reliever. Between 1984 and 1990, his last season with the Yankees, Righetti never appeared in fewer than 53 games, and during his most prominent years, he routinely appeared in 60 or more games. In 1986, Dave Righetti set the then Major League record for saves in a single season with 46. Righetti was voted to two All-Star games and twice was named the American League's top reliever. He left the Yankees after the 1990 season as their all-time leader in games pitched and saves. He now stands as second in those categories behind legendary closer Mariano Rivera.

BOSTON RED SOX at NEW YORK YANKEES

Friday, September 30, 1960 (Yankee Stadium)

	1	2	3	4	5	6	7	8	9		R	H	E
BOS	0	0	1	0	1	2	0	1	0		5	9	2
NY	0	0	1	0	0	0	1	1	3		6	11	1

BOS		AB	R	H	RBI	NY		AB	R	H	RBI
Green	SS	4	2	1	0	Kubek	SS	5	1	1	1
Tasby	CF	5	0	2	1	Lopez	LF	5	1	2	1
Wertz	1B	3	1	1	1	Maris	RF	5	1	2	1
Nixon	C	3	1	2	0	Mantle	CF	2	0	0	0
Malzone	3B	3	1	1	1	Pisoni	CF	1	0	0	0
Runnels	2B	3	0	2	2	Cery	PH/CF	2	0	1	2
Coughtry	PR/2B	1	0	0	0	Berra	C	3	0	0	0
Hardy	LF	3	0	0	0	Blanchard	C	1	0	0	0
Clinton	RF	4	0	0	0	Skowron	1B	3	0	2	0
Monbouquette	P	4	0	0	0	Johnson	3B	1	0	0	0
Brewer	P					Boyer	3B	1	0	0	0
Stallard	P					Long	PH/1B	2	0	0	0
						Richardson	2B	4	1	1	0
						Ditmar	P	1	0	0	0
						Hunt	PH	1	0	0	0
						Shantz	P				
						Duren	P				
						Gonder	PH	1	1	1	1
						Stowe	P				
						Maas	P				
						McDougald	PH	1	1	1	0

BOS	IP	H	R	BB	SO	NY	IP	H	R	BB	SO
Monbouquette	8	8	4	1	8	Ditmar	4	5	1	0	0
Brewer - L	0.1	3	2	0	0	Shantz	2	4	3	1	3
Stallard	0	0	0	0	0	Duren	1	0	0	0	0
						Stowe	1	0	1	1	0
						Maas - W	1	0	0	1	1

Hal Stowe

Courtesy of the Univ. of Pennsylvania
Archives

CHAPTER TWENTY
WALTER BERNHARDT (1918)

In the years before 1920, numerous players came to the Major Leagues from prestigious colleges and universities. Today, a much smaller percentage of players come from these elite institutions. For example, 21 of the 33 Major Leaguers who came from Harvard played before 1925. Princeton's record is no different. Nineteen of the 31 players from Princeton who played big league ball played in 1925 or earlier. For Yale, it is a similar story—half of the players from that school, 15 out of 30, played in 1925 or earlier.

Walter Bernhardt, Larry McClure, and Tom (Alex) Burr were all *Least Among Them* ballplayers who were Yankees during this time period. They each came from prestigious colleges; Bernardt from the University of Pennsylvania, an Ivy League school. McClure attended Amherst College, and Burr went to Williams College. Both Williams and Amherst Colleges are ranked among the finest in the nation.

Walter Bernhardt literally walked off the Ivy League campus of Penn where he was a star pitcher (having pitched for the varsity team in 1917 and 1918) right into the Major Leagues. The Yankees signed him in late June, on the same day future Hall of Famer Dazzy Vance (who, years later, would enjoy most of his Major League success with the Brooklyn Dodgers rather than the Yankees) also reported to the team after spending time in the minor leagues.

Bernhardt's one opportunity to pitch came on July 16, 1918 at the Polo Grounds, then the home of the Yankees, as they battled the Detroit Tigers. The teams played a doubleheader that day. Bernhardt pitched in the first game, recording the final two outs in a game the Tigers won 12-1. Bernhardt faced two batters and got them both out. First, he faced Oscar Stanage, a catcher, and struck him out. One can't imagine a better way to begin a Major League career. Next, Bernhardt faced the opposing pitcher Hooks Dauss who popped out to the second baseman Del Pratt. Hooks Dauss is often forgotten today, but in his time, from 1912 to 1926, he won 223 games, all with the Tigers.

Bernhardt was one of a number of players signed by big league teams to help fill out their rosters that were beginning to thin out due to the draft and "work or fight" orders for World War I. The Courier-News of Bridgewater, New Jersey (June 22, 1918) chronicled this fact perfectly noting, "With the fate of baseball very much in doubt for this season because of the draft, local managers have been engaged... with the business of keeping their team in the fighting." All told, it has been estimated that thirty-eight percent of Major League players served the United States military during this period.

The Detroit squad that Bernhardt faced was suffering through a difficult season. Nonetheless, there were two future Hall of Fame players on the field that day for the Tigers—Harry Heilmann (first base) and Ty Cobb (center field). The Tigers manager, Hughie Jennings, was also later enshrined in Cooperstown.

Sometime after the game, Walter Bernhardt went off to serve in the war. Since he had studied to be a dentist at the University of Pennsylvania, his war service consisted of working with the Army Dental Corps. After the war, Walter Bernhardt became practicing dentist in Rochester, New York.

He wasn't the last future doctor to play for the Yankees...

Courtesy of the Univ. of Pennsylvania Archives

Extra Innings
Doctors Who Played for the Yankees

In the history of the Yankees, there have been nine players who were called or known as Doc. Not all of these "Docs" though went on to a life in medicine.

Luther "Doc" Cook was a right fielder who played 288 games over four seasons as a Yankee (1913-1916). Spending his entire career with the Yankees, Cook batted .274.

Dwight "Doc" Gooden earned his nickname not from studying medicine, but from being a strikeout artist in his youngest days in the big leagues as a hard-throwing right-handed pitcher with the New York Mets. He was Dr. K. (Doctor Strikeout). The practice of fans hanging signs with the letter K following each strikeout originated with Gooden. He later etched his name in the Yankees' record books when he threw a no-hitter against the Seattle Mariners on May 14, 1996. Gooden pitched for the Yankees in 1996-97 and 2000. His career, once filled with promise, was derailed by substance abuse. In his sixteen-year career, Dwight Gooden won 194 games against 112 losses.

"Doc" Edwards was a catcher who played in the majors from 1962 through 1965 with a brief return to the big leagues in 1970. Edwards earned his nickname by serving as a Navy Medic with the United States Marines. Edwards played most of his career for the Cleveland Indians and the Kansas City Athletics, but appeared in 45 games for the Yankees, batting .190, in 1965. In his return to the majors in 1970, Edwards played for the Philadelphia Phillies. After his playing days, Edwards became a manager. He managed for 33 years, mostly in the minor leagues, but he was the manager for the Cleveland Indians from 1987 through 1989. Edwards' first opportunity as a minor league manager came with the Yankees organization when he piloted the West Haven Yankees in 1973 and 1974.

The first player in Yankee franchise history to become a doctor was Doc Adkins who pitched two games for the Yankees in 1903. During his playing days, he attended Johns Hopkins where he studied medicine and picked up his nickname. Adkins later become a coach at Trinity College in North Carolina. That college is now known as Duke University.

During the 1905 season, the Highlanders had two "Docs" on the team. Mike "Doc" Powers, a catcher and first baseman, who enjoyed an eleven-year playing career from 1898 through 1909, and Doc Newton, a left-handed pitcher, who had an eight-year career that went from 1900-1902 and again from 1905-09.

Doc Powers spent the majority of his career with the Philadelphia Athletics, but in 1905 he was with the Highlanders for eleven games. Powers was a medical doctor who studied at the College of the Holy Cross, the University of Notre Dame, and the Louisville Surgical College. His life was cut short during the 1909 season as he suffered from a rare intestinal condition. Doc Powers was a beloved player who left behind a family with three sons. The Philadelphia Athletics held a tribute day in honor of Powers in 1910 to raise money for his family. This day consisted of a skills competition and an exhibition game between the Athletics and other baseball stars of the day and was one of the first such days in baseball's history.

Doc Newton was a practicing dentist, but as a ballplayer, it seems he had a penchant for drinking alcohol. He supposedly believed that he performed better the more he drank. Newton pitched for various teams and was a Highlander for five seasons, from 1905 through 1909. The manager of the Highlanders, Clark Griffith, believed that Newton's inability to stay in shape cost his team the 1906 pennant. Before joining the Highlanders, Newton pitched the first no-hitter in the history of the Pacific Coast League.

Edward "Doc" Farrell was an infielder who played in the Major Leagues for nine seasons between 1925 and 1935. Farrell came up with the New York Giants and also played for the Boston Braves, the Boston Red Sox, and the Yankees. He is the only player in baseball history to play for the two Boston and the two New York City Major League teams. He was a Yankee in 1932 and

1933 appearing in 179 games. In 1934-35 Farrell played for the Yankees' Double-A Newark Bears franchise and was originally included in the trade between the Yankees and the San Francisco Seals for Joe DiMaggio. Farrell refused to report to the Seals. Instead, he played his final four games with the Red Sox in 1935 before beginning a career in dentistry. Like Walter Bernhardt, Farrell also attended the University of Pennsylvania.

The most notable Yankee to become a doctor was Bobby Brown who played for the Yankees from 1946-1954. For four seasons, Brown was the team's regular third baseman. He ended his career with a lifetime batting average of .279 over 548 games. Bobby Brown played on four World Series championship teams. His career was put on hold by his serving in the United States military during the Korean War where Brown was assigned to the 160th Field Artillery Battalion. In this duty, Bobby Brown headed the battalion aid station. He also served at Tokyo Army Hospital. Before his big league days, Brown had served in the Navy during World War II. After his playing days, Brown earned his degree in medicine from Tulane Medical School. Dr. Bobby Brown began serving as a cardiologist in 1958. Brown, though, never ventured too far from the game. In the 1970s, he served as the interim president of the Texas Rangers and from 1984 through 1994, Brown was the president of the American League. Dr. Bobby Brown has been honored throughout his lifetime both in sport and in medicine. An excellent ballplayer, a multiple world champion, a veteran of two wars, and a cardiologist, Dr. Bobby Brown stands as one of the most honored and respected Yankees of all time.

In the 1970s, the Yankees had a right-handed pitcher named George "Doc" Medich. Medich was drafted by the Yankees in 1970 and rose through the minor leagues, making his first Major League appearance in 1972 to begin an eleven-year Major League career. As a Yankee, Doc Medich won 49 games against 40 losses in four seasons through 1975. His greatest contribution to the Yankees though was being the centerpiece of the trade with the Pittsburgh Pirates that landed the Yankees star second baseman Willie Randolph and two other players, including pitcher Dock Ellis. Medich began medical school at the University of Pittsburgh the day after his Major League debut in 1972. He graduated in January 1977 while still an active player. There are three documented instances where Doc Medich used his medical skills in conjunction with his playing. He twice went into the stands to administer CPR to fans, saving a fan's life in 1978. Medich also tended to Yankee legend Whitey Ford after Ford collapsed following pitching a batting practice session in May 1975.

While not the centerpiece of the Willie Randolph trade, the Yankees did acquire Dock Ellis in that trade with the Pirates. Ellis had also been a star pitcher. In 1971, Ellis pitched to a 19-9, 3.06 record for the Pirates. He also pitched in the All-Star Game that year. Ellis achieved less than positive notoriety for pitching a no-hitter while under the effects of LSD in 1970. Ellis' career with the Yankees lasted slightly more than one season. In 1976, he went 17-8 for the American League champions. This performance earned him the American League Comeback Player of the Year Award. But, in 1977, after only three games, he was traded to the Oakland A's. Dock Ellis spent twelve seasons in the Major Leagues, pitching for five different clubs. Interestingly, the careers of Doc Medich and Dock Ellis ended up being similar. In their careers, both pitched for the Yankees, Pirates, A's, Rangers, and Mets. They were teammates on the Oakland A's in 1977 and with the Texas Rangers in 1978 and 1979.

Dock Ellis is the only player in this short history to not have the nickname "Doc." His given name was Dock Phillip Ellis.

DETROIT TIGERS at NEW YORK YANKEES

Tuesday, July 16, 1918 (Polo Grounds)

	1	2	3	4	5	6	7	8	9		R	H	E
DET	0	2	0	0	0	0	5	2	3		12	16	1
NY	0	0	0	0	1	0	0	0	0		1	7	2

DET		AB	R	H	RBI	NY		AB	R	H	RBI
Bush	SS	4	1	1	0	Gilhooley	RF	3	0	2	0
Jones	3B	5	1	2	2	Peckinpaugh	SS	3	0	1	1
Cobb	CF	4	2	3	2	Ward	PH/SS	1	0	0	0
Veach	LF	4	2	2	3	Baker	3B	4	0	1	0
Heilmann	1B	5	1	1	1	Pratt	2B	3	0	1	0
Harper	RF	5	2	2	0	Pipp	1B	4	0	0	0
Coffey	2B	4	1	2	1	Bodie	LF	4	0	1	0
Stanage	C	4	2	2	1	Miller	CF	4	0	0	0
Dauss	P	4	0	1	2	Hannah	C	3	0	0	0
						Caldwell	P	3	1	1	0
						Vance	P				
						Bernhardt	P				

DET	IP	H	R	BB	SO	NY	IP	H	R	BB	SO
Dauss - W	9	7	1	1	2	Caldwell - L	7	9	7	4	1
						Vance	1.1	7	5	1	0
						Bernhardt	0.2	0	0	0	1

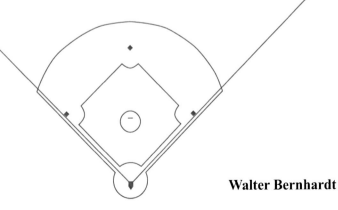

Walter Bernhardt

CHAPTER TWENTY-ONE
JACK ENRIGHT (1917)

Jack Enright earned his chance to pitch in the Major Leagues on September 26, 1917 in the Yankees' 149th game of the season. The 1917 Yankees were not a great team as they won only 71 games against 82 losses and finished sixth in the eight-team league. That finish marked the last time they would finish that poorly (exempting the 1925 season which was famous for Babe Ruth's bellyache) until 1965. This was a franchise that was slowly moving to respectability and eventual legendary greatness.

The journey Jack Enright took to reach the majors was the path followed by most players, but it began at a unique location. As a child, Enright attended (and later graduated from) the Carlisle School for Indians, one of the very first prep schools formed for Native Americans. The legendary Jim Thorpe also attended this school which was also where much of professional football as we know it was designed.

Enright, like so many before and since, began his professional career in the minor leagues climbing through the levels before his eventual Major League opportunity. Sometimes perseverance and determination pay off. Jack Enright proved this to be the case as his minor league career was nothing special.

Enright's career began in 1914 pitching for the San Antonio Bronchos of the Class-B Texas League. He did not fare well that first season winning only one game while losing eight. It seems that he was out of baseball in 1915. Records indicate that Enright returned to the bush leagues in 1916 pitching to a 6-18 record for the Double-A Newark Indians. The 1917 season wasn't much better as he won only 11 games while losing 19 pitching for the Richmond Virginians of the Double-A International League. It was at the conclusion of that minor league season that this pitcher with a lifetime record of 18-45 was called by the Yankees to start a late-season game against the Detroit Tigers on September 26. It might have been determination or perseverance... or maybe the Yankees just needed a pitcher. Nonetheless, Jack Enright had reached the big leagues.

The 1917 Tigers were very similar to the 1918 squad that Walter Bernhardt faced. There were three eventual Hall of Famers on that squad: Harry Heilmann, Sam Crawford, and Ty Cobb. In spite of their contributions, this was a thoroughly mediocre team that would finish the season with a 78-75 record, good enough for only fourth place.

Enright's one big league game was held at the Polo Grounds in New York. He pitched five innings and allowed five runs on five hits and three walks. Enright struck out just one batter. The Tigers did most of their damage in the third inning when they plated four of their five runs. Two of those scored on a bases-loaded double by Cobb. Of note, Jack Enright did pick off Cobb at second base after that double. Earlier in the game, Cobb had hit a sacrifice fly.

After five innings, Enright was relieved by Slim Love, the tall left-handed pitcher who threw for the Yankees, Tigers, and Senators over a six-year career. The Yankees offense was virtually nonexistent in this game as they lost 5-1.

Over the following two seasons, Jack Enright pitched for five teams at various levels of the minor leagues. He won ten games and lost fifteen before calling it a career.

Jack Enright's five-inning pitching performance was one of the longest for these *Least Among Them* Yankees.

Extra Innings
Babe Ruth and Ty Cobb Compete at Golf

T y Cobb's hitting helped make the difference against Jack Enright and the Yankees in this contest. This was no surprise as Cobb batted a lifetime .373 against the Yankees. Interestingly, over his career, Ty Cobb also hit better at the Polo Grounds than almost any other stadium. In 105 career games at the Polo Grounds, Cobb batted a remarkable .395. Cobb only bettered this in Washington where he batted .404 at Griffith Stadium which was the only ballpark where Cobb had a lifetime batting average over .400.

Cobb was widely regarded as the game's best hitter throughout the early years of baseball history. His style of play was the norm as he hit the ball hard, ran the bases with abandon, and played this aggressive style of baseball better than any player before him. Ty Cobb's .366 lifetime batting average is the highest of all time. He was considered baseball's greatest player until Babe Ruth began swatting baseballs over the fence for the Yankees in the 1920s. Ruth's style was a different brand of baseball than the game that Ty Cobb played. This difference led to a rivalry that continued throughout their playing days as these two vastly different approaches to baseball played out. Of course, it was Ruth's approach, the one focused on the long ball, that won out and totally changed the game. Because of Ruth, baseball became enamored with the home run.

The rivalry between Ruth and Cobb lasted after their playing careers ended (Cobb retired after the 1928 season, Babe Ruth in 1935). These legends were considered the game's two greatest players and debates raged over who was the greatest. Neither player was also above feuding with the other. It seems that even in retirement, Ruth and Cobb were rivals.

In 1941, many years removed from the game of baseball, Babe Ruth and Ty Cobb battled once more, this time on a golf course. They battled for pride, for fun, and to see just who was really the greatest between them. They also used this contest to raise money for various charities.

Heading into the contest, Ruth was the favored contestant as he carried a handicap of about seven and Cobb's handicap was about double Ruth's. Yet Cobb, a very wealthy man who had invested wisely with Coke-a-Cola and General Motors was a member of the prestigious Augusta National Golf Club and he had received lessons from Bobby Jones, the legendary golfer.

The first match took place in Newton, Massachusetts. Of the two, Cobb seemed to be the more serious. It was said that Ruth tried to engage him in chatter, but Cobb would have none of it. His focus and determination allowed him to finish the course at 81 two strokes fewer than The Babe. Cobb may have been the older contestant, he was 55 compared to Ruth's 46, but he was always the athlete and in better shape. In the end, Cobb remarked that he had never battled so hard in an athletic competition. For his efforts and the victory, Ty Cobb earned a silver cup trophy donated by the famous actress Bette Davis.

Babe Ruth and Ty Cobb with the trophy at the first match.
Courtesy of the Boston Public Library, Leslie Jones Collection

The second match took place at Fresh Meadow in Flushing, New York. This became a grueling affair lasting three hours and thirty minutes. Cobb, ever the perfectionist, spent a great deal of time, seemingly at every hole, pondering and practicing before pitching or putting. These delays caused Ruth great consternation. The battle between these two legends went stroke for stroke with the lead changing hands often and both players making some impressive shots. After eighteen holes, the two giants of baseball were tied. This forced a playoff. On the nineteenth hole, Ruth shot a five, Cobb a six. Babe Ruth had won the match 90-91.

The final match between these two legends was played in Detroit, Michigan. Over 2,000 spectators were in attendance to witness this contest. Ruth won the first hole 5-6. But after four holes, the match was tied at 20 strokes each. Cobb then went on a run. He won each of the next four holes by just one stroke each, but he was building an impressive lead heading into the game's second half.

Throughout the match, Cobb stayed true to form, deliberating on each and every shot. On two occasions, Ruth rested on the ground on his back crossing his arms across his chest and pretending to sleep as the match dragged ever onward. Maybe the resting worked as Ruth picked up his game and started catching up. As they shot holes eleven through fifteen, Babe Ruth held a one-stroke advantage. Because of this, he had cut into Cobb's overall lead and was down just three strokes after 15 holes. But due to the pace of the game, as play entered its fourth hour, the sun began to recede.

After the players both shot fives on the sixteenth hole, play was called. Cobb was the declared winner 78-81.

Babe Ruth called this battle "The Left-Handed Has-Beens Golf Championship of Nowhere in Particular," and it was a fitting name. In this final match, both players shot well over par, but in the course of play, these two formal rivals came together with graciousness and good spirits to help others and to remember the fire of competition that still burned, if a little less brightly, at their inner core.

DETROIT TIGERS at NEW YORK YANKEES

Wednesday, September 26, 1917 (Polo Grounds)

	1	2	3	4	5	6	7	8	9		R	H	E
DET	1	0	4	0	0	0	0	0	0		5	7	2
NY	0	0	0	1	0	0	0	0	0		1	5	2

DET		AB	R	H	RBI	NY		AB	R	H	RBI
Bush	SS	5	2	2	0	Miller	CF	5	0	2	0
Vitt	3B	3	1	2	1	Ward	SS	5	0	0	0
Cobb	CF	3	1	1	3	Baker	3B	2	1	0	0
Veach	LF	2	0	0	1	Pipp	1B	3	0	1	0
Heilmann	RF	4	0	1	0	Lamar	LF	4	0	1	0
Ellison	1B	3	0	0	0	Vick	RF	4	0	0	0
Young	2B	4	0	1	0	Fewster	2B	4	0	1	1
Stanage	C	4	0	0	0	Ruel	C	3	0	0	0
Boland	P	4	1	0	0	Nunamaker	PH	1	0	0	0
						Enright	P	1	0	0	0
						Gilhooley	PH				
						Love	P	1	0	0	0
						Hendryx	PH	1	0	0	0

DET	IP	H	R	BB	SO	NY	IP	H	R	BB	SO
Boland - W	9	5	1	4	7	**Enright - L**	5	5	5	3	1
						Love	4	2	0	0	2

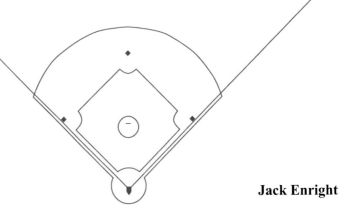

Jack Enright

CHAPTER TWENTY-TWO
LARRY MCCLURE (1910)

L arry McClure's lone Major League appearance came not necessarily because he was at the right place at the right time, but probably because another player was not at the right place when the time came. McClure was another of the *Least Among Them* Yankees who originally hailed from a prestigious college, in his case Amherst College, where he made quite a name for himself as a pitcher before entering professional baseball.

Amherst College is located in central Massachusetts. It was founded in 1821 when the president of Williams College, also in Massachusetts, took some of the teaching faculty, fifteen students (about twenty percent of the total student population at that time), and, as legend has it, a large percentage of the Williams College library to form Amherst College. From that moment on, the two colleges, both highly regarded institutions, began a fierce rivalry. Tom Burr, the focus of Chapter 23, attended Williams College.

Small of stature, Larry McClure stood just 5 feet, 6 inches and weighed only 130 pounds, but he was a top-notch pitcher at Amherst. During the 1909 season, as a junior, McClure threw no-hitters against Navy (Annapolis), Army (West Point), and (it just fits too nicely) Williams College. Along with that impressive display he added a one-hitter against Yale. In 1910, McClure once again no-hit the Williams College team. It was after graduation that Larry McClure was signed by the New York Highlanders.

Researchers have found only one account of a minor league pitching appearance by Larry McClure, for Toronto of the International League. On July 9, 1910, McClure pitched seven innings in relief, acquitting himself well in what must have been his pro baseball debut. The lack of appearances may have been due to the fact that McClure was suffering from arm troubles. Nonetheless, Larry McClure was with the Highlanders and in the Major Leagues on July 26, 1910 for his one big league appearance. If nothing else, that appearance was enough to get McClure a mention in Bill James' famed *Historical Baseball Abstract* in which he was classified as the lightest big league player of the 1910s.

On that day, the Highlanders were playing at home against the Detroit Tigers. This game was most likely played at Hilltop Park, the home of the Highlanders, but one source (the SABR Bio Project) notes that the game was played at the Polo Grounds.

Managed by Hall of Famer Hughie Jennings, the 1910 Tigers were one of baseball's strongest teams having won the American League pennant in each of the previous three seasons. The team was led by future Hall of Famers "Wahoo Sam" Crawford (who, in 1910, led the league in triples with 19, and runs batted in with 120) and Ty Cobb, one of baseball's greatest players, who would lead the league that year in runs (106) and batting average (.383). In 1910, Cobb was just coming into his own. The .383 average he put up that season was his best to date, but he would hit over .400 in each of the next two seasons, 1911 (.420) and 1912 (.409).

The surprising second-place finishers in the American League in 1910 were the New York Highlanders. This second-place finish was the last time they would finish this high in the standings until 1921 when they would, as the Yankees, win the American League pennant. Interestingly, no players from this Highlanders team has been enshrined in Cooperstown.

The most notable player on the 1910 Highlanders was Hal Chase who may have been the greatest fielding first baseman of all time. A Highlander since 1905, Chase was the first true homegrown star of the New York baseball franchise. He was a solid hitter and an exceptional fielder, but Chase was also known as a gambler. Stories persist that he had been involved in numerous betting incidents while playing and he was suspected as being involved, possibly as a "middle-man," in the notorious 1919 Black Sox scandal. Chase went to his grave denying his direct involvement while also admitting that he knew about the "fix" in advance.

In this game against the Tigers, Larry McClure did not have to wait long before his opportunity arrived. With two outs in the top of the first inning, Ty Cobb batted and roped an extremely hard-hit ball to right field. As the Highlanders' right fielder, Harry Wolter reached for the ball, it broke his finger and the ball skipped by him, going all the way to the wall. During this action, Cobb raced around the bases for an inside-the-park home run.

Because of the injury, Wolter was unable to continue in the field. For whatever reason reserve outfielder Charlie Hemphill was out of uniform at that moment. Knowing that McClure had played some outfield at Amherst, manager George Stallings made some defensive shifts to place McClure in the outfield. The half-inning soon ended with McClure failing to record any chances in the field.

In the bottom of the inning, McClure had an opportunity to bat since he replaced Wolter who was the number two batter in the lineup (and because Charlie Hemphill was still not ready to play). In his only Major League at-bat, Larry McClure struck out.

After the game, McClure was sent to a team in Jersey City. It does not appear that he played due to his sore arm. McClure went to spring training with the Highlanders in 1911, but again never appeared in a game. McClure may have also played with the Huntington, West Virginia Blue Sox for a time, possibly as an infielder. What is known is that he did attend West Virginia University where he coached the baseball team and earned a degree in law. Larry McClure then spent the remainder of his life as an attorney.

Extra Innings
The Shortest Yankees All-Stars

L arry McClure was one of the smallest Yankees of all time. Throughout their history, the Yankees have had numerous players who were short in stature. Currently there are nine players in the Baseball Hall of Fame who are listed at 5 feet 7 inches or shorter. Three of these players were notable Highlanders/Yankees.

The smallest player in the Hall of Fame is the appropriately nicknamed "Wee Willie" Keeler who played for the Highlanders from the franchise's first year in 1903 through the 1909 season. Wee Willie Keeler stood only 5 feet, 4 inches, a full two inches shorter than Larry McClure. A lifetime .341 hitter, Keeler was one of baseball's first great ballplayers. His adage, *"Hit 'em where they ain't"* is still uttered on ball fields across the country. The term "Baltimore Chop" was also derived from Keeler's (and his teammates' on the late 1890's Baltimore Orioles) unique ability to hit a ball into the ground making for a high bounce that would allow them to reach base safely. In his career, Keeler amassed 2,932 hits. He led the league in batting in 1897 (.424) and 1898 (.395). He also led the league in hits three times and runs once. In 1897, Keeler enjoyed a 44-game hitting streak which was the Major League record until 1941 when Joe DiMaggio hit in 56 consecutive games. Willie Keeler played fourteen of his nineteen big league seasons in New York boroughs playing for Brooklyn, the New York Giants, and the Highlanders. He also spent five seasons in Baltimore. In spite of the fact that he spent more games as a Highlander than with any other franchise, Wee Willie Keeler is pictured with a Brooklyn hat on his Hall of Fame plaque.

Joe Sewell, who stood only 5 feet, 6 inches, is another Hall of Fame player who enjoyed time with the Yankees, albeit only for the final three years of his noteworthy fourteen-year career, spent mostly with the Cleveland Indians, from 1920 through 1933. It was the Yankees, though, that played an indirect yet significant role in Sewell's ascension to the Major Leagues in 1920.

The 1920 season is known, in part, because the first and only on-the-field fatality took place that season. The fateful day was August 16, 1920. The first-place Cleveland Indians were visiting the Yankees at the Polo Grounds on a dark and rainy afternoon. In the fifth inning, Yankees' hurler Carl Mays, an underhand thrower known for pitching inside, hit star Cleveland shortstop Ray Chapman in the head with a pitch. Chapman fell to his knees with blood coming from his left ear. Two doctors came onto the field, and while Chapman was able to be escorted from the field, he died the next morning in the hospital. After his passing, it was Joe Sewell who was brought to the Major Leagues to replace him at shortstop. In twenty-two games to finish the season, Sewell hit .329 helping Cleveland win the pennant. Over the next nine seasons, Joe Sewell would hit .300 or better every year, except 1922 when he batted .299.

Joe Sewell's greatest skill was his ability to put the bat on the ball. He was the toughest batter to strike out in the history of baseball. Between 1925 and 1933, he never struck out more than nine times in a season. In 8,333 lifetime plate appearances, Joe Sewell struck out only 114 times. Joe Sewell spent his final three seasons, 1931-1933, with the Yankees playing as a third baseman. Sewell was a member of the 1932 world championship squad. In that World Series, Sewell batted .333. In the first inning of Game 3, he walked and then scored on a home run by Babe Ruth. In the fifth inning, Sewell grounded out to shortstop before Ruth hit his second home run of the game (and the last World Series home run of his storied career)—the legendary "Called Shot" into the center-field bleachers at Wrigley Field in Chicago.

The final diminutive Yankees Hall of Famer was their legendary shortstop Phil "Scooter" Rizzuto. In the annals of Yankee history, Rizzuto looms larger than life as he was a member of the Yankees' family as a player and broadcaster for forty years.

Phil Rizzuto was one of the cornerstone players on the Yankees teams that seemingly won every season. Rizzuto played on nine American League championship teams. Seven of those teams won the World Series including the five consecutive World Series from 1949 through 1953. The great Ted Williams of the Boston Red Sox once quipped that Phil Rizzuto was the single difference between the two teams in the standings. Later in life, it was Ted Williams who spoke passionately about Phil Rizzuto to the Hall of Fame's Veterans Committee helping Rizzuto gain election to Cooperstown in 1994.

As a player, Phil Rizzuto, who stood 5 feet, 6 inches, was a standout defensive shortstop and a solid hitter who was also a master at bunting. After playing in the 1941 and 1942 seasons, and earning Most Valuable Player votes both years, Rizzuto left baseball to serve in the United States Navy during World War II. He returned to the Yankees in 1946 and played with them until his retirement during the 1956 season. Phil Rizzuto's greatest season was 1950 when he won the American League's Most Valuable Player Award (he had been the runner up to Ted Williams in 1949). During that season, Rizzuto batted a career-high .324.

Rizzuto was the league leader in double plays and total chances per game three times. He twice led the league in putouts and in assists once. Rizzuto was involved in 1,217 double plays as a shortstop, which, factored over his innings played came to 89 double plays per 1,000 innings—the highest rate in baseball history. Yankee manager Casey Stengel once said of Rizzuto, "He's the greatest shortstop I have ever seen. Honus Wagner was a better hitter, but I have seen this kid make plays Wagner never did."

As a broadcaster, Phil Rizzuto was also legendary. His voice is still heard in archival footage calling some of the most famous events in Yankees history including Roger Maris' 61st home run in 1961, Chris Chambliss' American League pennant-winning home run in 1976, and Dave Righetti's no-hitter in 1983. Rizzuto was known for his friendly style on the airwaves, often talking about friends and family, and at times missing some of the play-by-play, but that was part of his charm. His last season in the broadcast booth coincided with Derek Jeter's first full season, 1996. The announcer's voice on Jeter's Opening Day home run that season is Rizzuto's. Jeter would play for twenty seasons and eventually replace Rizzuto as the greatest shortstop in Yankees history.

DETROIT TIGERS at NEW YORK HIGHLANDERS

Tuesday, July 26, 1910 (Hilltop Park)

	1	2	3	4	5	6	7	8	9		R	H	E
DET	1	0	0	0	0	0	0	0	0		1	8	1
NY	0	0	0	0	0	0	0	0	0		0	5	1

DET		AB	R	H	RBI	NY		AB	R	H	RBI
McIntyre	LF	4	0	0	0	Daniels	LF/CF/LF	3	0	0	0
O'Leary	2B	4	0	0	0	Wolter	RF				
Cobb	CF	4	1	2	1	McClure	LF	1	0	0	0
Crawford	RF	4	0	1	0	Hemphill	RF	3	0	0	0
Lathers	3B	4	0	2	0	Knight	1B	4	0	3	0
Bush	SS	4	0	2	0	Cree	CF/RF/CF	2	0	1	0
Jones	1B	3	0	1	0	Gardner	2B	3	0	0	0
Schmidt	C	3	0	0	0	Roach	SS	4	0	1	0
Donovan	P	3	0	0	0	Austin	3B	4	0	0	0
						Mitchell	C	3	0	0	0
						Warhop	P	3	0	0	0

DET	IP	H	R	BB	SO	NY	IP	H	R	BB	SO
Donovan - W	9	5	0	5	4	Warhop - L	9	8	1	0	3

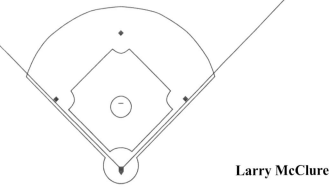

Larry McClure

CHAPTER TWENTY-THREE
TOM BURR (1914)

Alexander Thomas Burr's one-game career was similar in a number of respects to that of Larry McClure. Known throughout his life as Tom Burr, this pitcher from a prestigious northern college, played his only game as a Yankee in the outfield.

Tom Burr attended Williams College in Williamstown, Massachusetts before becoming a Major League player. Interestingly, Burr never played baseball at Williams, instead his legend grew as a high school baseball player where he starred for Choate, a prep school in Connecticut. Burr was a tall and strong pitcher, standing 6 feet, 3 inches. It was said that in high school he never lost a game. As a senior, he pitched in eleven games, allowing only 32 total hits and no earned runs. This dominance may have been due to his stature which allowed him to throw hard, but it also might have come from a deformity to his pitching arm. It seems Burr, who at times was called "The Man with the Bowlegged Arm," had a unique natural bend to his right arm which allowed him to throw a natural curveball. Due to his dominance at Choate, Burr was scouted and pursued by the Philadelphia Athletics, the Chicago White Sox, the Boston Red Sox, and the New York Yankees. It was the Yankees who signed him in January of his freshman year at Williams College before their baseball season got underway.

Tom Burr went to spring training with the 1914 Yankees and impressed their player/manager Frank Chance enough to keep him with the big club to begin the season. He was on the team, but Burr's only chance to play came in the fourth game of the season, in New York, against the Washington Senators.

The Senators were a strong team in 1914 having finished in second place in each of the two previous seasons. Their manager was Clark Griffith, an eventual baseball lifer and Hall of Famer. He had been the first manager of the New York Highlanders. The most notable player on that Senators team was the great Walter Johnson, the future Hall of Fame pitcher, who, by 1914, was in the fifth year of a ten-year streak in which he won at least 20 games every season. Johnson did not appear in this game because he had pitched the previous one.

The 1914 Yankees were a somewhat forgettable squad, eventually finishing in sixth place. Their only eventual Hall of Famer was manager Frank Chance who didn't even last the season as the skipper. He was replaced after 134 games by Roger Peckinpaugh.

Like Larry McClure, who was also a standout pitcher, Tom Burr's one Major League appearance came as an outfielder, but his appearance was even more short-lived than McClure's.

Through eight innings, the Senators were leading the Yankees 2-0, but in the bottom of the ninth, the Yankees mounted a comeback. In that frame, manager Frank Chance sent up a pinch hitter and two pinch runners, one of them being himself as he brought the team back to tie the game at two runs each. (This would be the last time Frank Chance would ever appear in a game as a player.) Now needing players in the field, Chance sent Tom Burr out to patrol center field for the 10th inning. Burr did not field any chances, and then, in the bottom of the frame, before his chance to bat, the Yankees scored the game winning run.

It was over that quickly.

By May, Burr was sent to New London in the Eastern Association and then Jersey City of the International League. Again, working as a pitcher, Burr struggled. He had difficulty finding the strike zone. In seven games, he walked 20 batters in only 19 innings bringing his professional career to an end.

Burr returned to Williams College. He never had an opportunity to graduate, though, as he enlisted in the United States Armed Forces in 1917 to serve in World War I. He became a member of the 31st Aero Squadron of the American Aciation Corps. On October 12, 1918, just about a month before the end of the war, Burr's airplane collided with another plane during a training exercise that killed both of the pilots.

Eight men, who had played Major League Baseball died in

World War I in service to their country. Interestingly, most of the eight had very brief careers as ballplayers. Five of the eight, including Tom Burr, played in only one season. This includes Bun Troy who died just one week before Burr. Bun Troy was a *Least Among Them* Detroit Tiger as his career was just one game for that franchise. The longest tenured Major Leaguer to die in World War I was Eddie Grant, an infielder who played primarily for the Phillies, Giants, and Reds during a ten-year big-league career. Sadly, six of those eight players died during the final two months (October and November 1918) of the war. Harry Glenn, a catcher who played six games for the St. Louis Cardinals in 1915 also died on October 12, 1918. Glen had been learning to fly airplanes, but he died from pneumonia after contracting the Spanish Flu.

Extra Innings
Sad Tales of Airplanes and Yankees

Tom Burr's life ended much too quickly in that terrible plane crash. Airplanes have been involved in numerous accidents that have taken the lives of Major League players. In the history of baseball, seven active players died in plane crashes including Ken Hubbs of the Chicago Cubs in 1964, and most notably, Roberto Clemente, in 1972. Clemente, one of the greatest players of the 1960s, and an eventual Hall of Famer, died while on a mission to bring needed supplies to the people of Nicaragua following a devastating earthquake. Clemente wasn't just one of baseball's great players, he was also a great humanitarian.

The history of the Yankees includes two players who died in airplane crashes during their playing days. Most recently, on October 11, 2006, pitcher Cory Lidle crashed a plane he was piloting into an apartment on New York's Upper East Side. Lidle had been acquired by the Yankees earlier that season from the Philadelphia Phillies. He pitched in ten games for the Yankees including an appearance in their final playoff game, a loss to the Detroit Tigers. In 2007, the team wore a black armband on their uniform sleeve to signify the loss of their teammate.

The most devastating plane crash in the history of the Yankees occurred on August 2, 1979 when star catcher and team captain Thurman Munson died while practicing takeoffs and landings near his home in Canton, Ohio. That day was an off day between a series in Chicago (where the Yankees had swept the White Sox) and a seven-game homestand. Munson had purchased an airplane because he wanted to be, more and more, with his family. The off day gave him an opportunity to be home and to practice his flying skills. Although he was a veteran player and a leader on the baseball field, Munson was still a novice as a pilot, having been flying for only eighteen months. The jet he was flying, a twin-engine Cessna Citation, was a model he was not, at that point in his flying career, ready or able to fully handle in all circumstances. An error in judgment on a landing pattern cost Munson his life and the Yankees their captain.

Munson's first full season with the Yankees was 1970, a year in which he hit .302 helping lead the team to a second-place finish. His performance earned him the American League Rookie of the Year Award. Munson would be the Yankees catcher from that point until his death. As a homegrown star, he was the heart of soul of the Yankees throughout the 1970s. A seven-time All-Star, Thurman Munson appeared in the mid-summer classic in every full season he played after his rookie year except 1972. Munson was a leader on the 1976 American League championship and the 1977-78 world championship teams. Munson batted over .300 five times and drove in over 100 runs for three consecutive years (1975-1977). He was recognized as the American League's Most Valuable Player in 1976. Known for his abilities as a clutch hitter, Munson batted .357 over six postseason series. In a losing effort in the 1976 World Series, Munson batted .529.

Munson was also an exceptional fielder, at least early in his career. In the 1971 season, for example, he made only one error—and that was on a play where he was knocked unconscious. Munson won the American League Gold Glove Award for catchers in 1973, 1974, and 1975.

On Monday, August 6, 1979, the Yankees played the Baltimore Orioles in a game televised across the nation as part of a program known as "Monday Night Baseball." Earlier that afternoon the team had flown to Canton, Ohio for Munson's funeral where one of Munson's best friends, teammate Bobby Murcer, delivered a eulogy. Yankees manager Billy Martin offered to let Murcer sit out the game that evening, but he refused. In an emotional game, Murcer had two hits, including a home run and drove home all five of the Yankees' runs. It was Murcer's two-run single in the bottom of the ninth inning that won the game for the Yankees.

WASHINGTON SENATORS at NEW YORK YANKEES

Tuesday, April 21, 1914 (Polo Grounds)

	1	2	3	4	5	6	7	8	9	10			R	H	E
WASH	0	0	1	0	1	0	0	0	0	0			2	6	1
NY	0	0	0	0	0	0	0	0	2	1			3	11	3

WASH		AB	R	H	RBI	NY		AB	R	H	RBI
Moeller	RF	5	0	0	0	Maisel	3B	5	1	3	0
Foster	3B	4	0	1	0	Hartzell	2B	5	0	2	1
Milan	CF	4	0	1	1	Walsh	LF	3	1	0	0
Gandil	1B	4	0	2	0	Williams	1B	3	0	0	0
Morgan	2B	3	0	0	0	Reynolds	PH	1	0	1	0
Shanks	LF	4	0	0	0	Warhop	PH/RF		1		
Henry	CF	4	0	0	0	Holden	CF	4	0	2	1
McBride	SS	4	1	1	0	Chance	PR/1B				
Boehling	P	4	1	1	0	Cook	RF	3	0	0	0
						Keating	PH	1	0	0	0
						Burr	CF				
						Peckinpaugh	SS	3	0	1	0
						Sweeney	C	4	0	1	1
						Fisher	P	2	0	1	0
						Boone	PH	1	0	0	0
						Cole	P	1	0	0	0

WASH	IP	H	R	BB	SO	NY	IP	H	R	BB	SO
Boehling - L	9.1	11	3	2	6	Fisher	8	6	2	2	2
						Cole - W	2	0	0	0	3

Tom Burr

CHAPTER TWENTY-FOUR
HERMAN "HEINIE" ODOM (1925)

It must be wonderful to be perfect. Not many people would know this feeling, and as has been seen throughout this text, most of the players who appeared even for the briefest of moments as Yankees were not often successful. Small sample size be damned; it is extremely difficult to be perfect. Yet, in his Major League career, in game action at least, Herman "Heinie" Odom's statistics are perfect. His lifetime statistics show a perfect batting average and a perfect fielding percentage. To add to the magic of his one day, Odom was able to achieve this feat while facing future Hall of Famers. The only problem with this narrative is that Heinie Odom wasn't as perfect in another area of the game.

Heinie Odom came to the Yankees after starring as shortstop for the University of Texas where he was recognized as an all-conference player during each of his final three collegiate seasons. Like many others, it seems the Yankees offered Odom a chance to travel and experience life with the big club before sending him to begin his minor league career. It was during this brief experience with the Yankees that Odom enjoyed his one taste of the Major Leagues.

Odom's opportunity came in the Yankees' seventh game of the 1925 season during the Washington Senators' home opener. This was a special affair as the Senators were celebrating their world championship from the previous season. Baseball Commissioner Judge Landis was in attendance, but he was not the most important dignitary. In the audience were Secretary of the Treasury Andrew Mellon and Secretary of State Frank B. Kellogg. Also in attendance were President Calvin Coolidge and the First Lady Grace Coolidge. As part of the season's opening celebration,

Secretary of State Kellogg raised the American flag and President Coolidge threw out the first pitch. The Senators' world championship banner was also raised as a marching band played on. It was a joyous beginning to the new baseball season in Washington.

The 1925 Washington Senators were a powerful team. There were five eventual Hall of Fame players on this squad: Sam Rice (right field), Goose Goslin (left field), Bucky Harris (manager/second base), and pitchers, Stan Covelski and Walter Johnson. One can't overestimate the magnitude of this early-season battle as the Yankees and Senators were the two teams that battled for American League supremacy throughout much of the 1920s. From 1921 through 1928, every American League pennant was won by either New York (1921, 1922, 1923, 1926, 1927, 1928) or Washington (1924, 1925).

The 1925 Yankees featured a collection of legendary players themselves. Five players on the 1925 squad would gain enshrinement in the Hall of Fame. These included Earle Combs (center field) and pitchers Waite Hoyt and Herb Pennock. The Yankees right fielder on this day was none other than a twenty-two-year-old rookie who was beginning in his first full Major League season. That player was Lou Gehrig. Gehrig was playing right field for two reasons; Wally Pipp was the team's star first baseman and Babe Ruth, the regular right fielder, was ill, nursing his famous "bellyache heard round the world." Ruth would not appear in a game until June 1. Interestingly, that June 1 game, also against the Senators, was significant for another reason. It was in the bottom of the eighth inning of that game that Gehrig pinch hit for shortstop Pee Wee Wanninger beginning his famous streak of 2,130 consecutive games played. From that day on, Lou Gehrig would not miss a game again until May 2, 1939.

Heinie Odom's opportunity to play came in the bottom of the seventh inning with the Yankees trailing 10-1. From the start, the Yankees were never in this game. The Senators had scored lone runs in each of the first three innings followed by three runs in the bottom of the fifth inning and four runs in the bottom of the sixth inning. By the end of the game, every Washington batter would have at least one hit and six different Senators would have at least one run batted in. Further, the Washington hurler was Walter Johnson, one of the greatest pitchers of all time. In short, by the time Heinie Odom appeared, the game, for all intents and purposes, was over.

In the bottom of the seventh inning, Odom entered as a defensive replacement taking over for the Yankees' regular third baseman Joe Dugan. With two outs in the inning, Sam Rice, a masterful batter hitting about .350, hit a ground ball to Odom who fielded it cleanly to end the inning. One play, one out... a perfect fielding percentage.

Heinie Odom then led off the top of the eighth inning. Batting against Walter Johnson, Odom singled to right field. One at bat, one hit... a perfect batting average!

If only that was where the story ended. Unfortunately, while the next batter Hank Johnson was striking out, Odom was picked off first base. No balls were hit to Odom in the bottom of the inning and the Yankees went down quietly in the ninth. With the final out, the ballgame and Heinie Odom's Major League career, were both over.

Heinie Odom eventually went to the St. Paul Saints of the American Association for the 1925 season. He played 25 games at third base that year, batting .250. In the field, he was far from perfect making eight errors. Odom hung around in the minor leagues through the 1929 season, never rising above Double-A and playing mostly as a reserve third baseman.

Extra Innings
The True Story of Wally Pipp's Headache

Much has been written about Wally Pipp and the famous headache that caused him to take a seat on the bench, seeming to never play another day of baseball as Lou Gehrig took over his position forevermore. As the false story goes, Pipp may have even been exaggerating his headache. The tale is sometimes told to warn people about taking it easy or missing a day of work. The cautionary tale implies that by missing a game or a day of work a person could be replaced by the next Lou Gehrig. This narrative, though, isn't accurate. Too often Wally Pipp is remembered, not for his great play on the diamond, but as a soft player who sat out a game and got his just desserts. None of that is true. In fact, Wally Pipp was an integral part of the Yankees' early success, playing on, and starring for three pennant-winning teams including the Yankees' first world championship squad.

Wally Pipp was the Yankees' starting first baseman from 1915 to 1924. He was a power hitter in the days before Babe Ruth revolutionized the game and what power hitters looked like. In 1916, Pipp led the American League in home runs with 12. In doing this, Wally Pipp was the first Yankee to ever lead the league in home runs. The next year, 1917, Pipp's nine home runs also led the league making him one of only three Yankees, along with Babe Ruth and Mickey Mantle, to lead the American League in home runs in back-to-back seasons. Wally Pipp also collected double figures in triples (the true power stat of the day) seven times. In 1924, Wally Pipp led the league in triples with 19. A strong middle-of-the-order batter, Pipp drove in 90 or more runs five times. In this period, Pipp also batted over .290 five times achieving a high of .329 in 1922 when he received some support for the Most Valuable Player Award. Rather than being a soft player, Wally Pipp was an everyday hardnosed early star for the Yankees. Back when baseball seasons consisted of 154 games, Wally Pipp played in 150 or more games a year for the Yankees six times. He was a rock of consistency.

The story of Wally Pipp's benching has been exaggerated over the years. It does not seem that he asked out of the line-up that fateful day in June 1925. Rather, because the team was slumping (at the time of his "benching," the Yankees were in seventh place in the eight-team league) manager Miller Huggins juggled the entire lineup. Much of the Yankees' poor play was the result of Babe Ruth missing the first months of the season with his famous "bellyache," but no player on the team was doing particularly well. Pipp was not the only starting player who was replaced in the lineup the day Lou Gehrig's consecutive games playing streak began. Second baseman Aaron Ward and catcher Wally Schang were also benched that day. It must also be noted that Gehrig wasn't exactly setting the world on fire before he had this opportunity to start. Through June 1, 1925, his batting average stood at a meager .167.

In this game though, Gehrig had three hits in five at bats including a double. But in the next two games, Gehrig went hitless. While Wally Pipp would never start another game as the Yankees' first baseman, on five occasions during that month he replaced Lou Gehrig at first base during the game.

What was unfortunate for Wally Pipp was that Lou Gehrig eventually began hitting and hitting well. In his first month of regular play, Lou Gehrig hit .348 with six home runs and 14 runs batted in. Gehrig then hit .305 in July, which was solid, but there were reports of manager Miller Huggins being less than pleased with his overall performance, especially against left-handed pitching. For example, on July 5, 1925, against left-handed pitcher Tom Zachary of the Senators, the Yankees started Fred Merkle (not Gehrig) at first base. Lou Gehrig's famous playing streak may have ended in its infancy that day, if not for the fact that he had a pinch-hit appearance late in the game. Later that month, on July 19, the Detroit Tigers started left-hander Dutch Leonard against the Yankees. Gehrig also began that day on the bench in favor of

Merkle. Later in that game, Gehrig did appear amassing three hits including a home run.

By August of 1925, Lou Gehrig was tearing the proverbial cover off the ball. That month, he hit .350 with five more home runs. For the season, Lou Gehrig batted .295 with 20 home runs and 68 runs batted in. Of course, he was only just getting started.

The truth is that Lou Gehrig may never had had the chance to amass the consecutive games streak if not for a terrible situation that happened to Wally Pipp that history has inaccurately recorded as the "headache" that took him out of the lineup. On July 2, 1925, Wally Pipp was severely beaned in the head during batting practice. This beaning actually knocked him unconscious. It was so severe that he was hospitalized for about two weeks. Rather than just a headache, Wally Pipp may have suffered from a skull fracture.

One testament to Wally Pipp's toughness was the fact that he returned to the team and was playing again, albeit not starting, by early August. Over the season's last two months, Wally Pipp appeared in twelve games, mostly as a pinch hitter or pinch runner.

With Gehrig firmly established at first base, the Yankees sold Pipp to the Cincinnati Reds prior to the 1926 season. In Cincinnati, Wally Pipp demonstrated his resiliency, and toughness. He batted .291 for the season appearing in 155 games. His performance earned him some support for the National League Most Valuable Player Award that season. Pipp played with Cincinnati through the 1928 season. In 1929, he played first base for the Newark Bears of the International League where he hit .312.

Rather than being "soft," Wally Pipp was a hard-nosed, high-quality player. He was an important star on the first pennant-winning teams in the history of the Yankees. Even after being replaced by one of the baseball's greatest players, and suffering from a potentially career-ending beaning, Wally Pipp was able to successfully play baseball at its highest levels.

NEW YORK YANKEES at WASHINGTON SENATORS

Wednesday, April 22, 1925 (Griffith Stadium)

		1	2	3	4	5	6	7	8	9		R	H	E
NY		0	0	0	0	0	1	0	0	0		1	7	1
WASH		1	1	1	0	3	4	0	0	X		10	14	2

NY		AB	R	H	RBI	WASH		AB	R	H	RBI
Dugan	3B	3	0	0	0	Leibold	CF	3	1	1	0
Odom	3B	1	0	1	0	McNeely	PH/CF	1	1	1	0
Combs	CF	3	1	2	0	Harris	2B	4	1	1	0
Johnson	P	1	0	0	0	Rice	RF	4	2	2	1
Meusel	LF	4	0	1	1	Goslin	LF	4	2	2	2
Gehrig	RF	3	0	1	0	Judge	1B	2	0	1	1
Pipp	1B	4	0	0	0	Bluege	3B	5	2	2	2
Ward	2B	1	0	0	0	Peckinpaugh	SS	3	1	1	2
Shanks	2B	3	0	1	0	Ruel	C	4	0	2	1
Scott	SS	2	0	0	0	Johnson	P	4	0	1	1
Wanninger	PH/SS	1	0	0	0						
O'Neill	C	3	0	0	0						
Bengough	C										
Shocker	P	2	0	1	0						
Francis	P										
Witt	PF/CF	1	0	0	0						

NY	IP	H	R	BB	SO	WASH	IP	H	R	BB	SO
Shocker - L	4.1	11	6	2	2	Johnson - W	9	7	1	1	4
Francis	1.2	2	4	3	0						
Johnson	2	1	0	0	3						

Heinie Odom

CHAPTER TWENTY-FIVE
CLEM LLEWELLYN (1922)

L ike so many *Least Among Them* Yankees, Clem Llewellyn earned his trip to the Major Leagues after an extremely successful college career as a pitcher. A North Carolina native, Llewellyn had an impressive high school record at Oak Ridge Military Academy. He earned an academic scholarship to the University of North Carolina at Chapel Hill. After his freshman year, Llewellyn left school to help support the country's efforts in World War I by working in a munitions plant and later by joining the United States Navy, although he saw no military action in the war. After returning to college in 1919, Llewellyn began a three-year period when his record was almost unmatched. A standout pitcher who helped lead North Carolina to three consecutive North Carolina State Baseball Championships, Clem Llewellyn's record for those three years was 23-2. Both his losses came during his sophomore year.

The Yankees signed Llewellyn out of college and brought him to New York to be with the big league squad. On June 18, 1922, Llewellyn was afforded his chance to pitch in the Major Leagues in a mop-up role against the Cleveland Indians.

The 1922 Indians were considered one of the strongest teams in the American League. Beginning in 1917, when they finished in third place, the Indians were always at or near the top of the standings. In 1920, the Indians had been baseball's world champions. The 1922 team employed three players who would later earn enshrinement in the Hall of Fame: pitcher Stan Covelski, infielder Joe Sewell (who also later played for the Yankees), and outfielder Tris Speaker. All three appeared in the game in which Llewellyn pitched.

The 1922 Yankees, of course, were also a powerful squad.

They entered the season as the American League champions and would once again win the pennant in both 1922 and 1923. It was the 1923 squad that won the Yankees' first world championship. Three Yankees players, third baseman Frank "Home Run" Baker (playing in his final big league season), pitcher Waite Hoyt, and outfielder Babe Ruth would also become Hall of Famers.

The game on June 18 was played at Dunn Field in Cleveland, Ohio. The Yankees came into the game as part of an extremely long road trip that lasted most of the month of June. They had already played four games in Chicago against the White Sox, four games in St. Louis against the Browns, and four games in Detroit against the Tigers. This game was the first of four in Cleveland, which would then be followed by trips to Boston (five games), Washington (two games), and Philadelphia (two games). The Yankees were also not playing their best ball as they arrived in Cleveland having lost each of their previous six games.

This game featured the two future Hall of Fame pitchers on each squad battling each other—Covelski versus Hoyt. Unfortunately for the Yankees, they got off to a poor start and it never got better. In the bottom of the first inning, the Indians scored four runs on six hits to begin the onslaught. The Indians scored four more runs in the bottom of the fourth inning followed up by two more runs in the seventh. In the top of the eighth inning, the Yankees were finally able to plate two runs. Trailing 9-2, Yankees manager Miller Huggins called upon Clem Llewellyn to pitch.

Llewellyn's first challenge was Cleveland's second baseman Bill Wambsganss. Two seasons earlier Wambsganns become famous for turning an unassisted triple play in the World Series. Llewellyn retired Wambsganns on a pop out to the third baseman. The legendary Tris Speaker then came to bat and grounded out to short. The next batter, Indians third baseman Larry Gardner, proceeded to hit a clean single to left field bringing up shortstop Joe Sewell. Sewell hit a ground ball to Wally Pipp, the Yankees' first baseman who threw to shortstop Everett Scott to record the final out of the inning and of Clem Llewellyn's Major League career.

Records indicate that Clem Llewellyn stayed with the Major League club for the next month or two. It was said that Llewellyn was Babe Ruth's favorite batting practice pitcher, which was quite an honor. Eventually, Llewellyn, who, in a pregame accident endured several broken ribs, was sent to the Buffalo Bisons of the Double-A International League. Llewellyn pitched in 16 games for Buffalo winning six and losing six. The next year, 1923, saw him returning to his roots in North Carolina playing at a much lower level of baseball for the Class-A Atlanta Crackers and the Class-B Greenville Spinners. Llewellyn enjoyed some moderate success playing for Greenville in the Class-B South Atlantic League through 1925.

Once his "legitimate" professional career ended, Clem Llewellyn began an interesting second baseball life as a player, manager, front office executive, and league president, first in the legendary Outlaw Carolina Baseball League. This was a league created by textile owners in North Carolina who wished to cash in on baseball's popularity. They signed professional players to play for them instead of teams that were part of the National Association of Professional Baseball Leagues. As such, this league, the North Carolina Independent League, was considered an outlaw league. Llewellyn returned to organized baseball with the North Carolina State League (Class D) and the Tri-State League (Class B). He used his degree in law from North Carolina to be elected as a judge.

Extra Innings
The Least Among Them Managers

After his professional career, Clem Llewellyn enjoyed success in various capacities in baseball including serving as a manager. As a manager in the Outlaw Carolina League, Llewellyn was known as a strong and effective leader.

The history of the Yankees also includes a long list of outstanding managers who are an extremely important part of the story of the Yankees' success. Through the 2020 season, thirty-three different men have served as a manager of the Yankees. Ten of the men who served as a Yankee manager are enshrined in the Baseball Hall of Fame, although some are enshrined for their contributions as a player rather than their work as a manager. These ten Hall of Famers are: Yogi Berra, Frank Chance, Bill Dickey, Clark Griffith, Bucky Harris, Miller Huggins, Bob Lemon, Joe McCarthy, Casey Stengel, and Joe Torre. Huggins, McCarthy, Stengel, and Torre earned a great deal, if not all of their Hall of Fame support due to their accomplishments as managers of the Yankees. These four leaders were at the helm for 21 of the Yankees' 27 World Championships. Casey Stengel and Joe McCarthy each had seven world championships, Joe Torre earned four, and Miller Huggins won three. The only other Yankees manager with multiple World Series championships was Ralph Houk who won two. Bucky Harris, Billy Martin, Bob Lemon, and Joe Girardi have each won one World Series as manager of the Yankees.

Of course, not all Yankees' managers achieved success. In the history of the Yankees, four managers held the reins for less than a half-season. These four field leaders could be considered the Yankees' *Least Among Them* managers.

The shortest tenure of any Yankee manager belongs to Art Fletcher who guided the team for just eleven games at the very end of the 1929 baseball season. Fletcher came to this post under very unfortunate circumstances as he was appointed manager following the death of the great Miller Huggins who passed away that season. Fletcher had been a coach with the Yankees since 1927 and was a highly regarded baseball thinker. Prior to coaching, Fletcher had enjoyed a successful thirteen-year playing career as a shortstop spent primarily with the New York Giants. Known more for his glove than his bat, Art Fletcher was a tough, hardnosed ballplayer. His style of play exemplified the rough and tumble aspects of the Giants teams in the early decades of the 20th Century. As a player, he appeared in four World Series with the Giants. Following his playing career, Fletcher managed the Philadelphia Phillies for four seasons but was never able to get his club out of the second division. His fortunes changed when he came to the Yankees as a coach beginning in 1927. During his years as a coach between 1927 and 1945, the Yankees appeared in ten World Series, winning nine. Accounts seem to indicate that Art Fletcher would have been considered to serve as the Yankees manager following the 1929 season, but it seems that he preferred being a coach to having managerial responsibilities. It seems he made a good choice. In his career, Fletcher appeared in uniform in fourteen different World Series—an amazing total that is all but forgotten today.

The man who managed the Yankees for the second fewest games was Johnny Neun who held the position for a mere 14 games in 1946. That season was one in which the Yankees employed three different managers. First was Joe McCarthy, one of the Yankees great managers who, after piloting the team for the previous sixteen years, retired in May. McCarthy cited health reasons for his retirement, but some speculated that he was not happy working with Larry MacPhail, the team's new president. McCarthy was replaced by the team's legendary catcher Bill Dickey. The Yankees enjoyed a winning record under Dickey (57-48) during his brief tenure, but when MacPhail refused to provide him with a vote of confidence for the 1947 season, Dickey resigned with just fourteen games left in the season. This was the environment in which Johnny Neun assumed managerial duties.

Neun had coached in the Yankees' minor league system between 1935 and 1943. He managed teams to league finals six times. In 1944, Neun became a Major League coach and was still with the team in 1946. Also of note, Neun was one of the few players in baseball history who, as a player, turned an unassisted triple play (a story recounted in Chapter Five).

The Yankees won eight games during Neun's brief term as manager. Following that tumultuous 1946 season, Neun also resigned. In 1947, Neun became the manager of the Cincinnati Reds. He remained in that position until the 1948 season when he was replaced after 100 games.

Roger Peckinpaugh, who was also one of the Yankees' first captains, served very briefly, as player/manager in 1914. He remains the youngest man to serve as a Major League manager as he was only twenty-three years old at the time. He managed the final twenty games of the season guiding the team to ten wins against ten losses. Bill Donovan replaced Peckinpaugh as the manager for the 1915 season and Peckinpaugh returned to being a fulltime player. Peckinpaugh remained a player with the Yankees, Washington Senators, and Chicago White Sox through the 1927 season. In 1925, Peckinpaugh was named the American League's Most Valuable Player. Following his playing career, Roger Peckinpaugh managed the Cleveland Indians from 1928 through 1933 and again in 1941.

The final *Least Among Them* manager was Clyde King who was the Yankees manager for a brief time in 1982. The 1982 season was also a tumultuous one for the Yankees. Following the Yankees' defeat in the World Series to the Los Angeles Dodgers in the 1981 World Series, 1982 saw the Yankees employ three managers. First, Bob Lemon lasted only fourteen games when he was

Roger Peckinpaugh, Library of Congress, Prints & Photographs Division [LC-DIG-ggbain-13194]

fired with a record of six wins against eight losses. Lemon had managed the Yankees previously, including in 1978 when they won the World Series. He was replaced by Gene Michael who managed the team for a mere 86 games that year despite an overall winning record at 44-42. The final Yankees' manager in 1982 was King.

Clyde King had previously managed the San Francisco Giants (1969-1970) and the Atlanta Braves (1974-1975). King had been the Yankees' pitching coach in 1978 and again in 1981 and into 1982 before he was named as the manager. King served as the Yankees' manager for a mere 62 games to close out the 1982 season. The Yankees won 29 games under King and lost 33. In 1983, the Yankees replaced King when they brought Billy Martin in for his third (of five) term as manager. After leaving the managerial position, King remained with the organization, first as a scout, and beginning in 1984, as the general manager. He later held various positions with the franchise until his death in 2010.

NEW YORK YANKEES at CLEVELAND INDIANS

Sunday, June 18, 1922 (Dunn Field)

	1	2	3	4	5	6	7	8	9		R	H	E
NY	0	0	0	0	0	0	0	2	0		2	7	0
CLE	4	0	0	3	0	0	2	0	X		9	17	1

NY		AB	R	H	RBI	CLE		AB	R	H	RBI
Witt	CF	2	0	0	0	Jamieson	LF	5	1	2	0
Skinner	CF	3	1	1	0	Wambsganss	2B	5	1	2	0
McNally	3B	3	1	2	0	Speaker	CF	5	2	3	1
Ruth	LF	2	0	0	0	Gardner	3B	5	1	2	1
Meusel	RF	3	0	1	1	Sewell	SS	5	2	3	3
Llewellyn	P					McInnis	1B	4	2	2	0
Pipp	1B	4	0	2	0	Graney	RF	2	0	0	0
Ward	2B	4	0	0	0	O'Neill	C	4	0	3	4
Scott	SS	4	0	1	0	Coveleski	P	4	0	0	0
Hofmann	C	4	0	0	0						
Hoyt	P										
Murray	P	2	0	0	0						
McMillan	PH/RF	2	0	0	0						

NY	IP	H	R	BB	SO	CLE	IP	H	R	BB	SO
Hoyt - L	0.2	6	4	1	0	Coveleski - W	9	7	2	3	8
Murray	6.1	10	5	1	1						
Llewellyn	1	1	0	0	0						

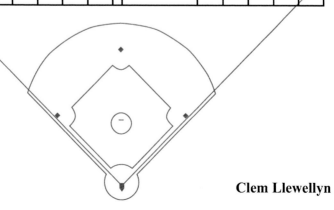

Clem Llewellyn

Photo from the author's collection.

CHAPTER TWENTY–SIX
GEORGE WASHBURN (1941)

Pitcher George Washburn came to the Yankees following the more traditional path than many of the players
chronicled in this text. Rather than getting his cup of
coffee as a result of a great career in college ball that led directly
to the big leagues, or in a walk-on appearance, seemingly out of
nowhere, Washburn worked his way through the minor leagues,
step-by-step.

Washburn began playing baseball professionally as a sixteen-
year-old in the Eastern Maine League and immediately became a
starting player. (Late in life, Washburn was elected to the Maine
Baseball Hall of Fame.)

Washburn's journey with the Yankees began in 1935, when
as a twenty-year-old, after signing with the Yankees organization,
he was assigned to the Washington Generals of the Class-D

Pennsylvania State Association. In his first year in professional ball, Washburn pitched 170 innings in 29 games and finished with an 11-7 record. This was enough to earn him a promotion to the Akron Yankees of the Middle Atlantic League to begin the 1936 season. Washburn pitched well in 16 games there to earn an in-season promotion to the Norfolk Tars of the Class-B Piedmont League. For that 1936 season, Washburn again logged a grand total of over 170 innings, pitching to an 8-11 record against tougher and tougher opponents. Hiram Bithorn, the first Puerto Rican baseball player to reach the Major Leagues, was a teammate of Washburn's on the 1936 Norfolk Tars.

George Washburn (and Bithorn as well) earned promotions to the Single-A Binghamton Triplets of the New York-Pennsylvania League for the 1937 season. That year, Washburn pitched some of his best baseball to date. He recorded a 13-11 record in the 32 games and 188 innings he pitched. Following this, Washburn was promoted to the Kansas City Blues, a Double-A team, for the 1938 season. Washburn went 12-4 for Kansas City. His progression through the minors had been slow, but steady and he proved competent at each level.

By 1939, George Washburn had almost reached the Major Leagues. For the 1939 season, the Yankees assigned Washburn to their top minor league franchise, the Double-A Newark Bears. Washburn would pitch for Newark in both 1939 and 1940. Washburn's 1940 season was his best. He started 32 games, logged 233 innings pitched, and won 18 games while losing only 8. He was the ace of a pitching staff that included longtime future Major Leaguers Hank Borowy, Tommy Byrne, and Randy Gumpert.

Finally, in 1941, George Washburn was provided with his chance to pitch in the majors. His opportunity came on May 4, 1941 at Briggs Stadium in Detroit against the Tigers. The 1941 Detroit Tigers were the reigning American League champions who were looking to return to the fall classic after losing the World Series to the Cincinnati Reds in seven games. This was a team loaded with stars and three future Hall of Famers: Charlie Gehringer (second base), Hank Greenberg (first base), and pitcher Hal Newhouser.

The eventual 1941 world champion Yankees were no less

talented. In addition to their squad of All-Stars, six players from the 1941 Yankees would gain enshrinement in the Hall of Fame. These included Bill Dickey (catcher), Phil Rizzuto (shortstop), Joe Gordon (second base), pitchers Lefty Gomez and Red Ruffing, and the center fielder, the great Joe DiMaggio. The Yankees' manager Joe McCarthy would also be enshrined.

After the Yankees failed to score in the top of the first inning, Washburn, the starting pitcher, came out to begin his Major League career. Washburn retired the first two batters, shortstop Frank Croucher and center fielder Barney McCosky, both of whom were hitting over .350, on fly balls to left field. Next, he retired Gehringer on a ground out to first base. Washburn's first inning was perfect.

The Yankees scored a run in the top of the second inning on a home run by left fielder Charlie Keller. Washburn took to the mound in the bottom of the frame with a 1-0 lead. Unfortunately, that lead wouldn't last. The first batter, All-Star Rudy York, struck out. That brought up Hank Greenburg, one of the most powerful right-handed batters of all time. Greenberg had hit 172 home runs over the previous four seasons including 58 in 1938. One can't blame Washburn if he pitched carefully to Greenberg and he did. Greenberg walked. What happened next wasn't pretty. Washburn then walked right fielder Bruce Campbell and third baseman Pinky Higgins to load the bases. With catcher Billy Sullivan at bat, Washburn threw a wild pitch that allowed the tying run to score. He then walked Billy Sullivan. Tigers pitcher Bobo Newsom then singled home two more runs. The damage might have been worse, but Joe DiMaggio threw out Sullivan as he attempted to reach third base. Frank Croucher then flew out to left field to end the inning. The Yankees were fortunate to escape that inning trailing only 3-1.

Unfortunately for Washburn, his next inning was shorter than the previous inning, and not any better. Barney McCosky led off with a triple. When Gehringer walked, Yankees manager Joe McCarthy had seen enough. He removed Washburn, replacing him with Marv Breuer. Washburn, of course, would never pitch in the Major Leagues again. The Yankees lost this game 10-1. Soon after, Washburn, who walked five of the twelve batters he faced, was once again pitching in the minor leagues.

George Washburn pitched, and also played some outfield, in the minors through the 1952 season. After leaving the Yankees, he pitched in the Brooklyn Dodgers and Boston Red Sox organizations. From 1947 through 1952, Washburn was a player/manager for the Class-D Houma Indians, the Class-C Baton Rouge Red Sticks, and the Class-C Alexandria Aces.

Extra Innings
The End of Joe DiMaggio's Streak

When the 1941 baseball season is mentioned, most people recall two of baseball's greatest accomplishments: Ted Williams batting .406 and Joe DiMaggio's 56-game hitting streak. These marks have remained as two of baseball's most legendary and noteworthy feats.

No player since 1941 has hit .400 for a season. In fact, since that time, only four players have even hit better than .380 for a season—Tony Gwynn (.394, 1994), George Brett (.390, 1980), Rod Carew (.388, 1977), and Ted Williams himself (.388, 1957). Batting .400 for a full season seems like an impossible task in today's game, yet, when Williams hit .406, there was no indication that the number wouldn't be approached or passed again. Just eleven years earlier, in 1930, Bill Terry of the New York Giants batted .401. Also, during the 1920s, the .400 mark was reached no fewer than seven times. Williams himself believed that he would bat better than .400 again. It is only over the decades since Williams last eclipsed .400 that the number has grown in stature. With each passing year, Williams' .406 seems more and more remarkable. While it was an amazing accomplishment at the time, batting .400 was not seen as a mark that couldn't or wouldn't be reached again.

The same cannot be said for Joe DiMaggio's 56-game hitting streak. This feat was remarkable in its time because it shattered an already long-standing mark and was seen as something unique and wonderful, and possibly singular, in the history of the sport.

The previous consecutive game batting streak record was held by Wee Willie Keeler. In 1897, while a member of the Baltimore Orioles (of the National League), Keeler hit safely in 44 consecutive games. The American League consecutive games streak had also been set decades earlier in 1922, by George Sisler when he batted safely in 41 consecutive games. With his 56-game streak, these records weren't just eclipsed by DiMaggio, they were shattered. DiMaggio's streak was 27.3% longer than the previous record. In short, DiMaggio's 56-game hitting streak is one of baseball's most amazing accomplishments.

When the streak began on May 15, the Yankees were in fourth place, playing under .500 ball. By the time the streak was finished, more than two months later, on July 17 in Cleveland, the Yankees had not only captured first place, but they had built a seven-game lead over the second-place Indians. The Yankees won 41 of the 56 games they played during DiMaggio's epic streak. DiMaggio himself batted .408 during the streak with 15 home runs and 55 runs batted in.

DiMaggio's streak ended on July 17, 1941 due in large part to the tremendous defensive work of Cleveland Indians' third baseman, Kenny Keltner. DiMaggio didn't go quietly, rather Keltner made a pair of great plays to stifle DiMaggio and end the streak.

Keltner had been the Indians starting third baseman since 1938. During his first seven seasons (1938-1944), before his service in World War II, Keltner was a frequent All-Star and in the yearly discussions regarding baseball's best players. In fact, just a few weeks before he stopped the streak, Keltner was one of the players that ignited the rally that brought the American League to a late victory in the All-Star Game—a game in which Williams delivered the game-winning three-run home run.

The July 17 game that would see the end of DiMaggio's streak drew a crowd of 67,463 to Cleveland Stadium, the largest attendance at any baseball game that season. Left-hander Al Smith, a middling pitcher, who had his career season (15-7) the previous year, was Cleveland's starting pitcher.

When DiMaggio came to bat in the first inning, the Yankees were already leading 1-0. There was one out and Tommy Henrich was on second base. Due to rain earlier in the day, parts of the field, including the batter's boxes and baselines were still slightly wet. DiMaggio smashed Smith's second offering down the third-base line. The ball sped past the bag but was grabbed backhanded by Keltner deep behind the base. Keltner's strong and accurate throw beat DiMaggio to the bag for the out.

In the fourth inning, DiMaggio came to bat again. In this at-bat the count was worked to 3-2. After a foul ball, DiMaggio walked.

His next chance to continue his streak came in the seventh inning. Keltner was positioned deep at third base, again, playing very close to the foul line. Knowing that DiMaggio had never bunted for a hit during his streak, Keltner was confident that this would not be the time when he started. In a play remarkably similar to the one in the first inning, DiMaggio rocketed a smash down the third-base line. Keltner again made a sensational play on a ball that on most days would have been a double. His strong throw again caught DiMaggio by just a step. Joltin' Joe was 0 for 2.

DiMaggio did get one more at-bat that game. This time he faced Jim Bagby a right-handed pitcher who was brought in to face DiMaggio with one out and the bases loaded. DiMaggio again hit the ball squarely, only this time, right to shortstop Lou Boudreau, a future Hall of Famer, celebrating his 24th birthday. Boudreau fielded the ball and turned it into an inning ending 6-4-3 double play. Joe DiMaggio wouldn't bat again that day. With those hard-hit outs, the great streak came to a close.

From the moment the game ended, credit for stopping DiMaggio was given to Kenny Keltner. All in attendance believed that his two exceptional defensive plays on balls that DiMaggio hit down the line would have been hits on almost any other day.

While DiMaggio's legendary hitting streak came to an end, it must be noted that he did reach base that day, with a walk. DiMaggio would eventually reach base safely in 74 consecutive games that year which was also a Major League record. Following this game, DiMaggio collected at least one hit for sixteen more consecutive games.

DiMaggio's record, reaching base in 74 consecutive games, did not last very long. In 1949 a different player reached base safely in 84 consecutive games. That player was Ted Williams.

NEW YORK YANKEES at DETROIT TIGERS

Sunday, May 4, 1941 (Briggs Stadium)

	1	2	3	4	5	6	7	8	9		R	H	E
NY	0	1	0	0	0	0	0	0	0		1	5	3
DET	0	3	1	4	0	0	2	0	X		10	10	1

NY		AB	R	H	RBI	DET		AB	R	H	RBI
Rizzuto	SS	4	0	0	0	Croucher	SS	4	0	1	0
Rolfe	3B	4	0	1	0	McCosky	CF	5	2	2	0
Selkirk	RF	4	0	0	0	Gehringer	2B	4	1	1	0
DiMaggio	CF	4	0	1	0	York	1B	3	1	1	3
Keller	LF	4	1	1	1	Greenberg	LF	3	2	1	0
Gordon	1B	4	0	0	0	Campbell	RF	2	2	1	0
Dickey	C	3	0	1	0	Higgins	3B	3	1	0	0
Priddy	2B	3	0	0	0	Sullivan	C	3	1	2	1
Washburn	P	1	0	0	0	Newsom	P	4	0	1	2
Breuer	P	1	0	0	0						
Henrich	PH	1	0	1	0						
Peek	P										

NY	IP	H	R	BB	SO	DET	IP	H	R	BB	SO
Washburn - L	2	2	4	5	1	Newsom - W	9	5	1	0	4
Breuer	5	8	6	2	4						
Peek	1	0	0	1	0						

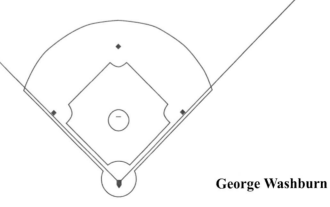

George Washburn

Courtesy of the Topps Company.

CHAPTER TWENTY-SEVEN
BOB DAVIDSON (1989)

B ob Davidson was a Major League pitcher, but he had the misfortune of playing for one of the most forgettable and worst Yankees teams in history. When he signed, he probably assumed that he'd be on a highly competitive team that had the potential to win a pennant. That wasn't the case. When he finally arrived in the big leagues, he played his one big league game for the 1989 Yankees, a team that won only 74 games and was never in the race.

Davidson was drafted by the Yankees in the 24th round of the 1984 players' draft. He was assigned to the Single-A Oneonta Yankees where he was being groomed as a relief pitcher. All twenty-four of his appearances that year came in relief. Davidson stayed with the Oneonta team in 1985 again pitching exclusively out of the bullpen. In 1986 and 1987, Davidson was shuffled between Single-A and Double-A with stops at Ft. Lauderdale (A), Prince William (A), and Albany-Colonie (AA). By 1988, Davidson earned a promotion to the Yankees top minor league team, the Triple-A Columbus Clippers. The Major Leagues were inching ever closer. It was during the 1989 season, after stops at Albany-Colonie (for the third year) and Columbus (for the second year) that Davidson had his opportunity to pitch for the Yankees.

In spite of being a less than impressive squad, the 1989 Yankees had three future Hall of Famers on the roster. The problem was that none of were playing anything like that. First was Rickey Henderson who hit only .247 in 65 games for the Yankees that year before being traded to the Oakland A's. The second eventual Hall of Famer was Rich "Goose" Gossage. Gossage came to the Yankees in August of that year after being released by the San Francisco Giants. At this point in his career, Rich Gossage was no longer a dominating pitcher, in fact he was just hanging on. The third Hall of Famer on that 1989 squad was Deion Sanders who hit just .234 that year and was eventually enshrined not in Cooperstown, but in Canton, Ohio, in the Pro Football Hall of Fame. (Dave Winfield, also a future Hall-of-Famer, was still with the Yankees in 1989, but he missed that season due to a herniated disc in his back.)

The other Yankees stars were all similarly flawed. Both Don Mattingly and Dave Righetti were just about past their peaks. Tommy John was pitching in his final season. Third baseman Mike Pagliarulo hit only .197. The only bright spots in the lineup were the young center fielder Roberto Kelly (.302) and second baseman Steve Sax (.315). Andy Hawkins (15-15, 4.80) was the only pitcher on the staff to win more than seven games.

Even though the 1989 Yankees lacked a lot of star power, Bob Davidson's lone appearance came on a day that was filled with Yankees stars and legends as his appearance occurred during Old-Timer's Day.

Unfortunately, by the time Davidson took the mound, the game against the Kansas City Royals was already out of hand. The 1989 Royals were a contending team, eventually finishing with 92 wins and in second place in the AL West. Much of this squad consisted of players from their 1985 world championship team including All-Stars Bret Saberhagen (pitcher), second baseman Frank White, and outfielder Willie Wilson. Eventual Hall of Famer George Brett was the ultimate star on this team. In 1990, Brett would lead the league in batting, becoming the only player to lead the league in batting in three different decades (1970s, 1980s, and 1990s).

Brett was one of the Yankees' biggest rival players throughout the 1970s and 1980s. His team was on the losing end to the Yankees in the 1976, 1977, and 1978 American League Championship Series. In the decisive Game 5 of the 1977 playoffs, Brett was involved in a fight with Yankees third baseman Graig Nettles after Brett slid hard into Nettles who then kicked him leading to a full on-field brawl between the teams. Remarkably, no players were ejected—a result that would play out much differently today.

Brett hit many big home runs against the Yankees. One, in the 1980 American League Championship Series, propelled the Royals to their first World Series appearance. Another Brett home run became famous for what occurred after he hit it and had circled the bases. On July 24, 1983, Brett hit a homer that appeared to have won the game for the Royals until he was called out by the home-plate umpire Tim McClelland for having too much pine tar on his bat. This game which has forever been known as the Pine Tar Game, was the subject of much controversy. American League President Lee MacPhail later overturned the decision and ordered the game be continued from the point of the home run. The game was resumed almost a month later, on August 18. The Yankees, upset by the decision, played left-handed Don Mattingly, at that time a rookie, at second base, and star pitcher Ron Guidry in center field replacing Jerry Mumphrey who had since been traded. The resumed game was over quickly with the Royals earning the victory.

And so it was George Brett, who had numerous signature moments in Yankee Stadium would have the opportunity to add to his impressive career statistics against Bob Davidson. By the time Davidson entered the game to begin the ninth inning, the Yankees trailed 5-1. The first batter he faced, Willie Wilson, grounded out to second base. Davidson then walked Royals third baseman Kevin Seitzer on four consecutive pitches. That brought up George Brett. After two more pitches out of the strike zone—of the first eight pitches thrown by Davidson—seven were balls, Brett zoned in on a fastball and sent it into the late-afternoon sky for a two-run home run. This was Brett's fifteenth of the seventeen home runs he would hit against Yankees pitching in Yankee Stadium.

Following the home run, Davidson coaxed ground outs out of Danny Tartabull and Jim Eisenreich to end the inning. When the Yankees, now trailing 7-1, went down in order in the bottom of the ninth inning, Bob Davidson's Major League career drew to a close.

Davidson pitched the remainder of the 1989 season and all of the 1990 season with the Columbus Clippers. In 1991 he played for the Triple-A Louisville Redbirds before retiring from baseball.

Extra Innings
Position Players Who Pitched

The aforementioned "Pine Tar Game" resulted in one of the most unique endings to a baseball game in Yankees history. As a form of protest, the Yankees played Don Mattingly, a first baseman, at second base, and Ron Guidry, a pitcher, in center field in the resumption that took place more than a month after the original game. Mattingly and Guidry were not involved in any defensive plays.

Probably the most common situation that involved a team purposely using a player out of position is when a non-pitcher is brought into a game to pitch. This usually happens when a team is trailing by a significant amount of runs and either does not have any other pitchers it can use or chooses not to. The Yankees, like every team, have had to employ this strategy numerous times in their history. Over the years, some notable position players have appeared as pitchers for the Yankees.

Wade Boggs was an eventual Hall of Fame third baseman who played five seasons as a Yankee from 1993 through 1997. One of baseball's premier hitters, Boggs amassed over 3,000 hits in his distinguished career. On August 19, 1997, Boggs appeared in a game, not as third baseman or as a hitter, but as a pitcher. In that game, against the Anaheim Angels, Boggs pitched the bottom of the eighth inning in a game the Yankees were losing 12-4. With the game out of hand, Boggs, who knew how to throw a knuckleball, was brought in to pitch the final defensive inning for the Yankees and actually fared well. After walking leadoff batter Luis Alicea, Boggs retired power-hitting outfielder Tim Salmon on a force out. Garrett Anderson, another excellent hitter, also grounded out and Todd Greene struck out. Boggs allowed no runs and no hits with one walk and one strikeout—an impressive performance!

Yankees executive Gene Michael has been given a great deal of credit for building the successful Yankees teams of the 1990s and early 2000s. Long before those days, though, Gene Michael was an excellent fielding, although poor hitting, shortstop. He was summoned to the pitcher's mound on August 26, 1968 in the second game of a doubleheader against the California Angels. The first game of this twin bill was a rescheduled game that was postponed due to the funeral for Rev. Dr. Martin Luther King, Jr. Michael was brought into a contest in the seventh inning with the Angels leading 5-1. In his first inning of work, Michael faced three batters and retired each. The eighth inning did not go as well. It began with shortstop Ruben Amaro making an error. Michael would allow four hits and also hit a batter as the Angels scored five runs in the inning. Remarkably, Michael also pitched the ninth inning of that game when he allowed a leadoff double before securing three outs in a row.

Then there was the occasion when a position player was brought in to pitch in the middle of a game, pitched well, and was replaced by a "real" pitcher in a game the Yankees ultimately won. That unique game took place on August 25, 1968. The Yankees were in such short supply of pitchers because they were playing in an extraordinary string of four doubleheaders scheduled over five days. The Yankees played nine games in those five days, and because of this, they needed people to take the mound.

In the first game of that day's doubleheader against the Tigers, starting pitcher Steve Barber lasted only 3.1 innings and allowed seven hits, three walks, and five runs. That's when Yankees manager Ralph Houk summoned Rocky Colavito to pitch. Colavito was a power hitter playing in the final season of his All-Star career. He entered the game with two runners on base and future Hall of Famer Al Kaline due to bat. Colavito coaxed Kaline into grounding out. He then faced the powerful Willie Horton who he retired on a fly out. In the fifth inning, Colavito faced five batters, walking two and retiring the other three without allowing a run. He also pitched the sixth inning. After retiring the first two batters, Colavito again faced Kaline. This time, Kaline doubled. Horton though lined out to end the inning. In the bottom of that frame, the Yankees plated five runs to jump ahead 6-5. With a

214

slim lead, pitcher Dooley Womack was called in to relieve Rocky Colavito. Lindy McDaniel pitched the final innings to secure the win for the Yankees—a game in which Rocky Colavito was named the winning pitcher!

Only two Yankees position players have ever taken the mound more than once. Former catcher Rick Cerone was summoned to pitch twice during the 1987 season. Cerone performed admirably in both appearances. His first appearance came on July 19 against the Texas Rangers, in a game the Yankees lost 20-3, Cerone pitched one inning and retired all three batters he faced. Interestingly, Cerone had been the catcher that day so when the pitching change was made, in the middle of the inning with runners on base, Cerone had to change out of his catcher's equipment before taking the mound. Mark Salas replaced Cerone behind the plate. While he didn't allow a hit, Cerone did commit a balk with a runner on third that allowed the Rangers to plate their 20th run of the game.

A few weeks later, on August 9, Cerone took the mound in a game the Tigers would win 15-4. Cerone again pitched the bottom of the eighth inning. As in his previous pitching appearance, Cerone had been catching that day, although in this instance he began the inning as the pitcher. Cerone faced four batters walking one and retiring the other three.

The only other Yankees position player to appear on more than one occasion as a pitcher was Babe Ruth. Before becoming the Yankees greatest player, Ruth was a star pitcher with the Boston Red Sox. On five different occasions during his Yankee career, Babe Ruth took the mound. He usually did this, especially later in his career, as a way to bring some excitement to a game and probably as a way to see if he could still do the job. Babe Ruth's record in those five games was 5-0.

One remarkable game that Ruth pitched took place on June 13, 1921. He pitched five innings that day against the Detroit Tigers. He then played center field for the final four innings in a game the Yankees would win 13-8. Ruth had two hits in five plate appearances and walked twice. Both of his hits were home runs.

Of special note was Ruth's last pitched game. That contest occurred on October 1, 1933, at Yankee Stadium against the Red

Sox. Ruth and the Yankees jumped out to a 6-0 lead after five innings of play assisted, in part, by another Ruth home run. In the top of the sixth inning, the Red Sox battled back, scoring four times. He might have been tiring, but Ruth stayed in the game. In the top of the eighth inning, he allowed one more run to trim the lead to one run. He would not allow another as the Yankees won 6-5. Ruth pitched nine innings and allowed twelve hits and walked three batters. Remarkably, Ruth recorded no strikeouts. This complete game victory was the last pitching win of Babe Ruth's illustrious career.

KANSAS CITY ROYALS at NEW YORK YANKEES

Saturday, July 15, 1989 (Yankee Stadium)

	1	2	3	4	5	6	7	8	9		R	H	E
KC	1	0	0	0	0	0	0	4	2		7	10	0
NY	0	0	1	0	0	0	0	0	0		1	5	0

KC		AB	R	H	RBI	NY		AB	R	H	RBI
Wilson	CF	5	1	3	0	Polonia	LF	4	1	2	0
Seitzer	3B	3	2	0	0	Brookens	2B	3	0	0	0
Brett	1B	4	2	2	2	Mattingly	1B	4	0	0	0
Tartabull	RF	4	1	1	3	Hall	DH	4	0	1	1
Eisenreich	LF	4	1	1	0	Barfield	RF	4	0	1	0
Tabler	DH	4	0	1	0	Pagliarulo	3B	2	0	0	0
Palacios	PR/DH					Slaught	C	2	0	0	0
Boone	C	3	0	1	1	Espinoza	SS	3	0	0	0
White	2B	4	0	1	0	Kelly	CF	3	0	1	0
Pecota	SS	4	0	0	0						

KC	IP	H	R	BB	SO	NY	IP	H	R	BB	SO
Aquino - W	9	5	1	3	2	Cary	7	2	1	5	2
						Guetterman - L	0.1	5	4	0	0
						Mohorcic	0.2	2	0	0	0
						Davidson	1	1	2	1	0

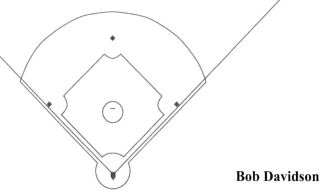

Bob Davidson

Courtesy of the Topps Company.

CHAPTER TWENTY-EIGHT
LOYD COLSON (1970)

L oyd Colson was drafted by the Yankees in the 28th round
of the 1967 Amateur Baseball Player Draft. A pitcher
from Bacone College in Oklahoma, Colson helped lead
his college to the 1967 NJCAA Baseball Championship.

After signing with the Yankees' organization, Colson's first
stop in the minor leagues was with Johnson City in the Rookie
Level Appalachian League. At Johnson City, Colson pitched in
twelve games, starting eleven, and earned a modest, but successful record of 3-1. This was good enough to earn him a promotion
to Single-A Fort Lauderdale for the 1968 season where he pitched
mostly out of the bullpen appearing in 21 games but logging only
43 innings and ending the season with an unspectacular 2-5 re-

cord. Colson stayed at Single-A for the 1969 season appearing in 45 games, throwing 120 innings and earning a 10-6 record. He seemed to have turned it around. That winter, the Yankees invited Colson to pitch in the Florida Instructional Winter League where he was used as a starting pitcher.

In 1970, Colson continued to climb the ladder. He pitched in 48 games for the Manchester Yankees of the Double-A Eastern League. Throwing over 100 innings, he went 7-5 and earned 16 saves. At the end of this successful season, Colson was brought to the Major Leagues.

Colson's lone Major League appearance came on September 25, 1970 at Yankee Stadium against the Detroit Tigers. The Yankees squad was on its way to winning 93 games and finishing in second place, their best finish between 1965-74. Young stars such as Bobby Murcer and Thurman Munson provided hope that the Yankees would once again return to their past glory after suffering through a series of second-division finishes to close out the 1960s.

The Tigers team he was facing was completing a disappointing season that saw it finish in fourth place. The Tigers had won the World Series only two years earlier and were the American League runners-up in 1969. There were numerous stars on the Detroit roster including Willie Horton, Bill Freehan, and Norm Cash, but their star was Al Kaline who was in the last seasons of a career that would see him reach the Hall of Fame.

Colson's appearance came in the first game of a doubleheader. Yankees manager Ralph Houk called on Colson to pitch in the top of the eighth inning with the Yankees trailing 2-1. Colson faced second baseman Dalton Jones, who flew out to center field. Third baseman Don Wert then singled. Catcher Gene Lamont doubled home Wert to extend the Tigers' lead to 3-1. Before the inning could get out of hand, Colson then struck out Elliott Maddux and pitcher Mickey Lolich. In the bottom of the eighth inning, the Yankees failed to score. Possibly buoyed by Colson's end-of-inning performance, Houk sent him out for the ninth inning. Colson did not disappoint. He struck out Dick McAuliffe to start the inning. Then, after a single by Mickey Stanley, Colson retired both Jim Northrup and Norm Cash.

LOYD COLSON

Courtesy of TCMA Ltd.

In the bottom of the ninth inning, the Yankees staged what looked to be a game-winning comeback. Jim Lyttle singled with one out. Gene Michael then reached on an error by Jones. This brought up the pitcher's spot, but, with the game in the balance, Houk pinch hit Roy White for Colson ending Colson's day... and career. White struck out and Horace Clarke lined out to end the 3-1 Tigers' victory.

Colson pitched well, allowing one run on three hits and struck out three consecutive batters in his two innings of work.

In 1971, Colson once again found himself in the minor leagues. In both 1971 and 1972, he pitched for the Triple-A Syracuse Chiefs. In 1972, he also dropped a rung pitching for the Double-A West Haven Yankees. By 1973, Loyd Colson was back in the lowest levels of the minors. He finished his career that year pitching one inning for the Kinston Eagles of the Single-A Carolina League, his one Major League game a distant memory.

Extra Innings
The First Designated Hitter

The Yankees did not fare well with their 77 picks in the 1967 Amateur Baseball Player Draft. Of that group, only eight made it to the Major Leagues. Only two of those eight players had distinguished careers. One was Steve Rogers who became a standout pitcher with the Montreal Expos. After being drafted, Rogers did not sign with the Yankees and instead attended the University of Tulsa. He later became the fourth player selected in the 1971 draft. The other player who made a mark in the Major Leagues was the first player they selected in the entire draft, first baseman Ron Blomberg. While Blomberg did not become the superstar the Yankees envisioned when they drafted him, he did make Major League history by becoming the game's first designated hitter.

Before reaching the majors, Ron Blomberg was a teammate of Loyd Colson's at Johnson City (1967) and Syracuse (1971) as they both progressed through the Yankees' farm system. Blomberg's minor league journey was relatively quick. He spent one year at each level demonstrating enough with his bat to earn a promotion the following season. By 1969, Blomberg earned his first taste of Major League Baseball after being promoted from the Double-A Manchester Yankees. He then spent the next season and a half with the Triple-A Syracuse Chiefs before he was promoted to the Yankees for good in 1971.

Ron Blomberg's calling card was his outstanding hitting ability. The Yankees envisioned Blomberg being a strong presence in their lineup for many years. After his call-up in 1971, Blomberg batted .322 in 64 games. Unfortunately, for Blomberg and the Yankees, he was never able to sustain that high level of play. Injuries seemed to be a constant for Blomberg, limiting his playing

Courtesy of the Topps Company

time and his effectiveness. In 1972, Ron Blomberg played in just 107 games and hit a disappointing .268.

Ron Blomberg's greatest season was 1973. Playing in only 100 games, Blomberg batted .329 with 12 home runs. It was at the start of that season that Ron Blomberg made history and entered the record books as baseball's first ever player to appear as a designated hitter.

In January 1973, the owners of the American League teams voted to introduce the designated hitter for a three-year trial period beginning that season. Because of this new rule, the first American League game played in 1973 would be the first to feature a designated hitter. The games that were first played to begin the season were the two afternoon games on the East Coast. The first featured the Yankees playing in Boston against the Red Sox. With a 1:37 p.m. starting time, it was all but assured that the first designated hitter would step to the plate in this game. The other East Coast game featured the Baltimore Orioles hosting the Milwaukee Brewers. That game, though, had a starting time of 2:17 p.m.

Blomberg was penciled in as the Yankees' designated hitters and slated to bat sixth in the lineup. The Red Sox put future Hall of Famer Orlando Cepeda in their lineup to be their first DH. Cepeda would be batting fifth.

Luis Tiant took the mound for the Red Sox that day. The first batter he faced was Yankees' second baseman Horace Clarke who singled. Left fielder Roy White struck out. Clark had attempted to steal second base on the final pitch to White and was promptly thrown out. As quickly as the game had started, there were two outs and the prospect of Blomberg, hitting sixth in the line-up, coming to bat that inning seemed remote. Right fielder Matty Alou though followed with a double. Bobby Murcer, the center fielder, then walked. That brought up Graig Nettles, the Yankees new third baseman, who also walked. As Nettles trotted to first, Ron Blomberg stepped up to the plate as baseball's first designated hitter with the bases loaded...

It is somewhat anticlimactic that Blomberg also drew a base on balls. That walk forced in the Yankees' first run of the game. Blomberg became baseball's first DH, the first DH to reach base, and first to "drive" home a run. Felipe Alou followed Blomberg with a double of his own scoring two more runs. The inning ended for the Yankees when catcher Thurman Munson popped out to first base.

Cepeda did not get to bat for the Red Sox until the top of the second inning. In his first at-bat, he struck out against Yankees' pitcher Mel Stottlemyre.

Blomberg came to bat in the bottom of the third inning following a two-out home run by Nettles (his first as a Yankee). Blomberg singled making him the first designated hitter to collect a base hit.

For the day, Ron Blomberg went one for three, with the aforementioned walk and RBI. Cepeda went hitless in six plate appearances with two strikeouts. In the game, the Red Sox rallied from their difficult start to beat the Yankees 15-5.

After that 1973 season, his best in a short career, Blomberg never appeared in as many as 100 games in a season again. In 1974, he batted .311 with 10 home runs in 90 games. In 1975, injuries limited him to only 34 games. Following the 1975 season, Blomberg would only play one more game as a Yankee due to lingering injuries.

Demonstrating his resolve, Ron Blomberg did make it back to the Major Leagues, in 1978, with the Chicago White Sox. That year he batted .231 in 61 games to close out his career—one that began with such great promise.

DETROIT TIGERS at NEW YORK YANKEES

Friday, September 25, 1970 (Yankee Stadium)

	1	2	3	4	5	6	7	8	9		R	H	E
DET	0	0	1	1	0	0	0	1	0		3	11	2
NY	0	0	0	0	1	0	0	0	0		1	7	1

DET		AB	R	H	RBI	NY		AB	R	H	RBI
McAuliffe	3B/SS	4	1	1	1	Clarke	2B	5	0	1	0
Stanley	CF	5	0	2	0	Mitchell	CF	3	0	0	0
Northrup	RF	5	0	1	0	Munson	C	4	0	3	0
Cash	1B	5	0	0	0	Cater	1B	4	0	0	0
Jones	2B	4	0	0	0	Ellis	3B	4	0	0	0
Brown	LF	2	1	2	0	Woods	LF	3	0	0	0
Wert	PH/3B	2	1	2	0	Lyttle	RF	4	0	1	0
Lamont	C	4	0	2	1	Michael	SS	4	0	0	0
Gutierrez	SS					Kline	P	1	0	0	0
Maddox	PH/3B/LF	4	0	2	1	Hansen	PH	1	1	1	1
Lolich	P	2	0	0	0	Jones	P				
						Murcer	PH	1	0	1	0
						Colson	P				
						White	PH	1	0	0	0

DET	IP	H	R	BB	SO	NY	IP	H	R	BB	SO
Lolich - W	9	7	1	2	3	Kline - L	5	6	2	1	3
						Jones	2	2	0	1	2
						Colson	2	3	1	0	3

Loyd Colson

CHAPTER TWENTY-NINE
TWO WHO MIGHT BE
JOINING THE TEAM (2015)

The 2015 Yankees employed two pitchers, who seem to have joined the roster of *The Least Among Them* Yankees, but it is still a little too early to tell. As the years pass, there will be more members of this elite squad, but enough time must pass before the players can be included on this roster. In the annals of baseball there have been players who returned to the Major Leagues again after seemingly leaving the game for good including Jim Bouton, a former Yankees' pitcher.

Left-hander Matt Tracy pitched in one game for the Yankees on April 11, 2015, mopping up in an 8-4 loss to the Red Sox. When Tracy came into the game, the Yankees were losing 5-1. He gave up three runs in his first inning of work. In his second inning, he allowed no runs. In the game, the Yankees mounted a comeback of sorts, but fell short.

Tracy returned to the minor leagues where he toiled for numerous organizations including the Florida Marlins, the Minnesota Twins, and the Toronto Blue Jays. He pitched in the minors through the 2018 season.

As this book entered into its final editing stages, Matt Tracy joined the Blue Jays organization as a minor league pitching coach.

Jose DePaula, also a left-handed pitcher, had his one day with the Yankees on June 21, 2015 when he toiled 3.1 innings to close out a game the Yankees lost to the Detroit Tigers 12-4. In his outing, Jose DePaula walked four batters, allowed two hits (including a home run) and struck out two batters.

Following that game, DePaula returned to the minor leagues

where he finished out the season pitching for Scranton/Wilkes-Barre in Triple-A. Since 2015, Jose DePaula has pitched in Japan's Baseball Challenge League (an independent minor league program), in the Mexican Baseball League, and in 2020 he pitched in the Chinese Professional Baseball League. If he remains a *Least Among Them* Yankee, DePaula will be the one who has played in the most professional baseball leagues around the world.

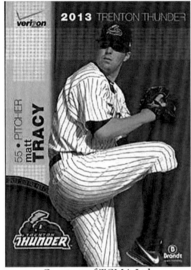 

Courtesy of TCMA Ltd.   Courtesy of the Topps Company.

Extra Innings
An Amazing Comeback

T he career of Jim Bouton was one that was unlike any other. Bouton reached the Major Leagues in 1962, right at the tail end of one of the great Yankees' dynasties. Even though they reached the World Series in 1963 and 1964, the 1962 season would be the last that would see the Yankees become world champions until 1977.

By 1963, Jim Bouton had become one of the most reliable pitchers on the team as he won 21 games against only 7 losses. The next year, Bouton was again terrific winning another 18 games in the regular season and two more in the 1964 World Series.

And then it all fell apart. Bouton had arm problems that destroyed his effectiveness and his career. In 1965, he won but four games and lost fifteen. He'd never win even that many games again for the Yankees, but somehow he stuck with the club through the 1968 season.

In 1969, Jim Bouton became a member of the expansion Seattle Pilots. Knowing that his career was just about over, he decided to take a gamble and chronicle what might be his last journey as a big leaguer. The notes he took became *Ball Four*, the most famous baseball book of all time. This diary of Bouton's 1969 season with the Seattle Pilots and the Houston Astros (the team he was traded to during the season) rocked the baseball world. This was baseball's first-ever "tell-all" that took readers way behind the scenes into the clubhouses and bullpens to tell the story of how baseball players thought, talked, and acted. If that wasn't enough, Bouton chronicled stories that took place on the team buses and airplanes and shared secrets from bars, restaurants, and hotel rooms. The book was a sensation and is still considered one of the most influential books (not just sports books) of the twentieth century.

Major League Baseball's reaction to the book was one of shock and outrage. Bouton had told secrets by giving a true, intimate look at the teams and players. In his writing, he shattered myths. Because of *Ball Four*, baseball would never be the same. Nor would Bouton's life. To some, he became a hero, to others, especially those within the game, he became a pariah. The year the book came out, 1970, would be Jim Bouton's last in the big leagues. In writing this best-selling book, Bouton stamped what was the end of his playing career. He was done as a ballplayer at the age of 31.

Or so it seemed.

After enjoying the fame and notoriety of being a famous author, Bouton found himself as a sports anchor on the local network news in New York City. He also authored two subsequent books. But this didn't completely satisfy him. As he wrote in *Ball Four*, "You spend a good piece of your life gripping a baseball and in the end it turns out that it was the other way around all the time." Like so many of us, the game of baseball never left Jim Bouton.

In 1975, Bouton hooked up with a Single-A baseball team attempting a comeback. It didn't work out. In 1977, he tried again pitching in the Mexican League and then again in the lowest levels of the minor leagues. He had only middling success.

By 1978, Jim Bouton was a 39-year-old has-been major-leaguer. He had one last chance to make it back to the majors by signing with the Atlanta Braves organization, the only team that gave him an opportunity.

Remarkably, he defied the odds and on September 10, 1978, eight full years after he last pitched in the Major Leagues, he started a game for the Braves against the Los Angeles Dodgers. Bouton lost the game, giving up six runs in five innings. But then, on September 14, he got a second chance, this time starting against the San Francisco Giants. In that game, Bouton pitched six innings allowing just three hits, and only one run. He ended up as the winning pitcher completing what was one of the game's most unlikely of comebacks.

BOSTON RED SOX at NEW YORK YANKEES

Saturday, April 11, 2015 (Yankee Stadium)

	1	2	3	4	5	6	7	8	9		R	H	E
BOS	0	1	0	1	0	0	3	3	0		8	9	0
NY	0	1	0	0	0	0	0	3	0		4	5	3

BOS		AB	R	H	RBI	NY		AB	R	H	RBI
Holt	CF	5	1	4	3	Gardner	LF	4	1	1	0
Pedroia	2B	5	0	1	2	Young	CF	4	1	1	3
Ortiz	DH	5	0	0	0	Beltran	DH	4	0	0	0
Napoli	1B	4	1	0	0	Rodriguez	1B	4	1	1	0
Sandoval	3B	5	1	1	0	Headley	3B	4	0	0	0
Craig	RF	4	0	0	0	Jones	RF	3	0	1	0
Nava	LF	3	1	2	2	Murphy	C	3	0	0	0
Bogaerts	SS	4	2	1	0	Gregorius	SS	2	0	0	1
Hanigan	C	2	2	0	1	Petit	2B	3	1	1	0

BOS	IP	H	R	BB	SO	NY	IP	H	R	BB	SO
Kelly - W	7	1	1	2	8	Warren - L	5.1	5	2	2	1
Ogando	0.2	3	3	0	1	Wilson	0.2	0	1	1	1
Varvaro	0.1	0	0	0	1	Martin	1	2	2	0	0
Ross	1	1	0	0	1	**Tracy**	2	2	3	2	1

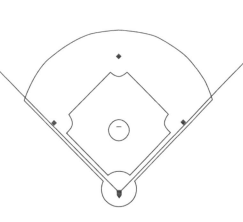

Matt Tracy

DETROIT TIGERS at NEW YORK YANKEES

Sunday, June 21, 2015 (Yankee Stadium)

	1	2	3	4	5	6	7	8	9		R	H	E
DET	4	2	0	0	1	5	0	0	0		12	15	0
NY	0	2	0	0	0	0	1	0	1		4	9	1

DET		AB	R	H	RBI	NY		AB	R	H	RBI
Davis	CF/LF	5	1	1	0	Gardner	CF	3	0	0	0
Kinsler	2B	5	0	0	0	Flores	LF	2	0	0	0
Castellanos	3B					Gregorius	SS	4	0	1	0
Cabrera	1B	3	2	2	0	Rodriguez	DH	4	0	1	0
Wilson	3B/2B	1	0	0	0	Teixeira	1B	3	0	1	0
V. Martinez	DH	6	2	3	4	Murphy	C	1	0	0	0
Cespedes	LF	5	2	1	1	McCann	C/1B	4	1	2	1
Gose	CF					Jones	RF	4	0	0	0
J.D. Martinez	RF	5	3	3	6	Young	LF/CF	4	1	1	0
Holaday	C	5	0	2	0	Drew	2B	3	2	2	2
Romine	3B/1B	4	1	2	1	Ryan	3B	3	0	1	1
Iglesias	SS	3	1	1	0						

DET	IP	H	R	BB	SO	NY	IP	H	R	BB	SO
Sanchez - W	7	7	3	2	5	Tanaka - L	5	10	7	2	6
Hardy	1	1	0	0	1	Burawa	0.2	3	4	1	1
Soria	1	1	1	0	0	**De Paula**	3.1	2	1	4	2

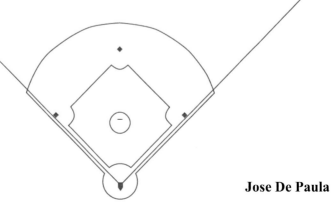

Jose De Paula

CHAPTER THIRTY
ANDY O'CONNOR (1908)

The tale of the *Least Among Them* players ends as it began, with a complete game. Elvio Jimenez had the great fortune to maximize his only Major League experience playing the entire game in a thirteen-inning affair. While Andy O'Connor's experience did not last beyond nine frames, he is the only other player in this history to participate in a complete game. For Andy O'Connor, his complete game was a nine-inning pitching performance against the Boston Red Sox. Interestingly, O'Connor's mound opponent, Henry "Doc" McMahon also threw a complete game IN his only opportunity in the Major Leagues. Doc McMahon is a *Least Among Them* Red Sox.

Andy O'Connor arrived with the Highlanders after an undistinguished career in the minor leagues. Except for his one big league game, Andy O'Connor never pitched above B-Level in the minor leagues. In 1906 and 1907, O'Connor pitched for the Syracuse Stars, and in 1908 he threw for the Trenton Tigers.

As noted, Andy O'Connor's one Major League game came on October 6, 1908 in Boston against the Red Sox. That Boston squad contained future Hall of Famers Cy Young (who was nearing the end of his career) and Tris Speaker (whose career was just beginning). The Highlanders also had two future Hall of Famers, pitcher Jack Chesbro and outfielder Willie Keeler. While the 1908 Red Sox finished under .500, these Highlanders were the doormats of the league. They won only 51 games against 103 losses.

O'Connor threw a complete game lasting eight full innings, with no need for the Red Sox to bat in the ninth as they dominated the scoring and won the game 11-3. O'Connor allowed 14 hits and walked seven. Of the eleven runs that scored against O'Connor, nine were earned. On the plus side, he did record five strike-outs. Interestingly, the Highlanders also knocked out 14 hits, but Doc McMahon of the Red Sox allowed no free passes in his complete-game win.

In 1909, O'Connor played for four different teams, with three of them; the Trenton Tigers, the Johnstown Johnnies, and the Altoona Mountaineers all part of the Tri-State League. O'Connor's career ended after the 1910 season pitching for the Lynn Shoemakers in the Class-B New England League.

When Andy O'Connor passed away on September 26, 1980 at 96 years old, he had achieved a noteworthy honor. At the end of his life, Andy O'Connor had been the oldest living former Major League Baseball player. In that sense, at least for a short while, Andy O'Connor was the most among them.

Extra Innings
A "Casey At The Bat" Moment

Throughout baseball history, the greatest rivalry between two teams has always been considered between the Yankees and the Boston Red Sox. These two teams have battled over the years for supremacy in the American League.

In the early years of the American League, the Red Sox were the premier franchise. The Boston team won baseball's first ever World Series in 1903 (over the Pittsburgh Pirates). The Red Sox were also world champions in 1912, 1915, 1916, and 1918. They were a powerhouse. In fact, the Highlanders/Yankees were not much of a contender in those years. In their first eighteen years of existence, they never had a first-place finish. Only three times (1904, 1906, and 1910) did the Highlanders finish as high as second. Only in 1904, were the Highlanders locked in a battle for the pennant with the Red Sox. The greatest rivalry in sports was very slow in developing although the initial sparks were set with that 1904 pennant race.

That 1904 pennant race has been largely forgotten, but it was the first epic battle between the Highlanders and the Red Sox, then known as the Boston Americans. That season ended with these teams playing the season's final five games, including two doubleheaders, against each other to determine the league's champion. This final series was also the final games of the year for both teams as the National League champion New York Giants had already let it be known that they were not going to play any team from the new American League in any "World Series." This was only the American League's fourth season. The previous year, the Boston team had won the first ever World Series embarrassing the long-standing National League. So as to not be placed in a similar situation, the Giants, with an insurmountable lead in the National League, had already declared themselves the champions of baseball.

The Highlanders entered the first of the final five games just a half-game behind the Americans. In that game, played in New York, the Highlanders' ace pitcher Jack Chesbro outdueled Norwood Gibson of Boston and won 3-2. With the victory, New York was in first place with just four games to play.

The first of the final two doubleheaders to finish the season was scheduled to be played on Saturday, October 8. These games had been scheduled to be played in New York, but the Highlanders' owner, Frank Farrell had already rented the ballpark to Columbia University for its football game against Williams College. (Columbia would win 11-0.) As such, the teams traveled to Boston to play the doubleheader.

Chesbro, winner of 41 games, was the Highlanders' unrivaled ace so they turned to him again for the first game of the doubleheader. Happy Jack did not bring his best stuff and the Highlanders took a painful loss 13-2. In the second game, the hard-throwing right hander Cy Young defeated the Highlanders 1-0. It was a sweep for the Bostonians. All they needed was one win the next day to secure the American League pennant.

The teams returned to New York for the season's final games on Monday, October 10, 1904. For the first game, the Highlanders, again, turned to Chesbro. Since October 1, Chesbro appeared in four games and had pitched 31 innings, but the Highlanders needed him one more time. The Red Sox called upon Big Bill Dinneen. This would turn out to be one of baseball's great games. Heading into the bottom of the seventh inning, New York held a 2-0 lead. Boston came back due, in part, to some poor defensive play by Jimmy Williams, the Highlanders' second baseman, who made a throwing error that allowed two runs to score.

In the top of the ninth inning and the score tied, Boston was able to get the go-ahead run to third base with two outs. Then, with two strikes on the batter, Jack Chesbro let loose a wild pitch that allowed the Red Sox to take the lead, 3-2. This is often where the story stops, but in reality, since the game was played in New York, the Highlanders had one last chance to tie or win the game and with this came a *"Casey at the Bat"* moment as Patsy, Mighty

234

Patsy, would advance to the plate.

Patsy Dougherty was one of early baseball's great clutch hitters. In 1902, for Boston, Dougherty batted .342, fourth best in the league. The next year, again with Boston, he hit with even greater abandon. Dougherty led the league in hits (195) and runs (107) while batting .331. In the 1903 World Series, Dougherty hit two home runs in Game 2 and two triples in Game 5 to help Boston win the first ever World Series. After only two seasons in the Major Leagues, Patsy Dougherty was becoming a legend in Boston.

In the early days of the league, there were machinations that seemed to indicate that American League President Ban Johnson was working to strengthen the New York franchise. His hand may have helped the Highlanders acquire a number of their early stars. He may also have been behind a June trade that sent Patsy Dougherty from Boston to New York in exchange for Bob Unglaub, a rookie who was hitting only .211 at the time and was, by at least one report, in the hospital suffering from alcohol poisoning. If Ban Johnson wasn't behind the deal, it sure didn't seem like a great exchange for Boston. The newspapers reported this as a major story. The SABR Biography Project reports that the Boston Herald's headline "DOUGHERTY AS A YANKEE" is considered the first ever time the New York franchise was referred to as the Yankees in print.

New York's success that season can be attributed, in large part, to Patsy Dougherty's arrival. No American League team played better for the rest of the season than Dougherty's High-landers who won 64 games against only 38 losses. Dougherty belted 128 hits in 106 games with the "Yankees." Just as impor-tantly, he scored 80 of his league-leading 113 runs.

And so we return to that fateful game in New York—the game that would determine the American League champions. The bot-tom of the ninth inning arrived with the Boston team leading 3-2. The bottom of the New York's order, the sixth, seventh, and eighth hitters, were due to bat. Then there was the pitcher's spot. Since he was the leadoff hitter and due to bat fifth that inning, there seemed but little chance of Patsy getting to the bat.

But, with one out, the third baseman Wid Conroy worked

a walk. And then, after another out, Deacon McGuire, the forty-year-old catcher, pinch hitting for Chesbro, also worked a walk.

When the picture came into view,
when they saw what had just beckoned,
Old Deacon was at first
and Conroy a huggin' second.

And with that, Patsy, Mighty Patsy advanced to the bat. By this time, the epic poem *Casey At The Bat* was already sixteen years old having been written and published in 1888. There had to be people in the ballpark that day who were familiar with the story.

Big Bill Dinneen was still on the mound for the Red Sox. This was an era in which the starting pitchers finished their games. Dinneen would throw 335 innings that year and not even lead his team in that category as Cy Young threw 380 innings. But even that total paled in comparison to Jack Chesbro's 454.2 innings of work that season.

There was ease in Patsy's manner as he stepped into his place,
There was pride in Patsy's bearing, and a smile on Patsy's
face...

It was apparent that this battle between Dinneen and Dougherty would be the one that would settle the 1904 pennant race once and for all.

Four pitches were thrown from the pitcher to the batter,
Four pitches to determine which fans' hearts would be shat-
tered.

Dinneen delivered two strikes right and quick
But also two balls that made a Boston fan's heart somewhat
sick.

Big Bill stood tall on the mound that day
But Patsy, the batter, would no ground give away.

The pitcher, he threw, the best his arm would allow
And Patsy swung hard just like he always knew how.

Oh, somewhere in that big city hearts surely felt light
People were laughing and enjoying the sights
Under an autumn sky two lovers might have kissed
But at Hilltop Park, Patsy Donovan swung… and missed.

NEW YORK HIGHLANDERS at BOSTON RED SOX

Tuesday, October 6, 1908 (Huntington Avenue Baseball Grounds)

	1	2	3	4	5	6	7	8	9		R	H	E
NY	0	1	0	0	0	0	0	0	2		3	14	5
BOS	1	5	0	0	0	0	1	4	X		11	14	1

NY		AB	R	H	RBI	BOS		AB	R	H	RBI
Cree	CF	5	1	2	0	McConnell	2B	5	2	3	2
Gardner	2B	5	1	4	0	Lord	3B	5	2	3	1
LaPorte	LF	5	0	3	2	Speaker	CF	4	1	1	2
Moriarty	1B	5	0	1	0	Hoey	RF	5	1	0	0
O'Rourke	SS	4	0	2	0	Cravath	LF	1	1	0	1
Blair	RF	4	0	0	0	Wagner	SS	3	1	2	0
Donovan	3B	4	1	1	0	Niles	PH/SS	1	1	1	1
Sweeney	C	4	0	1	1	Stahl	1B	3	1	1	3
O'Connor	P	3	0	0	0	Donahue	C	3	1	1	1
Wilson	PH	1	0	0	0	McMahon	P	5	0	2	0

NY	IP	H	R	BB	SO	BOS	IP	H	R	BB	SO
O'Connor - L	8	14	11	7	5	McMahon - W	9	14	3	0	3

Andy O'Connor

CHAPTER THIRTY-ONE
THE MOST FAMOUS LEAST AMONG THEM PLAYERS (1947)

In the 1930s there was an entire team of baseball players who began playing together as a unit. This squad performed together for decades. Remarkably, except for the positions of shortstop and right field, the rest of the team always appeared together as one. Seven of the players stayed together for their entire careers. There are also no documented instances of those seven players ever appearing on a baseball diamond with different teammates other than the shortstop and right fielder.

This team of players began playing together in the lowest levels of the minors, and early on were performing for a number of managers before they were adopted by a partnership that kept hold of these players until the ends of their collective careers. As one might predict, since they all went through the bush leagues together, at the end, they also retired together.

The first documented appearance of this squad was in 1937 when they were said to be playing for a team in Hollywood, California. They began to be known locally on a small circuit. It was the legendary singer Kate Smith who, in 1938, helped bring this team of unknowns to national prominence. While not much is known about the players' abilities, and while no statistics were kept on any of the players, ever, what is known is that baseball fans truly adored this squad.

The team also played together through the 1940s. In 1945, there is archival footage that documents, very specifically, that the players were members of the St. Louis Wolves, a heretofore little-known team.

The team came together as New York Yankees for one day on

April 10, 1947. It seems that Joe DiMaggio was also on that squad. Since DiMaggio was recovering from a foot operation, he was unable to start the season. Remarkably, DiMaggio sent a telegram to a player named Lou Costello who had played for the Cookamonga Wild Cats, to "take my place on the New York Yankees until I recover." No film footage exists of these players for that April 10th game, but audio tapes survive that indicate that the game they played was broadcast nationally on the radio. Lou Costello seems to have a great deal of influence on the Yankees because the tapes from the broadcast indicate that he brought a partner, a certain Bud Abbott, with him to the Yankees to serve as a coach. Bucky Harris, the Yankees' manager gave Abbott a job as coach for as long as Costello was on the team. What is also remarkable is that Abbott already knew the players' names and had to teach them to Lou Costello.

After that one appearance as New York Yankees, the squad left the Major Leagues, but they continued to play for appreciative audiences well into and throughout the 1950s. It is known that they once played for a team that was sponsored by the Colgate Corporation. They also came together to play, in what was possibly a charity event, at the Retired Actors' Home. When their part-time catcher and presumed right fielder, Lou Costello passed away on March 3, 1959, the team disbanded and never played together again.

The names of these players, who were only mentioned once in relation to a Major League team, are familiar to almost every baseball fan. These players were the eight best known *Least Among Them* New York Yankees of all time. Since they only played together, they will be listed in positional order beginning with their most famous member, their first baseman, who has one of the most recognizable baseball names of all time.

Here are those one-time Yankees in the order in which they appear:

1B   Who
2B   What
3B   I Don't Know
LF   Why

CF   Because
P   Tomorrow
C   Today
SS   I Don't Give A Darn

Of course, these are the imaginary players from the famous Abbott and Costello routine, *Who's on First*. In this writer's research, he can find no instances when Abbott and Costello refer to the players as being part of any Major League team other than the Yankees. Their April 10, 1947 radiocast was a show designed entirely around the theme of baseball. *Who's on First* was the skit that ended their performance that night.

The skit that mentions the Yankees begins with the premise that Lou Costello would be replacing Joe DiMaggio on the team. In that skit, all of the other players were all named including the center fielder, DiMaggio's regular position. In this scenario, one would have to assume that DiMaggio, the only player not named in the skit, and the only position not listed, would be the right fielder. Since, he was signed to replace DiMaggio, Lou Costello would have also been the right fielder on that team.

The St. Louis Wolves are the team most associated with the *Who's on First* routine because the most famous archival footage comes from the Abbott and Costello 1945 movie *The Naughty Nineties*. It is the clip from this film that is shown as a part of a permanent exhibit at the Baseball Hall of Fame in Cooperstown, New York.

In the various renditions of the skit, performed over many decades, the shortstop is known as "I Don't Care," "I Don't Give A Darn," and, depending on the audience, "I Don't Give a Damn."

It is amazing, and quite wonderful that the *Who's On First* players are all *Least Among Them* Yankees.

NOTES, SOURCES, AND REFERENCES:

In the course of writing this book I used a plethora of sources to supplement my own knowledge of the history of the Yankees. The following sources were utilized in my research for this book.

ON-LINE SOURCES:
The following on-line sources were integral components of my research:
Ancestry.com
Baseball-Almanac.com
Baseball-Fever.com
Baseball Hall-of-Fame.com
Baseball-Reference.com
BR Bullpen
Find A Grave.com
Retrosheet.com
Rotoworld.com
The SABR Baseball Biography Project

BOOKS AND MAGAZINES:
Appel, Marty. (2012). *Pinstripe Empire.* Bloomsbury, New York.

Frommer, Harvey. (1997). *The New York Yankees Encyclopedia.* Simon & Schuster Macmillan Company, New York.

Gallagher, Mark & LeConte, Walter. (2000). *The Yankee Encyclopedia (4th ed).* Sports Publishing Inc., Champaign, Illinois.

Gentile, Derek. (2001). *The Complete New York Yankees.* Black Dog & Leventhal Publishers, New York.

Gutman. Bill. (2010). *Yankees By The Numbers.* Skyhorse Publishing, USA.

James, Bill. (2001). The New Bill James Historical Baseball Abstract. The Free Press, New York.

Johnson, Lloyd &Wolff, Miles. (1993). *The Encyclopedia of Minor League Baseball.* Baseball America, Durham, North Carolina

Lee, Bill. (2003). *The Baseball Necrology.* McFarland & Company, Inc., Jefferson, North Carolina.

MacLean, Norman (Ex.ed). (1990). *All-Time Greatest Who's Who in Baseball (1872-1990).* Who's Who In Baseball Magazine Company, New York.

Okkonen, Marc. (1991). *Baseball Uniforms of the 20th Century.* Sterling Publishing Co., Inc, New York.

Solomon, Bert. (2001). *The Baseball Timeline.* Avon Books, New York.

Stout, Glenn. (2002). *Yankees Century.* Houghton Mifflin Company, New York.

Spatz, Lyle. (2000). *Yankees Coming, Yankees Going.* McFarland & Company, Inc., Jefferson North Carolina.

Vancil, Mark & Mandrake, Mark. (2002). *One Hundred Years – New York Yankees: The Official Retrospective.* Ballantine Books, New York.

Whittingham, Richard (ed). (1989). *The DiMaggio Albums (Vol. 1 and 2).* G.P. Putnam's Sons, New York.

OTHER:

The National Baseball Hall-of-Fame Individual Player Archives, Cooperstown, New York.

The Letters of Bill Haber contained in the National Baseball Hall-of-Fame Individual Player Archives

SPECIFIC CHAPTER-BY-CHAPTER SOURCES:

Note- Some of the newspaper accounts are from unidentified newspaper clippings found in a player's individual file in the National Baseball Hall-of-Fame player archives.

Chapter 1, Elvio Jimenez

Bat King Jimenez A Glove Whiz Too, The Sporting News. January 6, 1968

White, Roy & Berger, Darrell. (2009). *Then Roy Said To Mickey....:The Best Yankees Stories Ever Told.* Triumph Books, Chicago, Illinois.

Younger Jimenez Yankee Hopeful, The Monroe News-Star. January 21, 1964.

Chapter 2, Frank Verdi
Former Binghamton Triplets Manager Verdi Dies at 84, The Binghamton News. July 10, 2010.
Moonlight Graham Comes To The Bronx, leighmayo.com. 2015.
Orioles Cuba Trip Opens Old Wounds, New York Daily News. March 28, 1999.
1974 Denver Bears Program.
2008 International League Hall-of-Fame Program.

Chapter 3, Charlie Fallon
Moonlight Graham Comes To The Bronx, leighmayo.com. 2015.
Waddell Helps Team To Beat New York, The New York Times. July 1, 1905.
Tapper, Craig. *The Yankees' Moonlight Graham.* Yankees Magazine, Vol. 34, No. 3. May 2013.

Chapter 4, Art Goodwin
Art Goodwin personal letter. August 25, 1911.
This Day in 1914, The Troy Record. May 6, 1914.

Chapter 5, Phil Cooney
Boxerman, Burton A. & Boxerman, Benita W. (2007). *Jews And Baseball.* McFlarland & Company, Inc., Publishers, Jefferson, North Carolina.
Horvitz, Peter S. & Horvitz, Joachim. (2001). *The Big Book of Jewish Baseball.* S.P.I. Books, New York.
1968 Old Timers A.A. of Greater Paterson, NJ National Sports Hall of Fame Program.

Chapter 6, Roger Slagle
Slagle Making His Pitch To Stay in New York, New York Daily News. September 9, 1979.
Tellis, Richard. (1998). *Once Around The Bases.* Triumph

Books, Chicago, Illinois.

Trucks, Rob. (2002). *Cup of Coffee.* Smallmouth Press, New York.

Chapter 7, Floyd Newkirk

Buddy Hassett, 85, Ballplayer, The New York Times. August 26, 1997.

https://illinoiscollegeathletics.com/honors/hall-of-fame/floyd-newkirk/9. The Official Website of Illinois College Athletics.

Elston, Gene. (2006). *A Stitch In Time.* Halcyon Press, New Orleans, Louisiana.

Floyd Newkirk, pitcher..., Article from unidentified newspaper. September 28, 1933.

Mayer, Ronald A. (1985). *The 1937 Newark Bears.* Rutgers University Press, New Brunswick, New Jersey.

Needs Only Few Digits, Article from unidentified newspaper. February 22, 1934.

Chapter 8, Honey Barnes

Bill Jurges Wounded By Girl He Rejects, The New York Times. July 7, 1932.

Bisons Start at Newark Today, Buffalo Courier-Express. April 13, 1926.

Baseball Magazine Biography Form. C. Ford Sawyer, Boston, Massachusetts.

Chapter 9, Steve Garrison

Ewing Township Native Garrison Taking Break From Baseball, nj.com. July 8, 2014.

Hideki Irabu Gave Us Night To Remember, espn.com. July 29, 2011.

Hun Product Steve Garrison Waits As The Yankees Search For A Lefty, The Trentonian. March 29, 2011.

New York Yankees' Steve Garrison, from Ewing, N.J., Shuts Down Mariners In Relief in MLB Debut, New York Daily News. July 26, 2011.

Yankees Get Rights To Irabu In Deal With Padres, The New York Times. April 23, 1997.

Yankees' Steve Garrison, a Ewing Native, Makes Major-League Debut, The Star Ledger. July 26, 2011.

Chapter 10, Eddie Quick
Bucky Dent. Baseball Nicknames: major-smolinski.com
Eddie Quick Dies; Was Omaha Pitcher, Omaha Daily Bee. June 23, 1913.
Eddie Quick Responds to Last Call, Rocky Ford Tribune. June 20, 1913.
New York To Play Detroit Today, The Times Dispatch (Richmond, VA). September 29, 1903.
Russo, Frank (2017). The Cooperstown Chronicles: Baseball's Colorful Characters, Unusual Lives, and Strange Demises. Roman & Littlefield Publishers. Lanham, Maryland.

Chapter 11, Homer Thompson
Lyons, Douglas. (2006). The Baseball Geek's Bible: All the Facts and Stats You'll Ever Need. MQ Publications, London, United Kingdom.
Moonlight Graham Comes To The Bronx, leighmayo.com. 2015.
Purdy, Dennis. (2006). The Team-By-Team Encyclopedia of Major League Baseball. Workman Publishing, New York.
Yanks' Niekro Changes Style And Wins 300th, The New York Times. October 7, 1985.

Chapter 12, George Batten
Jumped Ford At Start, The Philadelphia Inquirer. September 29, 1912.

Chapter 13, Harry Hanson
Article from Sporting Life, July 26, 1913.
Col. Harry F. Hanson (obituaries), Savannah Morning News. October 6, 1966.
Hanson-Col. Harry F. (funeral notice), Savannah Morning News. October 6, 1966.
(Untitled). Our Paper, Massachusetts Reformatory. August 2, 1913.

Roster of the Illinois National Guard & Illinois Naval Militia. California State Library. Sacramento, California.

Chapter 14, Jim Hanley
Reisler, Jim. (2002). Before They Were the Bombers: The New York Yankees' Early Years, 1903-1919. McFarland Publishing, Jefferson, North Carolina.

Box Score from San Francisco Call. July 4, 1913.

Manhattan College Basketball Team Nickname Stirs Mystery, The Wall Street Journal. March 19, 2014.

Question Box, The New York Times. September 9, 1985.

What's A Jasper?. Manhattan College website (manhattan.edu).

Chapter 15, Rugger Ardizoia
Rinaldo Ardizoia, the Oldest Living Yankee, Reflects On His Career, The New York Times. April 27, 2015.

(Untitled). World Telegram Clipping. December 6, 1939

Yankee Prospect Gets Going, unidentified newspaper. May 30, 1940.

Yankees Purchase A Hollywood Star; He's an Ace Hurler, unidentified newspaper. August 14, 1940.

Chapter 16, Stefan Wever
A Dream Unfulfilled, MLB.com. September 12, 2005.

Reaching The Height of Potential, Pinstripe Alley (pinstripealley.com). December 12, 2011.

Sunlight For A Moonlight Man, The Post Game (thepostgame.com). January 17, 2012.

They Were There: Stefan Wever, This Great Game (thisgreatgame.com). January 27, 2015.

Chapter 17, Sam Marsonek
The Best Prospect The Yankees Ever Had…For Six Weeks, River Ave Blues (riveravesblues.com). February 5, 2015.

Cambridge's Marsonek Steps Down; Texas Coach Takes His Place, Tampa Bay Times. May 21, 2013.

Former Jesuit Star and Yankees Pitcher Has Found A New

Calling, 10 News, CBS, Tampa Bay (wtsp.com). May 20, 2013.

Hinkey Haines: One For the Record Book, The Chronicle (Lycoming College). 2008.

Slade Heathcott's Journey From Teen Turmoil to Yankees Millions, New York Post. February 24, 2013.

Slade Heathcott's Path To Majors Took More Turns Than Most, New York Post. May 20, 2015.

Yankees Win First Game in Rebuilt Stadium, The New York Times. April 16, 1976.

Chapter 18, Christian Parker

Christian Parker, 1995 Goldpanners Scrapbook (goldpanners.com). 1995.

Untitled. New York Post (nypost.com/sports/Yankees/37499.htm

Parker Looking Like Yankees' Fifth Starter, Baseball Weekly (baseballweekly.com). March 24, 2001.

Parker Unravels In His Yankee Debut, The New York Times. April 7, 2001.

Who Will Be The Yankees' Fifth Starter?, CBS Radio (cbslocal. com). February 14, 2013.

Yankee Rook Gets Hooked Christian Thrown To Blue Jays' Lion, New York Daily News. April 7, 2001.

Chapter 19, Hal Stowe

Clemson Puts Ace In Relief, The Victoria Advocate. June 12, 1959.

O'Neil, Bill. (1994). *The Southern League: Baseball in Dixie, 1885-1994.* Eakin Press, Fort Worth, Texas.

Stowe Snags Win Without A Pitch, milb.com. May 11, 2007.

Tellis, Richard. (1998). *Once Around The Bases.* Triumph Books, Chicago, Illinois.

Chapter 20, Walter Bernhardt

Service Men Are To Be Admitted Free, The Courier-News. June 22, 1918.

Sunday Remembrance of Rangers Past: George "Doc" Medich, Postcards From Elysian Fields (trsullivan.mlblogs.com). February 19, 2015.

Warrington, Robert. A Ballpark Opens And A Ballplayer Dies: The Converging Fates of Shipe Park and "Doc" Powers, The Baseball Research Journal (SABR). June 2014

Chapter 21, Jack Enright
No additional accounts were located for Jack Enright.

Chapter 22, Larry McClure
Akin, William E. (2006). *West Virginia Baseball: A History, 1865-2000.* McFarland & Company, Jefferson, North Carolina.

Chapter 23, Tom Burr
Appel, Martin & Munson, Thurman. (1979). *Thurman Munson: An Autobiography.* Coward, McCann & Geoghegan, Inc., New York.

Lidle Dies After Plane Crashes into NYC High-Rise, ESPN (espn.com). October 12, 2001.

Moonlight Graham Comes To The Bronx, leighmayo.com. 2015.

When Wrigley Opened, Yanks Were Different. Well, Not Totally, The New York Times. April 20, 2014.

25 Years Later, Thurman Munson's Last Words Remain A Symbol Of His Life, New York Daily News. August 1, 2009.

Chapter 24, Heinie Odom
No additional accounts were located for Heinie Odom.

Chapter 25, Clem Llewellyn
A Storied Past, A New Beginning, YES Weekly (yesweekly.com). April 7, 2010.

Clement Manley Llewellyn, The Charlotte-Mecklenburg Story (cmlibrary.org) March 5, 2015.

Utley, R.G.. (2006). Outlaw Ballplayers: Interviews and Profiles from the Independent Carolina Baseball League. McFarland and Company, Jefferson, North Carolina.

Chapter 26, George Washburn
No additional accounts were located for George Washburn.

Chapter 27, Bob Davidson
No additional accounts were located for Bob Davidson.

Chapter 28, Loyd Colson
Bacone Honoring 1967 NJCAA Baseball Champions, Bacone Athletics (baconeathletics.com). March 15, 2015.

Lyons, Jeffrey, Lyons, Douglas B., Costas, Bob. (1998). Out of Left Field: Over 1,134 Newly Discovered Amazing Baseball Records, Connections, Coincidences, and More! Three Rivers Press, New York.

Chapter 29, Two Who Might Join the Team
No additional accounts were located for Matt Tracy or Jose DePaula.

Chapter 30, Andy O'Connor
Cups of Coffee: Andy O'Connor, Diamonds In The Dusk (diamondsinthedusk.com).

Obituary. From National Baseball Hall-of-Fame Player's File

Paul (right) with his son Ethan.

ABOUT THE AUTHOR

A lifelong educator, leader, and speaker, Dr. Paul Semendinger, is widely known for his deep knowledge of the history of baseball, specifically the New York Yankees. He is a member of the Internet Baseball Writers Association of America (IBWAA) and a regular contributor to their exclusive newsletter, "Here's The Pitch." Paul operates, writes for, and is the Editor-in-Chief of the extremely successful Yankees blog, Start Spreading the News, which has enjoyed millions of page views. He appears regularly on Northeast Streaming Sports' flagship program "The Mac and Jack Show" where Paul is known as their resident baseball expert. Paul is a regular guest on many baseball podcasts and programs including the "Bronx Beat Podcast." Paul still pitches in a competitive baseball league in New Jersey and even as he reaches his mid 50's, he still has the ability to pitch nine-inning complete games. Paul still holds out hope that the Yankees will call on him to pitch for the big club. He knows he can help them in their quest for their next championship.